Speakers' Illustrations for Special Days

EDITED BY CHARLES L. WALLIS

First reprinted 1975 by Baker Book House Company
with the permission of Abingdon Press

ISBN: 0-8010-9555-7

Library of Congress Catalog Card Number: 56-5373

Third printing, September 1991

Printed in the United States of America

Acknowledgments

Charles Scribner's Sons for extracts from *Invitation to Pilgrimage* by John Baillie, *Our Knowledge of God* by John Baillie, *How to Think of Christ* by William Adams Brown, *Communion Through Preaching* by Henry Sloan Coffin (Copyright 1952 Charles Scribner's Sons), *The Country House* by John Galsworthy, *The Spirit of St. Louis* by Charles A. Lindbergh (Copyright 1953 Charles Scribner's Sons), *High Country* by Alistair MacLean (Copyright 1952 Charles Scribner's Sons), *The Irony of American History* by Reinhold Niebuhr (Copyright 1952 Charles Scribner's Sons), *Too Late the Phalarope* by Alan Paton (Copyright 1953 by Alan Paton), *Beyond Anxiety* by James A. Pike (Copyright 1953 James A. Pike), *Dominations and Powers* by George Santayana (Copyright 1951 Charles Scribner's Sons), *Triumphant Believing* by John Short (Copyright 1952 by Charles Scribner's Sons), *The Shaking of the Foundations* by Paul Tillich.

Speakers' Illustrations for Special Days

Charles L. Wallis Library, 0-8010-9715-0

1010 Sermon Illustrations from the Bible, 0-8010-9552-2

Speakers' Illustrations for Special Days, 0-8010-9555-7

A Treasury of Story Sermons for Children, 0-8010-9556-5

The Funeral Encyclopedia, 0-8010-9539-5

TO *Charles L. Allen*

PREFACE

The preparation of any book is a co-operative venture in which many persons, directly or indirectly, determine the scope and quality. A book of the character of this volume reflects many minds and moods, many talents and insights. I am keenly aware of my many debts, and especially do I wish to acknowledge with appreciation the assistance of those persons who in response to my request have generously contributed original materials. Nearly one fourth of the items have not been previously printed. I have carefully checked with similar volumes and have eliminated those materials which have already been anthologized.

This book has twenty-four main divisions according to the days and seasons most widely observed in the church and civil calendars.

There are two indexes. The first lists names of contributors, and the second is a cross index of subjects and ideas.

CHARLES L. WALLIS

CONTENTS

BROTHERHOOD WEEK

LENT AND EASTER

FESTIVAL OF THE CHRISTIAN HOME

CHILDREN'S DAY

FATHER'S DAY

NATURE SUNDAY

INDEPENDENCE DAY

LABOR DAY

WORLD-WIDE COMMUNION

UNITED NATIONS WEEK

REFORMATION DAY

WORLD TEMPERANCE DAY

STEWARDSHIP DAY

THANKSGIVING DAY

NEW YEAR'S DAY

THE FORWARD LOOK

1. The future is with men of faith. There is a striking monument to General Gordon outside the city of Khartoum in Egypt. It is a statue of Gordon sitting on a dromedary, and his face is toward the desert. A visitor one day, looking at it, said to the guide, "The face should be toward the city, toward the Nile from whence re-enforcements were to come to his relief." "No, sir," said the Arab, "he is not looking toward the city, not toward the Nile, but toward the desert, toward the Sudan, for which he died. He is waiting, sir, for the morning to dawn." That is the attitude of faith.

—Hugh Thomson Kerr in *Design for Christian Living*. Copyright, 1953, by W. L. Jenkins, The Westminster Press. Used by permission.

2. There is a striking incident related by Sholem Asch in his book *Kiddush Ha-Shem.* It occurred during the terrible Jewish massacre in Russian Poland of the seventeenth century. The Jewish section of the city of Lublin had been laid waste. Men and women and children had been slain; families had been divided and destroyed. Only death seemed to be alive. One of the survivors was walking through the streets in the denuded, deserted town, trying to understand the meaning of it all. The more he observed, the sadder he became with a sadness akin to doubt. As he passed the market place he saw merchants with their booths already set up for selling articles of food and clothing. There was one booth, however, that hypnotically drew his attention. In it was an old Jew, dressed in rags. It looked empty and devoid of goods. The sorrow-stricken, despair-filled man marveled at this strange sight. In amazement he went up to the owner and asked: "But your booth is empty. What do you sell?" The old Jew looked at him with a pitying smile. Slowly he said: "I sell faith. I sell faith."

—Reprinted with permission of publishers from *The Power of Faith,* by Louis Binstock. Copyright, 1952, by Prentice-Hall, Inc., 70 Fifth Avenue, New York 11, New York.

3. Clare Boothe Luce quotes the motto of Marshall Foch, the hero of Verdun: "There are no hopeless situations; there are only men who have grown hopeless about them."

—*Europe in the Spring,* Alfred A. Knopf, Inc.

4. Open the Bible almost anywhere at random and you will find a sentence beginning with the word, *Behold.* It is calling upon the reader to use all his powers to *see* what rods and cones are bound to miss. We are being asked to see with "new eyes." This call to "behold" expresses surprise, wonder, thrill,

joy, admiration. It is an attitude which we express with the exclamation point. If we could learn how to *behold* with new eyes we could more often supplement the interrogation point with the exclamation point of wonder and awe.
—RUFUS M. JONES in *New Eyes for Invisibles.* Copyright, 1943. Used by permission of The Macmillan Co.

5. In my life of professional teaching, I have never endeavoured to make young men more efficient; I have tried to make them more interesting. If one is interested, one is usually interesting. The business of the teacher is not to supply information, it is to raise a thirst. I like to hang pictures on the walls of the mind, I like to make it possible for a man to live with himself, so that he will not be bored with himself. For my own part, *I live every day as if this were the first day I had ever seen and the last I were going to see.*
—WILLIAM LYON PHELPS in *Autobiography with Letters,* Oxford University Press.

6. A student from Maine attending Yale told in a class of the town of Flagstaff which was taken over as part of a hydroelectric development. The town in Maine would be submerged as a result of the dam that was being built. In the months before this was accomplished, all improvements and repairs to homes and other buildings came to a dead stop. What is the sense of painting a house if it is going to be covered with water in six months? Why fix anything? So week by week the little town became more and more bedraggled, forlorn, and shabby. It had gone to seed long before the deluge came. One man explained it in these words: "Where there is no faith in the future, there is no power in the present."
—DAVID A. MACLENNAN in *The Upper Room Pulpit.*

7. Marguerite Higgins, a war correspondent, received the much-coveted Pulitzer Prize for international reporting, for her coverage of the Korean struggle. In her articles she refers to many interesting and deep-seated experiences. One is mentioned in an account of the Fifth Company of Marines, which originally numbered 18,000, in combat with more than 100,000 Chinese Communists. It was particularly cold—42 degrees below zero—that morning when reporters were standing around. The weary soldiers, half frozen, stood by their dirty trucks, eating from tin cans. A huge Marine was eating cold beans with his trench knife. His clothes were as stiff as a board. His face, covered with heavy beard, was crusted with mud. A correspondent asked him, "If I were God and could grant you anything you wished, what would you most like?" The man stood motionless for a moment, then he raised his head and replied, "Give me tomorrow."
—G. CURTIS JONES in *What Are You Worth?* Copyright 1954, Bethany Press.

8. A few years ago one of our nation's newest submarines "turned turtle" and sank, trapping its entire crew in a watery prison. For a while it seemed as though rescue operations might be possible. Contact with those inside was established. Feverish efforts were made to save them, but time ran out. The last message laboriously tapped out before their oxygen failed was this: "Is there any hope?" That is the question always at the back of our minds. We can stand anything as long as we feel that there is hope.
—RAYMOND E. BALCOMB in *Pulpit Digest.*

9. Shortly after the death of Thomas Carlyle two friends met. "So Carlyle is dead," one said. "Yes," answered the other, "he is gone, but he did me a

very good turn once." "Did you ever see him or hear him?" was the natural question. "No, but once when I was almost through my apprenticeship and was just beginning life, I lost all interest in everything and everyone. I felt as though I had no duty of importance to discharge, that it did not matter whether I lived or not, that the world could do as well without me. This continued for more than a year. One gloomy night, feeling that I could stand my distress no longer, I wandered into a library where I found Carlyle's *Sartor Resartus* lying open on a table. My eye fell upon one marked sentence: "Do the duty which lies nearest thee; which thou knowest to be a duty! The second duty will already become clearer." That sentence was a flash of lightning in my dark soul. It gave me a new glimpse of human existence. It made a changed man of me. Carlyle, under God, saved me and put content and purpose and power into my life."
—John C. Wiley

10. Humanity certainly needs practical men, who get the most out of their work, and, without forgetting the general good, safeguard their own interests. But humanity also needs dreamers, for whom the disinterested development of an enterprise is so captivating that it becomes impossible for them to devote their care to their own material profit.
—Marie Curie from: *Madame Curie,* by Eve Curie. Copyright 1937 by Doubleday & Company, Inc.

THE ROAD WE TAKE

11. If you are acquainted with the city of Charlotte, North Carolina, you may remember the time when you first tried to find your way around in the section of the city known as Myers Park. It is a jumble of streets which curve and cross one another with no apparent design.

Later on you discover that the key to the puzzle is a thoroughfare named Providence Road. Providence Road begins at Fourth Street and runs on out into the country. If you know where Providence Road is, you can pretty well find your way around. If you are looking for an address on Oxford Place, say, you consult your map and notice that Oxford Place turns to the right off Providence Road at the 1100 block, and there you are.

Now for many of us life is pretty much like the puzzle that is Myers Park. It looks like a jumble of streets that do not make sense, and a conglomeration of blind alleys that lead nowhere. Is there a Providence Road running through this map of life which can provide our cue?
—John A. Redhead in *Getting to Know God,* Abingdon Press.

12. How often on a plane I have heard the hostess ask, "Destination, please?" And always the passengers have an answer. How true it is that each moment of the day is asking that question of us: "Destination, please?" Where are we going in this life?
—Roy A. Burkhart

13. There is an old story to the effect that once a traveler in ancient Greece had lost his way and, seeking to find it, asked directions of a man by the roadside, who turned out to be Socrates. "How can I reach Mt. Olympus?" asked the traveler. To this Socrates is said to have replied gravely, "Just make every step you take go in that direction." A man who can keep his eye on his goal and not waste undue time or energy in answering critics is well on the way to his own Mt. Olympus, however modest his particular peak may be.
—Elton Trueblood in *The Life We Prize,* Harper & Bros.

14. Rufus Jones told of a man who asked a lad for directions to reach his destination. Said the boy: "If you go on the way you are headed, it will be about 25,000 miles, but if you turn right-about-face, it will be about 3 miles." It is a great personal tragedy when a man persists in stumbling blindly along in his own sinful way which leads nowhere. . . . He will find his goal of life-abundant close at hand when he turns face about and faces God.
—CHARLES M. CROWE in *Sermons on the Parables of Jesus,* Abingdon Press.

15. One night in New York on the subway I asked a man, "What is the nearest station to 181st street? I am not too familiar with the stations up that way." He said, "I don't know." "You don't know? Do you ride this line regularly?" "I ride it every night." "Don't you know the nearest station to 181st street?" "No," he said, "I never go above 168th street." His daily world, he explained, was from 168th street to 34th street. If such a person is not careful he may get the 34th street to 168th street mind after a while. You can live in the greatest city in the world and become awfully little by allowing your horizons to shrink and your visions of the great world to shrivel.
—HUGH L. DRYDEN in *The Pulpit.* Copyrighted by the Christian Century Foundation and used by permission.

16. G. K. Chesterton once took a train trip and on the way became so engrossed in his reading that he forgot where he was going. At a station stop, he called up his wife and asked her, "Where am I going?" She replied, "Look at your ticket." The irony of today's living is not so much that we do not know where we are going but that we have even forgotten that we have a ticket to that destination. Modern folks seem to have lost the faith that God has a destination for us, a specific plan for each life.
—J. R. BROKHOFF

17. One day an old man lay very ill. A friend came to see him and, after talking for a while, asked him, "In your long life, have you any regrets?" The old man's mind was away back in the days of his childhood. "When I was a boy," he said, "I often used to play with my school friends out on the roadside. One day, after my chums had gone away, I found at the corner of the road an old rickety signpost. I twisted it in its socket, so that its pointer arms pointed the wrong way. Just today, for some reason or other, I've been wondering how many travelers I sent that day on the wrong road."

That is just what sin is. Sin is that which sends other people on the wrong road in life. Sin is that which makes it harder for other people to live well.
—KENNETH D. HARVEY in *The Upper Room Pulpit.*

FRONTIERS AND HORIZONS

18. Men grow when inspired by a high purpose, when contemplating vast horizons. The sacrifice of oneself is not very difficult for one burning with the passion for a great adventure.
—ALEXIS CARREL in *Man, the Unknown,* Harper & Bros.

19. At the top of one hill the winding road to the top of the next hill looks perpendicular, and you wonder if your car can possibly make it. Yet a few moments later you realize that the car has the required power and the incline is not as steep as it had seemed from afar. Along the road toward tomorrow the way looks forbidding, but the man of faith has at his command such un-

dreamed of reserves that he may move ahead with confident trust.
—Robert C. Newell

20. The past is gone and static. Nothing we can do can change it. The future is before us and dynamic. Everything we do will affect it. Each day brings with it new frontiers, in our homes and in our businesses, if we will only recognize them. We are just at the beginning of progress in every field of human endeavor.
—Charles F. Kettering

21. One day the wife of Robert Louis Stevenson went into his bedroom when he had been forced to put aside his writing materials to stanch the life blood that he was coughing away through wracking pain. "I suppose you will tell me that it is a glorious day," she said. "Yes," he replied, "strange, isn't it, that I was just going to say that?" Looking at the sunlight streaming through the window, he continued, "I refuse to let a row of medicine bottles be the circumference of my horizon."
—Frank A. Court

22. One of the persons whom I most admire is Helen Keller. She has lived a rich and an abundant life in spite of her handicap of blindness. Her home in Long Island was sold some time ago, and the purchaser was amazed to find that it was a house of many windows. The living-room and dining-room windows looked over Long Island Sound. He asked her why, since she could not see, she was so meticulous in having so many beautiful windows. Miss Keller replied that just because she was blind was no reason why she needed to live in a room with just four walls. She wanted a room that looked out upon beauty so that, even though she could not see, she could stand before the window knowing that without was beauty and the far view of a horizon and there sense that view by the hunger within to know the loveliness without.
—Frank A. Court

23. I talked to a woman who had cataracts on her eyes which had gradually narrowed her vision to a thin point of light. Then she had an operation, and her eyes could see the wide horizon again. Until her operation she was a very gloomy person. After the operation her vision was again wide; and she became a changed person, alert and bright. She said, "You have no idea how much difference it makes to have a wide vision."
—Ensworth Reisner

24. When Marian Anderson went with her God-given voice to sing for the composer Sibelius in his home, the composer listened and said with tears in his voice, "My roof is too low for you!" . . . This world has too low a ceiling for aspiring man.
—J. Wallace Hamilton in *Ride the Wild Horses,* Fleming H. Revell Co.

25. A society woman once went to consult a famous psychotherapist. He said at the first interview, "Now tell me all about yourself." She needed no second invitation. At the end of the hour the doctor said, "That will do now; I'll see you again tomorrow." The same formula was repeated several times a week for some weeks. Then one day the doctor said to his patient: "Madam, I can do no more for you now. I advise you to take the first train to Niagara Falls, and there take a long, lingering look at something bigger than yourself."
—John Trevor Davies in *Lord of All,* Abingdon Press.

26. The power of God is the worship he inspires. That religion is strong which in its ritual and its modes of thought evokes an apprehension of the commanding vision. The worship of God is not a rule of safety—it is an adventure of the spirit, a flight after the unattainable. The death of religion comes with the repression of the high hope of adventure.
—Alfred North Whitehead in *Science and the Modern World.* Copyright 1939. Used by permission of The Macmillan Co.

27. Edgar DeWitt Jones recalls a time years ago when standing with an uncle on the sand dunes of Cape Henry, he watched a small schooner move proudly down the bay and turn toward the misty deep. He said: "What an adventure! So small a ship, so great an ocean!" "No, not as much of an adventure as you think," said his uncle. "You see, the ocean is charted, there's a navigator on board and a pilot. The strong likelihood is that that ship will reach her port, despite thick weather, storms and rough waves." "Jesus charted this life," Jones concludes, "and the other life for us; and he is the Pilot whom we hope to see when we 'have crossed the bar.' "
—*Sermons I Love to Preach,* Harper & Bros.

28. We live in both space and time. In moving through space we look ahead. The driver of a car or a plane sits at the front and peers before him. But in moving through time we cannot see ahead. We move into our tomorrows like persons rowing a boat, that is, with our backs to the prow. At Lake Mohonk I did a little rowing for exercise. Desiring to get the most physical exercise in the shortest possible time, I tried to see how hard and fast I could row. But I did not go very straight. In fact, I was becoming almost a public menace to the other boats on the lake because I could not see where I was going. So I would turn around and see in which direction the lake was clear and then get my line with some tree on the shore I was leaving. Thus I steered by the wake of my boat. So in life we can guide ourselves by the wake. We can chart our course by landmarks behind us in time.
—Ralph W. Sockman

THE MEASUREMENTS OF TIME

29. The Christian must view time always in two ways, paradoxically. To the Christian *each instant* is a sacrament, an intense encounter with reality. . . . His life has that inner unity which gives meaning to his every activity, so that time is regarded always with reverence. On the other hand, we must, as Christians, view life with what Mabel Cratty used to call "the thousand-year-look." . . . The quality of perspective and proportion which comes from the thousand-year-look is like the poise of the astronomer and the anthropologist whose attitudes have tone and quality because they are rooted in millions of light miles and aeons of human life.
—Winnifred Wygal in *Reflections of the Spirit,* Whiteside, Inc.

30. Time is our destiny. Time is our hope. Time is our despair. And time is the mirror in which we see eternity. Let me point to three of the many mysteries of time: its power to devour anything within its sphere; its power to receive eternity within itself; and its power to drive toward an ultimate end, a new creation.
—Paul Tillich in *The Shaking of the Foundations,* Chas. Scribner's Sons.

31. Malcolm Ross has written a book called *The Man Who Lived Backward.*

The author carries his central character, Mark Selby, through a long career of living backward. His life is lived from World War II back to the closing days of the Civil War. There he makes an effort to save Lincoln from being shot.

Too often we want to do this. We like to retreat into some comfortable shelter that lives in our memory. We are afraid of the unknown future. We resist change. We like to measure the changing present by some fixed point in the past. This shows lack of faith. God has made change a necessary part of life. He gives us the ability to adapt to changing conditions.

—CHARLES M. CROWE in *The Sanctuary,* 1952, Abingdon Press.

32. The French artist Lhermitte has given us a painting, "Fish Market at St. Malo," which portrays an early-morning scene at an open market. A woman in the foreground is holding up her fish. A more prominent figure has her fish on a board. Her knife is poised, waiting the word of the customer that she may slice off the specified amount. Under the print, which I have seen, is this comment: "Lhermitte was interested in giving the spectator a realistic interpretation of the French peasants. . . . His work has some similarity to that of the Impressionists in its attempt to catch *an exact moment of time.*"

Think of some of the great moments of time. That portrayed by Lerolle in "The Arrival of the Shepherds"; by Hoffman in "Christ and the Doctors"; the moment when Christ said, "Arise, and take up thy bed, and walk"; when he said, "Father, into thy hands I commend my spirit"; when he said, "Mary," to the frightened and bewildered woman in the Garden. Or the moment when you chose Christ above all!

—HOMER J. R. ELFORD

33. Alan Paton in *Too Late the Phalarope* describes the first sermon of the young dominie with these words:

—That's the sickness of our times, he said, that we are afraid to believe it any more. We think of ourselves as men in chains, in the prison of our natures and the world, able to do nothing, but having to suffer everything. God's plan? Ah that's another thing that's done to us, history, and war, and narrow parents, and poverty, and sickness, and sickness of soul, there's nothing we can do but to suffer them.

—It's a lie, he said, and again he struck the wood with his hand. It's the lie we tell to ourselves to hide the truth of our weakness and lack of faith. Is there not a gospel of God's love, that God's love can transform us, making us creators, not sufferers? I knew a man that counted the days, each day, every day, tearing them off on the little block that stood on his desk. He was always looking at his watch, and saying, it's one o'clock or it's four o'clock or it's nine o'clock, as though it were something for satisfaction. . . . I never saw him on New Year's Day, but I suppose he would have said, the Old Year's gone; he was waiting for death, though he didn't know it, because he was afraid of life, though he didn't know that either.

The young dominee's voice rose.

—I am come that ye might have life, and have it more abundantly, saith the Lord.

34. Jesus of Nazareth was master of the art of spending time. He never let it master him. He did not give the impression of dashing about Palestine trying to save time and keep to a schedule. He

knew that his earthly working days were short. He said so. There was an air of urgency about him, but there was no feverish hurrying. He had time to sit and talk with individuals along the way. He paused to play with little children. He took time off to spend whole hours in prayer. But was it taking time off? Off from what? Ah, Jesus was not keeping to a calendar. He was fulfilling a life. And if we are to fulfill life, we must live our days to the full, so putting our whole selves into the present moment that the moment becomes a bit of eternal life.
—RALPH W. SOCKMAN

35. "Due to circumstances beyond our control we are unable to continue with the program originally scheduled for this time." These words are familiar to the radio listener who knows that the station will "mark time" by broadcasting recorded music. Life is full of circumstances beyond our control, but it is not necessary for us merely to mark time. Paul hoped to go to Bithynia and do great things "but the Spirit suffered them not." Circumstances beyond the control of Paul and his associates did not make them mark time. They went on to Troas, and it was from that city that Paul received the Macedonian call.
—E. PAUL HOVEY

36. Fulton Oursler tells of a town in Cape Cod where the telephone operator received a call every morning asking for the correct time. Finally, impelled by curiosity, she asked the inquirer, "Would you mind telling me why you call about this time every day and ask for the correct time?" "Sure, I'll tell you," he said. "I want to get the exact time because I'm the man who blows the whistle at twelve o'clock." "Well, that's funny, that is," said the girl, "because every day at the stroke of noon I set our clock by your whistle." Isn't that a parable of human life? Multitudes of men and women take their moral and spiritual time from one another; the nations of the world take their moral and spiritual time and their national policies from their neighbors, with resulting confusion and conflict. As surely as we live, there will be personal antagonisms and warfare until we find a higher reference than the standards of men.
—JOHN SUTHERLAND BONNELL

INVENTORY AT NEW YEAR

37. The New Year seems a proper time for appraisal. During the past year our sense of values may have become confused. Lloyd C. Douglas in *Time to Remember* tells of a youthful correspondence between his brother Clyde and a youngster named Sam Logan. The Logan boy once wrote: "Dear Clyde. How are you? Well I hope. We are alright here. Do you still have the white rat? Mind that pair of rabbits I had? I have lots of rabbits. School has took up again. I hate school. Your friend, Sam Logan. P. S. Pap died last night."
—MERVIN C. HELFRICH. Quotation published by Houghton Mifflin Co.

38. Harry Emerson Fosdick tells the story of a man who was rowing down the Niagara River past Buffalo. He could not make up his mind whether or not to get off at Buffalo. First he thought he would; then he thought he wouldn't. He was undecided. Ultimately he awoke at the foot of Niagara Falls to discover that he had decided not to get off at Buffalo. He had decided by indecision.
—HENRY P. VAN DUSEN in *Life's Meaning*, Association Press.

39. Do you remember the newspaper report about the eighteen-year-old girl who

killed herself on New Year's Day? Before she died, she had written a letter telling of an agreement she had made with God, or fate, or something, the year before. "I agreed that if something did not happen in the year to make life worth living, I'd quit living. That wasn't asking too much, was it?" She had laid down her own conditions for life without attempting to understand those conditions which God had already written into the nature of the universe.
—E. PAUL HOVEY

40. A good old mother duck, who having for years led her ducklings to the same pond, when that pond has been drained and nothing is left but baked mud, will still persist in bringing her younglings down to it, and walks about with flapping wings and anxious quack, trying to induce them to enter it. But the ducklings, with fresh instincts, hear far off the delicious drippings from the new dam which has been built higher up to catch the water, and they smell the chickweed and the long grass that is growing up beside it; and absolutely refuse to disport themselves on the baked mud and to pretend to seek for worms where no worms are. And they leave the ancient mother quacking beside her pond and set out to seek for new pastures —perhaps to lose themselves upon the way? Perhaps to find them? To the old mother one is inclined to say: "Ah, good old mother duck, you cannot see the world has changed? You cannot bring the water back into the dried-up pond! Mayhap it was better and pleasanter when it was there, but it has gone forever; and, would you and yours swim again, it must be in other waters."
—OLIVE SCHREINER in *Woman and Labour,* Ernest Benn, Ltd.

41. In museums we have all seen cords stretched across the arms of old chairs and small signs which read: "Do not sit in this chair." Long ago the chairs were sturdy enough to bear the weight of the heaviest guest, but now they are antiques and good only to look at in museums. What of the outmoded prejudices and outdated opinions, the antiques in our hearts and souls? Our hearts need signs which read: "Do not lean on this old custom." "Do not rely on this inadequate belief." How dangerous can be our use of antiquated customs and ideas!
—GLENN H. ASQUITH

42. Some years ago when oil was first discovered in the then Indian Territory, now Oklahoma, one of our eastern dailies sent a reporter down to get the story. In the course of his report he spoke of a visit to the farm on which the most productive well had just been opened. It had belonged to a family which had moved out a generation before from North Carolina and by great effort had won a livelihood on none too fertile soil. The sons and daughters as they grew up had to leave home and seek their livings elsewhere. Then one day a party of men had come along, made some investigations, and asked the farmer's wife for a drink. She had drawn up the bucket from the well, and was astonished to see them put some of the water in a bottle and take it off with them. A week or so later they had returned and offered the farmer a price for his land far in excess of what he had thought it worth. He sold it; and the reporter told of a well sunk just between the house and the barn, and of the startling gallons of oil pumped up daily. At the time of his visit, he found the elderly couple leaning on a fence watching the operation at the pump, and overheard the woman say to her husband:

"To think that all that was at our doorstep, and we never guessed it!"

In God we live and move and have our being. He in all his unsearchable richness is not far from any one of us, and yet—men and women live and die as orphans, and congregations appear weak and ineffective, and the church exists almost lifeless and inert.
—Henry Sloane Coffin in *Religion in Life.*

43. Life needs growth—growth of mind, heart, and experience. Every day should add a measure of breadth and depth to life. A story is told of a headmaster of a New England school who appointed a young man to be a department chairman. He was offered the position despite the fact that several of his colleagues had served the school for longer periods of time. When one of them remonstrated, the headmaster said: "In reality you haven't had twenty years' experience. You have had one year's experience twenty times over."

44. A New Yorker who prided himself on his knowledge of the intricacies of the city took his oriental friend from one point to another on the subway. Starting out with seats on a local train, he pulled his friend to the door at a given stop and propelled him across the crowded platform and into an express train, where they stood the rest of the way to their destination. As they hurried across the platform to the escalator, the New Yorker explained triumphantly to his oriental friend that by changing trains they had saved two minutes. And as they mounted the escalator the New Yorker heard the quiet question, "What significant thing shall we do with the two minutes we have saved?"
—Loring D. Chase in *The Pulpit.* Copyrighted by The Christian Century Foundation and used by permission.

45. A noisy little boy once became very quiet. His mother, wondering if he were in some mischief, searched for him and at last found him sitting in a chair doing nothing. She asked, "Maurice, what are you doing?" He indignantly answered: "Can't you see? I'm just livin'." When we stop what we are doing and relax, we will begin to live. In solitude and meditation we will find our life in God.
—J. R. Brokhoff

46. In the language of [China] there is hardly a more suggestive or challenging word than "crisis." It is made up of two characters, *way gee.* Each of these is half a word, the first being "danger" and the second "opportunity." Hence a "crisis" is literally a "dangerous opportunity."
—Earle H. Ballou in *Dangerous Opportunity,* Friendship Press.

47. It is the content of our lives that determines their value. If we limit ourselves to supply the means of living, in what way have we placed ourselves above the cattle that graze the fields? Cattle can live in comfort. Their every need is amply supplied. Is it not when one exercises his reason, his love of beauty, his desire for friendship, his selection of the good from that which is not so good, that he earns the right to call himself a man? I should be inclined to claim that the person who limits his interests to the means of living without consideration of the content or meaning of his life is defeating God's great purpose when he brought into existence a creature with the intelligent and godlike powers that are found in man. It is in living wisely and fully that one's soul grows.
—Arthur H. Compton in *The Human Meaning of Science,* University of North Carolina Press.

48. Antoine de Saint Exupéry in *Wind, Sand and Stars* tells about the rescue of his friend, Guillaumet, an air pilot whose plane had been forced down on a frozen crag of the Andes. Guillaumet, who was not equipped to face the cold and ice, had determined to die standing so that rescuers might find his body and his wife could claim their small insurance. When he was at last found, he mumbled through frozen lips: "I swear that what I went through, no animal would have gone through." The author adds: "This sentence, the noblest ever spoken, this sentence that defines man's place in the universe, that honors him, that re-establishes the true hierarchy, floated back into my thoughts."
—Harcourt, Brace & Co., Inc.

49. Dean Wicks of Princeton once told of a friend of his who took a victrola record of a Brahms symphony, bored a hole just off the center, and played the record. What should have sounded like heavenly music, when played on the off-center hole, sounded like the cracklings of fiends in hell. On what center will you play the record of your own life? . . . Try playing the record of your brief years on the center of the worship and love of God, and there will be harmony, for you will have hit upon that center which is the true center of your inmost being.
—Waldo Beach in *The Intercollegian.*

50. When Cortez disembarked his five hundred conquistadors upon the eastern coast of Mexico, he set fire to the ships. His warriors, watching their means of retreat burning in the harbor, knew that they were committed with their lives to the conquest of the new world for Spain. All doubt had been cauterized from their minds. Similarly, everyone who first sets foot on the shore of discipleship is called upon to burn his ships in the harbor.
—Dwight E. Stevenson in *Faith Takes a Name,* Harper & Bros.

51. I well recall the time Shailer Mathews, dean of the Divinity School of the University of Chicago, came to class a few minutes late. There was a twinkle in his eye as he explained his tardiness: "A reporter from one of the papers was calling to find out whether I have written or done anything lately that deserves space in my obituary!" This serves to remind us that obituaries, while published after death, are actually written in life.
—Harold A. Bosley in *Preaching on Controversial Issues,* published in 1953 by Harper & Brothers.

WEEK OF PRAYER

MEANING OF PRAYER

52. High prayer is an art. . . . Every art demands elimination. The pianist cannot risk his fingers in baseball. The painter cannot imperil his eyes for the sake of his appetite. The singer must scrupulously guard not only her throat but her general health as well. . . . If we want to be artists of the spirit we must set up some taboos in our . . . life. The dream of communion with God must have precedence over everything else. "This one thing I do."

Nor is that a sacrifice. It is a joy!

—ALBERT E. DAY in *An Autobiography of Prayer,* published in 1952 by Harper & Brothers.

53. Prayer is need finding a voice. Prayer is embarrassment seeking relief. Prayer is friend in search of friend. Prayer is a quest in the darkness of midnight. Prayer is knocking on a barred door. Prayer is communion through both darkness and closed doors. Prayer is shameless insistence in the name of another. Prayer is expecting and receiving all things whatsoever we need to meet the demands when Jesus our Friend calls on us.

—RALPH A. HERRING in *The Pulpit in the South,* Frank S. Mead, ed., Fleming H. Revell Co.

54. Marconi wrote as if wireless telegraphy made it easier for him to believe in profounder forms of communication: "Every scientist knows that there are mysteries which science will never be able to solve. . . . I am proud of saying that I am a Christian and a believer. I believe in the power of prayer. I believe in it not only as a devout Catholic but as a scientist. A wireless set no bigger than your hand can transmit messages across the ocean, but the human brain is something far more intricate than anything else devised by man. The wireless set sends out vibrations to their destinations; is it not reasonable to believe that this greater miracle, this superset, which is called the human brain, may send out vibrations in the form of prayer which, too, reach their destination?"

—From *Two Worlds for Memory,* by ALFRED NOYES. Copyright, 1953, by Alfred Noyes. Published by J. B. Lippincott Company.

55. When John Ruskin wanted his art students to enter into a genuine fellowship with color, he had them take an opal and stare at it intently from one angle and another daily, until, as he said, they came to "know it by heart." . . . The achievements of prayer demand a similar concentration—what the Bible calls a "mind stayed on Thee," and means when it exhorts us, "search with all your heart."

—ALBERT E. DAY in *An Autobiography*

of Prayer, published in 1952 by Harper & Brothers.

56. As we grow in the life of the spirit, a great simplification of life begins to settle upon us. Many things we once would have prayed for, and would have regarded as needful to our spiritual growth, now seem quite unessential or even unencumbering. The mother in André Gide's novel, *The Counterfeiters,* confides to her guest, "I have learned to ask less and less of life . . . and of myself, more and more." The result of much prayer is for us to be brought to this simplification of our needs, and this offering back of ourselves to God.
—John L. Casteel in *Rediscovering Prayer,* Association Press. Quotation published by Alfred A. Knopf, Inc.

TIME FOR RENEWAL

57. The scientist Michael Faraday concluded a successful lecture to a distinguished London audience. When the enthusiastic applause had subsided, the Prince of Wales proposed a motion of congratulation. This was seconded, and the motion was carried amid thunderous cheers. The uproar was followed, however, by a strange silence. The crowd waited anxiously for Faraday's reply, but he had vanished. He was later located at a little meetinghouse nearby where he served as an elder. The lecture had been concluded in time for him to attend, as was his custom, the midweek service.
—J. Calvert Cariss

58. I visited George Washington Carver's laboratory in Tuskegee, Alabama, and was shown the windows nailed shut with blinds or boards over them so that the curious could not peek in. Then I learned from a man who had been his assistant that Carver did that not only to keep the prying eyes of the curious away from his experiments but also that people would not know the hours of time he spent just standing at his laboratory bench in prayer.
—Ensworth Reisner

59. The Harvard Classics were published on the premise that if an individual would regularly give a few minutes a day to reading and study of the contents of the volumes, he would be familiar with much of the distilled wisdom of the race. The premise is sound. Spiritual growth, too, requires time each day given to meditation, to prayer, to honest thought about the purpose of life and how it best may be lived and as to the best way to accomplish those purposes.
—From *Personal Security Through Faith* by Lowell Russell Ditzen. Copyright, 1954, by Henry Holt and Company, Inc. Reprinted by permission of the publishers.

60. Often a sign near the front door reads, "Make all deliveries at the rear." It is because of those deliveries at the rear that we are able to maintain the house. It is the period of private devotions, the time of prayer and meditation, that enables the Christian to face all phases of life victoriously. Maintain your Christian poise by keeping the "service entrance" ever ready to receive the blessings of God which give us the power to face life.
—E. Paul Hovey

61. Anatole France told the story of a young French writer who suddenly became famous and brought all Paris to his feet. Thinking the experience might spoil him, France said, "You keep your head, young man," to which the youth responded: "Before I knew the drawing

rooms of Paris, I dwelt in the Louvre and the great cathedrals."
—FRED R. CHENAULT

62. There is an ancient story which relates that many men, having determined to build a community structure, went individually to the forests to secure timber. Some of the men returned tired and exhausted, but one man was refreshed and strong. Yet he had returned with the heaviest burden. He had cut down a fruit tree; and as he hauled it away, he occasionally paused to take nourishment from the fruit on the branches. In our struggle to build Christlike lives we find soul strength as we pause to nourish our spirits by prayer and meditation.
—ROBERT C. NEWELL

63. A clergyman on one occasion was in the course of a walk along a public highway and stopped to watch a stone breaker at work. He said to him, "Your job is rather like mine. You are busy breaking stones. I notice that you are always striking at the heart. Breaking stony hearts—that's my job too." "Yes," said the stone breaker, "but you will notice I always do my job on my knees."
—ROBERT MENZIES in *Fight the Good Fight,* Abingdon Press.

64. The most difficult thing in the life of a busy downtown city pastor is that of setting aside a period of time each day for the renewal of the inner man. A clergyman acquaintance set aside a time each day for such meditation and left word with his wife that he should be disturbed under no circumstances. One day an important official of the church insisted upon talking to him. Reluctantly his wife called him to the phone, and the official, starting the conversation, said, "I hope I didn't bother you." The clergyman replied, "No, no more than you would be bothering a surgeon in the midst of an important operation." We may not agree with the caustic manner with which he spoke, for there are times when the insistent call of someone is God's reply to our seeking him in meditation, but the story does emphasize the importance of our daily need to renew the inner man.
—ENSWORTH REISNER

65. J. C. Penney has told of a man who was packing his bag to spend a few days at a spiritual retreat. His young son heard him say that he was "making a retreat" that week end. Knowing best the language of war, the lad asked, "Retreat, Dad? Who is after you?" As Penney added, it is not so much who but what is after modern man.
—RALPH W. SOCKMAN

66. An old shepherd who offered prayer in a Welsh revival lamented his backsliding in these words: "Lord, I got among the thorns and briars, and was scratched and torn and bleeding. But, Lord, it is only fair to say it was not on that ground. I had wandered out of thy pasture."
—IRA M. HARGETT

THE LIFE OF PRAYER

67. Henry Sloane Coffin . . . tells of a great Scottish preacher in an earlier century who kept the congregation waiting for a long time while he tarried in the vesting room. At length some of those who had grown impatient sent the sexton [who] returned and said that his knock was not answered but that he heard the preacher . . . apparently talking to someone else. This other was not heard to answer, but the preacher kept saying to him, "I cannot go, I will not go, unless you go with me." And

the historian adds that when he did come forth and enter the church and climb up into the pulpit, "he was singularly assisted."
—Walter Russell Bowie in *Preaching,* Abingdon Press.

68. Jenny Lind always spent a few minutes alone in her dressing room before a concert. Her maid, who locked the door and stood guard over it, has told what happened in those last moments of preparation. Miss Lind would stand in the middle of the floor, her shoulders back and her head up, draw a deep breath, strike a clear, vibrant note, and hold it as long as her breath lasted. When the overtones had all died away, she would look up and say: "Master, let me ring true tonight!"
—James P. Wilbourn in *Pulpit Digest.*

69. In the Phillips Brooks House at Harvard there is a small bronze plaque under the bust of Brooks which reads: "This house is dedicated to Piety, Charity, and Hospitality." But directly underneath was tacked a white card which read: "No Trespassing. Unauthorized Persons are not Allowed in This Bldg." This is too often the case with our prayers. It does us no good to pray for God's will to be done when we are determined to have our own way.
—Charles M. Crowe in *On Living With Yourself,* Abingdon Press.

70. On the night of July 10-11, 1943, a vast armada of 3,000 ships containing 80,000 Allied soldiers sailed across the waters from Malta to the shores of Sicily in a great amphibious operation. General Eisenhower, surrounded by his staff officers, stood on a high hill overlooking Malta harbor. In the light of a full moon shining down on the sea he watched the troop-laden ships weigh anchor and sail out into the mists while squadrons of planes roared into the sky. Deeply moved, Eisenhower sprang to attention and saluted his heroic men. Then he bowed his head in silent prayer—his staff joining him in this brief act of devotion. Turning to an officer beside him, Eisenhower said: "There comes a time when you've used your brains, your training, your technical skill, and the die is cast and the events are in the hands of God, and there you have to leave them."
—John Sutherland Bonnell in *The Practice and Power of Prayer.* Copyright, 1954, by W. L. Jenkins, The Westminster Press. Used by permission.

71. A woman was asked, "What did you pray for today?" To which she replied, "Oh, I am passed that—just asking for things—I have taken the lid off my soul!"
—Louis H. Evans in *The Kingdom Is Yours,* Fleming H. Revell Co.

72. Once a mother heard her son praying. She noticed that what he was doing was telling God what he planned to do and seeking to direct God to help him. She said to him, "Son, don't bother to give God instructions; just report for duty."
—Robert O. Smith

73. Bernard Iddings Bell tells of a boy who went into a church to pray. The rector, observing that he had done this on several occasions, asked him what he said to the Lord in his prayer, and he answered with childlike simplicity, "Oh, I was just loving him awhile."
—Lynn James Radcliffe in *Making Prayer Real,* Abingdon Press.

74. Origen, the influential church leader of the third century, was a re-

markable scholar who made a unique contribution in the fields of Bible study and of theology. He wrote the first Christian philosophy of religion, and for centuries after him all Christian thought has been marked by his influence. But when Bishop Brooke F. Westcott writes of him, the most significant thing he says does not have reference to Origen's scholarship. He speaks of his saintly life and the intimacy of his communion with God in declaring: "His life was one unbroken prayer." Here was a man intellectually keen and highly educated, but the thing that was most outstanding about him was not his colossal contribution to Christian knowledge and thought; it was the fact that his life was lived in intimate fellowship with the Eternal.

—SANDFORD FLEMING in *The Upper Room Pulpit.*

ANSWERED PETITIONS

75. In Lloyd C. Douglas' novel *The Big Fisherman* a Roman officer prays for Peter's life. But Peter is condemned to die. "I have prayed for you, Peter," murmured Mencius, "but it hasn't done you any good." "I'm sure it has!" said Peter. "I haven't been afraid."

—Houghton Mifflin Co.

76. Much humility is needed if we are to pray effectively. We simply do not always know what is good for us. We may earnestly desire some particular good and yet, if it were granted, it might be disastrous. "I have never dared to ask worldly success for my children," says James I. Vance. "I have been afraid. I have seen too many ruined by prosperity." Realizing the limitation of his own outlook, Fénelon hesitated to make any specific request of God. "Lord," he prayed, "I know not what I ought to ask of thee; thou only knowest what I need; thou lovest me better than I know how to love myself. O Father, give to thy child that which he himself knows not how to ask."

—KARL H. A. REST

77. Men do not really pray until they are willing to work. Former Governor William E. Russell, of Massachusetts, had his boat to overturn about a mile from shore. He was not a good swimmer, and those on shore despaired of his life. When he finally reached safety, they exclaimed, "Mr. Russell, how on earth did you ever make it?" He replied, "I don't know. All I know is that I prayed to God, and kept my arms and legs in stroke." Here then is the secret of prevailing prayer.

—HERSCHEL H. HOBBS in *Cowards or Conquerors.* Copyright, 1951, by The Judson Press. Used by permission.

78. Answers to prayer often come in unexpected ways. We pray, for instance, for a certain virtue; but God seldom delivers Christian virtues all wrapped in a package and ready for use. Rather he puts us in situations where by his help we can develop those virtues. Henry Ward Beecher told of a woman who prayed for patience, and God sent her a poor cook. The best answers to prayer may be the vision and strength to meet a circumstance or to assume a responsibility.

—C. R. FINDLEY

79. A severe storm blew against the log cabin; and Esther Green, fearful that the single window and door would not withstand the winds, tossed and turned on her bed. Peace and sleep came when she heard the voice of God saying to her: "Haven't I always been with you? Have I ever left you alone? I am always

with you in the time of storm." On the morning following, when the clouds had passed and the sun was shining, she found one of her children sick and with a high temperature. She became fearful lest her child should die before a doctor could be called. Then the voice of God returned to her: "Trust me, for not only am I with you when the storm is outside your home, but I am with you when the storm is inside your house."
—Floyd Massey, Jr.

80. Fosdick tells the story of a father and his two sons who were caught in a fishing boat off the rugged coast of Maine during a storm. When it looked like all was lost, the father put his arms around his sons and said, "Over on the coast there is a little woman praying for the safe return of her husband and sons. To the riggin', boys, let's help her get that prayer answered."
—Gaston Foote in *Living in Four Dimensions,* Fleming H. Revell Co.

CLOSED CHANNELS

81. A man who was sprinkling his lawn became greatly disturbed when no water poured from the hose. The small boy at his side exclaimed, "Grandpa, you have your foot on the hose!" Our communion with God is perfected only when self-centered concerns are not allowed to close the spiritual channels of our lives.
—Aaron N. Meckel

82. My faithful and wise maid said in response to the question of what keeps people from praying, "Too stiff to bend, I guess."
—Theodore Parker Ferris, *This Is the Day* (Greenwich: The Seabury Press, 1954), p. 52. Used by permission of the publisher.

83. Sarah Vaughn's little niece was being told about prayers. They were explained to her as being like telegrams to God. "Is that why we send them at night," asked the child, "to get the cheaper rate?"
—Charles M. Crowe in *On Living With Yourself,* Abingdon Press.

84. John Henry Jowett told a story about two little girls. One was at the top of her class, and the other was at the bottom. The one at the bottom asked, "How is it that you are always at the top and I am always at the bottom?" The one at the top said, "I always ask Jesus to help me in my studies." The other girl said, "I'll try that too." A few days passed by, and nothing happened. So the one at the bottom said, "I thought you said if you asked Jesus to help you, he would." "Oh," said the other, "he will. How much do you study?" The little girl at the bottom said, "I never study. I thought if you asked Jesus to help, that was all you had to do."
—Gerald Kennedy

85. Once in London during the war I asked a group of young people if they would answer a question quickly, without reflection. "O.K.," they said. "The question," I said, "is this: Do you think God understands radar?" They all said "No," and then, of course, roared with laughter as they realized how ridiculous the answer was! But the "snap answer" showed me what I suspected—*that at the back of their minds* there was an idea of God as an old gentleman who lived in the past and was rather bewildered by modern progress.
—J. B. Phillips in *Plain Christianity.* Copyright 1954. Used by permission of the Macmillan Co.

86. A nine-year-old went to visit his grandparents in the country during Lent, and because no sitter was available on prayer-meeting night he went along to the meeting. He had a wonderful time. The minister read stories which he called parables and then he told other stories to match them. He made points about things that would be good for the world and then someone prayed about each point. It seemed to the boy that the world must soon be a much better place and he felt as if he were in on big business for the Kingdom. When he got home from prayer meeting he took the half hour before his bed time to write to his mother. On Easter his mother arrived for a visit. One of her first remarks was addressed to the child's grandmother. "My goodness! he looks well. I was a little worried about his going to so many parties on school nights." The grandmother was surprised. "Why, he never went to a party on a school night!" The child looked up from his Easter eggs, "Oh, I always wrote her I'd been to a party on Thursday night because she wouldn't understand what a prayer meeting was."

—MARGUERITTE HARMON BRO in *More Than We Are,* Harper & Bros.

87. When Herodotus, the ancient historian, wished to become a war correspondent, he was advised to consult the oracle at Delphi for permission. At the shrine he prayed. "O gods, which of you should be my patrons as I undertake this venture?" Like many another prayer of pagan and Christian, he did not ask concerning the advisability of the course of action; he asked rather for the gods' blessing upon his own decision.

—A. D. JOHNSON

88. A well-known American professor addressed an educational convention in New York not long ago. Speaking of the problem of teaching unco-operative youth, he remarked that it makes one "understand what a dynamo feels like when it is discharging into a nonconductor." . . . Immediately I thought of the immense generators and dynamos at Niagara Falls and the high-tension wires that span northern New York, carrying light and power to homes, stores, and the streets of towns and cities. Yet out on the open countryside there may still be found darkened homes. The wires are there, the power is there, but there is no conductor to carry the electric current into the homes. How like so many of our churches, homes, and lives! God's eternal power waits, but there are too many nonconductors frustrating his divine purposes.

—JOHN SUTHERLAND BONNELL in *The Practice and Power of Prayer.* Copyright, 1954, by W. L. Jenkins, The Westminster Press. Used by permission.

89. In the days when the British empire was a great colonial power, the Britisher, wherever he went, took his bath every day, dressed for dinner, and kept his body in good shape. He had a fear of "going native." There are stories of men who with less pride went native in strange countries and among unknown people. Their moral standards fell apart. They no longer read challenging books. Their bodies became dirty and unkempt. Something like this happens to Christians who, living in an environment without an inspiring spiritual climate, fail to maintain their Christian life and growth. They go native by mimicking the life about them.

—HERBERT W. HANSEN

MISSIONARY DAY

THE MISSION MIND

90. [Nurse Emma Haussknecht of the Lambaréné mission tells how] Dr. [Albert] Schweitzer still makes the last rounds of all the patients in the hospital every night, because two years ago one of them, in reply to his morning greeting, said that he had not slept at all the night before, "waiting for you to say good night." . . . "It is a privilege just to live in the neighborhood of such a man," Nurse Haussknecht exclaims. "There are so many different kinds of things to do, that you have to develop every gift you have. . . . Sometimes it is very difficult to live without any comfort at all. But I wouldn't have missed those years of my life."
—Courtesy *Time.* Copyright Time, Inc., 1954.

91. At the heart of the life of Albert Schweitzer there is the feeling of indebtedness to Almighty God. "I was stabbed awake one morning with the realization that I could not accept life's happiness as a matter of course," he has written. "I must give something in return. I was made to see the deeper meaning of the passage 'He that loseth his life shall find it.' " He gathered up his life philosophy in four unforgettable sentences:

"To know the will of God is the greatest knowledge.

To suffer the will of God is the greatest heroism.

To do the will of God is the greatest achievement.

To have the approval of God on your work is the greatest happiness."
—Frank A. Court

92. Albert Schweitzer has written of a conversation with a patient whose sickness had been healed: "Hardly had he recovered his senses when he glanced about him in amazement and repeated over and over again, 'It's stopped hurting! It's stopped, I tell you!' His black hand groped for mine and wouldn't let go. And I began telling him, and his friends, that it was our Lord's wish that the doctor and his wife should come out to the Ogowe. In Europe, I told them, there were other white men who had made it possible for us to come out and live among our patients. And then they asked me what manner of people these were. Who were they? Where did they live? How did they know that the natives were suffering? The African sun blazed down and lit up the darkened hut as it stood in its grove of coffee-shrubs. And we all, black men and white men alike, knew that we were bringing to life Christ's words: all men are brothers."
—Jacques Feschotte in *Albert Schweitzer,* Beacon Press.

93. In *The Unrecognized Christ* John Gardner tells of a friend who went as a

missionary to the Fly River region of New Guinea to take the place of the murdered James Chalmers. On a furlough he told Gardner of the type of people he found there. They seemed utterly devoid of moral sense. If a baby began to cry, the mother would throw it into a ditch and leave it to die. If a man broke his leg, he too would be left by the roadside to fend for himself. "Well, what did you do for people like that? Did you preach to them?" Gardner asked. "Preach! No, I lived!" was the reply. "When I saw a forsaken baby crying, I comforted it. When I saw a man with a broken leg, I mended it. When I saw people in distress, I took them in and pitied them. . . . And those people began to come to me and say: 'What does this mean? What are you doing this for?' Then I had my chance and I preached the gospel." Gardner asked, "Did you succeed?" The missionary responded, "When I left, I left a church."
—Herbert Booth Smith. Quotation published by Fleming H. Revell Co.

94. Francis Xavier Ford of the Maryknoll Society, first American Roman Catholic bishop and fourth American civilian known to have died in the prisons of Red China . . . neither courted martyrdom nor shirked it. On first arriving in China, he uttered this prayer: "Lord, make us the doorstep by which the multitudes may come to worship Thee, and if . . . we are ground underfoot and spat upon and worn out, at least we . . . shall have become the King's Highway in pathless China."
—Courtesy *Time*. Copyright Time, Inc., 1952.

95. One day I walked around the gray field-stone wall which encircles old Canterbury Cathedral in southern England. I kept saying to myself: "This wall has been rebuilt, but just imagine, it was first built by missionaries hundreds of years ago." The heroism of Christian pioneers moving into a new and pagan land to bring the good news—what power for missions there was in those days! Pilgrim monks tramped weed-grown Roman roads and made the out-of-doors their sanctuary. Later, in great halls, sat bearded, tawny kings of Saxon England, swords on knees, listening like little children to the story of Christ. Then slowly the wild old gods Woden and Thor left nothing behind them but the names "Wednesday" and "Thursday," as they crept into the twilight before the coming of the light.
—Gordon M. Torgersen in *Missions,* Vol. 151, No. 9, p. 37.

96. An African chief is said to have defined the problem of Christian education as similar to that of ivory hunting. "You go hunting ivory, . . . and you find that there is always an elephant attached." That precisely is the problem of the Christian frontier. You start out to educate people in Christian faith and discover that you must educate them for all of life.
—D. T. Niles in *That They May Have Life,* Harper & Bros.

97. A teacher helping in the Church School of Missions used a chart indicating the number of Christians in the world and the number of non-Christians by the simple means of black and white circles. The next day one of the parents phoned the teacher to say that before her little boy had gone to bed he had prayed: "Dear Jesus, help me to grow up to be a man, and when I get to be a man make me a good man, so I can make the black circle smaller and the white circle bigger."
—Margaret McCord Lee *in The Presbyterian Tribune.*

98. A member of the State Department was giving an address in a certain community. A woman in the audience asked such intelligent questions about the conditions in those countries that the speaker asked at the close of the meeting, "Was your husband ever in the State Department?" "No." "Was he ever in the Consular service?" "No." "Well, why are you so well informed about those countries?" "I am president of the missionary society in my church," was the modest reply.

—Warren D. Bowman in *The Upper Room Pulpit.*

A WORLD TO WIN

99. Across the desk of a leading Communist in New York is stretched in large letters this challenging inscription: *"A World to Win!"* It is a constant reminder to him and all who come to see him that there is nothing local or limited about the Communist goal. No matter how insignificantly placed they may be, their missionary aim is not two blocks or their own little environment. It is the *world!* Every move they make is a move for *all* mankind. Because of their global vision, they become ten times as effective in whatever area they find themselves. Where did the Communists get their broad-gauged vision? Why is it when they take a job it is seldom, if ever, a routine one? Why is it nearly always a creative post that touches the lives of the multitude, not merely the few? Why is it that every true Communist displays such driving purpose, enterprise and directions? Why is he willing to put up with endless delays, hard work, inconvenience, misunderstanding, boredom, setbacks, suffering, and even defeat, in his extraordinary allegiance to his cause? In the answer to these questions, there are many factors. But outranking them all, believe it or not, is the broad-visioned daring of Christ in which they have been thoroughly indoctrinated *—while at the same time schooled to REJECT his Truth.*

—James Keller in *You Can Change the World,* Longmans, Green & Co., Inc.

100. When Socrates was describing the ideal way of life and the ideal society, Glaucon countered: "Socrates, I do not believe that there is such a City of God anywhere on earth." Socrates answered, "Whether such a city exists in heaven or ever will exist on earth, the wise men will live after the manner of that city, having nothing to do with any other, and in so looking upon it, will set his own house in order."

—Rollo May in *Man's Search for Himself,* W. W. Norton & Co., Inc.

101. White men have often exploited and degraded the natives in colonial areas. Here is the first letter written in English by a Congo convert, named Ugalla, and addressed to the Archbishop of Canterbury: "Great and good chief of the tribe of Christ, greetings! The humblest of your servants kisses the hem of your garment and begs you to send to his fellow servants more gospel and less rum. In the bonds of Christ, Ugalla."

—Charles B. Foelsch in *The Pulpit.* Copyrighted by the Christian Century Foundation and used by permission.

102. Asked by a Hindu why he and his wife had come to India, a young missionary replied: "We are here because Christlike character is the highest that we know, because Christ gives men a free, full life, and, most important of all, he gives them God. And we do not know of anyone else who does do these things except Christ."

—Robert J. McCracken

103. Just before World War II, we visited various mission fields both in China and India. We went into schools both government and mission. One day I said to my guide, a missionary, "Is it prejudice on my part or do the children in the mission schools really have a different look from those of the government schools?" My friend answered, "Everyone who comes here observes the same difference. Christ and the Christian home makes all the difference."
—THOMAS TAYLOR FAICHNEY in *The Upper Room Pulpit.*

104. In the beginning of the Christian cause all were ministers. *Member* equaled *evangelist* equaled *missionary*. There was no place within the society for the observer, the mere supporter or the nominal member. This is the conclusion of Auguste Sabatier, on the basis of his monumental study of early Christianity, and as expressed in his definitive work of scholarship. "At this period," he says, "we find no trace of a division of Christians into clergy and laity. All formed the elect people, and conversely, this people was collectively a people of priests and prophets. There were no passive members. The most humble had their share of activity and were by no means least necessary."
—ELTON TRUEBLOOD in *Alternative to Futility,* Harper & Bros.

105. Our religion begins at home, but it does not stay at home. Jesus did not heal the last person in one town before he healed the first person in the next town. Ours is a begin-at-home religion but not a stay-at-home religion.
—ROLLAND W. SCHLOERB

106. Some years ago I asked a medical missionary in the Belgian Congo about the supply of doctors and nurses in a village of some 50,000 people. He said there was no doctor there at all. There were two overworked nurses and a hospital of some twenty beds. A neighboring doctor called once a week. "A doctor in that village," he said, "could save 10,000 lives that will otherwise die." That's a worthy ambition for some young man.
—GASTON FOOTE in *Living in Four Dimensions,* Fleming H. Revell Co.

107. Open your eyes and look for a human being, or some work devoted to human welfare, which needs from someone a little time or friendliness, a little sympathy, or sociability, or labour. There may be a solitary or an embittered fellow-man, an invalid or an inefficient person to whom you can be something. Perhaps it is an old person or a child. Or some good work needs volunteers who can offer a free evening, or run errands. Who can enumerate the many ways in which that costly piece of working capital, a human being, can be employed? More of him is wanted everywhere! Search, then, for some investment for your humanity, and do not be frightened away if you have to wait, or to be taken on trial. And be prepared for disappointments. But in any case, do not be without some secondary work in which you can give yourself as a man to men. It is marked out for you, if you only truly will to have it.
—ALBERT SCHWEITZER in *The Philosophy of Civilization.* Copyright 1949. Used by permission of The Macmillan Co.

108. F. W. Boreham relates that he was standing one day in St. Paul's before the original of Holman Hunt's familiar painting "The Light of the World." He remarked to his companion that he never understood why Hunt had put a lighted lantern in Christ's hand, since there was

ample light in the clearing before the door where he knocked. A third man, who had been standing unseen behind them, stepped forward. "I couldn't help overhearing your conversation," he said, "and may I point out one thing you may have missed. You will see that the cottage where Christ knocks is on the edge of a wilderness. There it is dark. So the artist was suggesting that when the door has opened and Christ has entered in, he expects that those who receive him will go, in turn, with him into the wilderness to bring light."
—GENE E. BARTLETT in *Missions,* Vol. 151, No. 5, p. 36.

109. Said a guide in a picture gallery: "Every time I try to explain these pictures, I see more to explain." This is true also in matters of faith. As we seek to win others to our faith in Christ, our faith is deepened and our knowledge of Christ is increased.
—KARL H. A. REST

HEARTS THAT ARE TOUCHED

110. A little Italian mission was started years ago in a small New Jersey city. After a few years it was abandoned. "It is a waste of money," the executive said. Some years later I encountered a colporteur distributing tracts and Bibles among the Italians in a Colorado mining town. This zealous soul said that he had been converted in that little mission in northern New Jersey. Subsequently, I fell into conversation with one of the officers of an Italian Protestant church in Rochester, New York. He told me that he got his start in the Christian life by reading a tract someone had given him in a mining town in Colorado. Years afterward I was in Sicily visiting some of the little Protestant congregations there. One of the leaders spoke English, and he told me that during ten years of residence in America he had lived in Rochester, where he had come under the influence of an Italian Protestant church, chiefly through the efforts of one particularly zealous church officer. What a glorious failure that little mission in New Jersey proved to be!
—KENNETH D. MILLER in *Man and God in the City,* Friendship Press.

111. In the year A.D. 410 the barbarian hordes from the north swept into the city of Rome and the light of civilization was dimmed for 600 years. Yet the true light still shone in the hearts of those whose hope lay beyond history—the light of the knowledge of the glory of God in the face of Jesus Christ. As Alaric and his tribesmen plundered Rome an aging bishop began to write a book. As Professor John Foster has pointed out, a man of sixty writing at such a moment might well have written: "Memoirs of the City of Rome." What Augustine wrote was *Concerning the City of God.*

"After the storming and the sack of Rome," he wrote, "my zeal was kindled for the house of God." From that kindling zeal was born, in the midst of calamity, a magnificent treatise in the Christian meaning of history. There was born also a new hope in the hearts of men and a new sense of mission in the life of the Church.

Among the barbarian tribes which invaded Rome and put out the light of Western civilization were some of my Anglo-Saxon ancestors. . . . A century and a half later there came a counterattack from the east. Missionaries from Rome were invading Britain and they were led by another Augustine. Modern Church historians have pointed out that the connection between the two Augustines is more than nominal and casual.

"The second Augustine came [to Britain] because the first had believed, taught, and stamped it upon the minds of his successors that the kingdoms of this world may change, but the city of God goes on abuilding."
—CHARLES W. RANSON in *The Intercollegian.*

112. J. J. Methvin was a pioneer preacher to the Kiowa Indians in the Southwest. One night Hunting Horse and other braves rode boldly into Methvin's brush arbor and announced they had come to scalp the missionary for preaching the white man's God to the Indians. As they approached him, with knives poised, the missionary explained he came to tell the Indians of their own God. The confused Indians ordered Methvin to preach and they would judge for themselves whether or not it was an Indian gospel. The terrified man of the cloth preached literally for his scalp. What a sermon it must have been! Then, when he invited the Indians to accept Christ, Hunting Horse stepped forward. "I didn't know it then, but God came into my heart that moment," Hunting Horse recalled. "I told the others, 'Stop and listen, for he tells the truth,' and they bowed their heads in shame." If you and I had to speak and act in the name of Christ for our scalps we would doubtless find life more exciting.
—Reprinted with permission of publishers from *You Can Master Life* by JOHN H. CROWE. Copyright, 1954, by Prentice-Hall, Inc., 70 Fifth Avenue, New York 11, New York.

113. A tribe on Mount Hagen in New Guinea offered a gift to a missionary if he would take his God and depart. They said that while he was there they could not go on practicing their pagan customs. But some of the young men disagreed with the tribe's request. "It is impossible to send this God away again," they said. "He lives in our own hearts. As soon as we want to do something a voice asks whether it is right before God. And we don't want him to go away. We don't want to return to paganism."
—GERALD KENNEDY in *With Singleness of Heart,* Harper & Bros.

114. A missionary friend on leave from his duties in the Belgian Congo showed me a photograph of a young girl who was suffering from an advanced form of leprosy. Her hands and feet were nearly gone. Yet there was a smile on her lips and happiness radiating from her face. Civil authorities had taken her to the leper colony where my friend held regular worship services. There she gave her heart to Christ and in the serenity of her new faith gave this testimony: "If I had not been a leper, I should never have heard about Jesus."
—FRANK R. SNAVELY

115. There was a time when the aristocracy would not employ a Methodist cook, for she would seek to convert the housemaid and the kitchenmaid and the parlormaid and the between-maid, and spend and be spent in the activity.
—LESLIE D. WEATHERHEAD in *When the Lamp Flickers,* Abingdon Press.

THE DISCIPLINES OF SERVICE

116. The missionary must be a man or woman of God, and recognizably so. The younger churches in India, Pakistan, and Ceylon are deeply and humbly conscious of their own spiritual poverty and their inadequacy to the task of winning one fifth of the human race for Christ. When a new missionary comes, they turn to him wistfully, saying, though not aloud, "Have not you, with your background of fifteen centuries of

Christian faith, something that we have not as yet attained? Can you not set us an example of Christian discipline? Can you not teach us, by example more than by word, to enter more deeply into the secret of prayer? Can you not show us more than we already know of the power of the Holy Spirit?" If they turn away disappointed, they may welcome the missionary and love him, but they will feel that he has failed them at the central point of all, that he has shown himself weak at the very point where they longed that he should be strong.
—STEPHEN NEILL in *Under Three Flags,* Friendship Press.

117. "My experience of prison-sitting," writes F. Olin Stockwell in *With God in Red China,* "leads me to conclude that the three essentials for such vocation are the New Testament, the grace of God, and a sense of humor. . . . . I can assure you that nothing became more real to me in prison than the certainty that I was not alone. Day after day when I should have been planning suicide or going crazy with loneliness, I would feel the sustaining power of God. . . . What was true of me was true of the others."
—Harper & Bros.

118. Years ago I heard an Englishman tell of going twice to speak in an English college, where he plead for recruits to go out to the mission field. The first time he went he asked for a man to go out to India. He told of the beautiful cities of India, of the salubrious climate, of the splendid social advantages, and of an adequate salary. He told his story and made his appeal. Not a man responded. They simply filed out of the hall. Several years later he went to the same school and stood in the same room and told his story. This time he was asking for a volunteer to go out to central Africa to take the place of a man who had died at his post. He painted the picture just as it was. He told them of the oppressive heat, of the tragic loneliness, of the deadly malaria, and the sleeping sickness. He told them of the five graves there under the equator of the men who had gone out to that lonely spot. Then he asked if there was a man there willing to go and carry on. "Perhaps," he said, "you will not come back." Ten young men rose to their feet and offered to go. Someone said recently: "If you wish to kindle the religious zeal of youth, give them something they can die for."
—STUART NYE HUTCHISON in *The Upper Room Pulpit.*

119. They asked a missionary about to return to Africa whether he liked his work. He turned to the questioner and said quietly, "Of course I don't like my work. We are people of average sensitivity and we don't like dirt and infestation and danger and isolation from our loved ones, but Heaven help our world if we only do for God what we *like* to do!"
—CHARLES B. TEMPLETON in *Life Looks Up,* Harper & Bros.

120. The captain of an ocean liner is charged with the safety of his passengers and his ship. He knows little rest or relief until port is reached. The passengers may splash in the swimming pool, loll in deck chairs, sleep late in the morning, and do as they please. But the captain, no matter how much he may envy their carefree lives, cannot cast aside his responsibilities. So it is with all who have accepted God's call to be stewards of his household and messengers of his gospel. Theirs is a fateful charge until life's journey is ended.
—GLENN H. ASQUITH

121. When the challenge is pressed vigorously for Christians to be witnesses of Jesus, no end of protests are heard. Our age prides itself on its frankness, its ability to speak straight from the shoulder. We moderns, for instance, speak about sex as casually as our forefathers spoke about the weather. But ask these moderns to talk to a friend or neighbor about the claims of Jesus Christ and with embarrassment they say: "Religion is a private matter, and no one should interfere with another person's belief." Even another person's lack of belief does not challenge most Christians to a forthright witness.
—Karl H. A. Rest

122. A Christian life is not Christian unless it witnesses. The mouth speaks what the heart is full of. If for us to live is to make God's fellowship real on earth, we are all by nature missionaries. There is a kind of polite agreement that religion and politics be left alone. The weather and the work are far safer topics. Yet no one can leave religion alone, leave witnessing to Christ alone, for whom *to live* is Christ. This involves speech, too. With the mouth confession is made to salvation. How can anyone be a real Christian without having won over to his way of believing at least someone else?
—Nels F. S. Ferré in *Pillars of Faith,* Harper & Bros.

UNDERGIRDING THE SERVANTS

123. Our missionary giving is more like a thermostat than a thermometer. A thermometer merely reflects the temperature in a room, whereas a thermostat determines it.
—Ralph M. Johnson in *Missions,* Vol. 150, No. 6, p. 336.

124. John Wanamaker, noted merchant and liberal Christian giver, made a trip to China to determine how well the moneys he had given for missions were being used. He came upon an old man plowing with a crude instrument that was being drawn by an ox and a young man hitched together. Wanamaker was surprised and asked for an explanation. The old man told how a chapel was being built in the village and how it needed a spire that would be visible for miles about. The members of the mission had prayed and had given all that they could, but it had not been enough. The old man's son had suggested to the father: "Let us give one of our two oxen. I will take the yoke of the ox we sell." Wanamaker said that when he heard that story, he immediately offered up a silent prayer, "Lord, let me be hitched to a plow, so that I may know the joy of such sacrificial giving."
—Armin C. Oldsen

125. Once the late Archbishop of Canterbury C. Y. Lang preached before his king, the late George V. Lang knew that his sovereign was, as we say, allergic to foreign missions and to sermons appealing on their behalf. Lang believed that he should present this essential element in the gospel to his sovereign. Afterward the king spoke crossly to him. "Am I to understand that, because I do not believe in foreign missions, I am not a Christian?" The archbishop quietly answered: "Sir, I am presenting the facts, not drawing conclusions."
—David A. MacLennan

126. The story is told of a man who seemed to be unusually happy as he watched a ship being loaded before sailing to the Orient. He revealed to a stranger standing at his side the cause of his interest and joy. The ship was to carry $20,000 worth of supplies to a Christian hospital in a heathen land. Having given himself to the Lord, he was giving $20,000. It was a splendid gift. But it suddenly sank in significance when he discovered that the stranger to whom he was speaking was sailing on the same ship. He was a missionary, who had also given himself to God. In fact, he had already given forty years of his life in strenuous labors in the foreign-mission field.

—ARMIN C. OLDSEN

127. A wealthy man watched a missionary nurse attending to lepers in China. He said to her, "I wouldn't do that for a million." And the nurse quietly replied: "Neither would I. But I do it gladly for the love of God."

—E. STANLEY JONES in *Growing Spiritually,* Abingdon Press.

128. When the Disciples of Christ were lingering overlong on the threshold of a genuine foreign missionary program . . . J. H. Garrison, one of the two leading journalists of the brotherhood at that time, was preparing to depart for the 1880 national convention in Louisville, Kentucky. . . . Two of his small sons and a girl cousin brought him the contents of their savings banks and said, "We want this to go to send the gospel to children who have never heard of Jesus." The amount of their contribution was exactly $1.13, but it was the beginning of Children's Day among the Disciples, which has financed scores of missionaries in ten foreign fields over a period of more than sixty years. [One of the sons is W. E. Garrison, formerly of *The Christian Century.*]

—DWIGHT E. STEVENSON in *Faith Takes a Name,* Harper & Bros.

LINCOLN'S BIRTHDAY

MEASURE OF THE MAN

129. There is a striking similarity between the Man of Galilee and the man from Illinois.

Both had obscure beginnings.

Each came to his own and they received him not.

Neither allowed difficulty to turn him from his central purpose.

Both prepared for responsibility through self-sacrifice and self-denial.

Both loved little children.

Both befriended the weak.

The common people heard each of them gladly.

Neither condescended, yet both loved all men as children of God.

Both hated the things which enslaved men.

Each had a passion for justice and truth.

Each took the pains of humanity as his own so that he was a "man of sorrows . . . acquainted with grief."

Neither made room for bitterness.

Each of them knew the loneliness of following the course of the heart rather than the dictates of men.

Both marched resolutely toward death for humanity.

Each of them died to set men free.

—K. MORGAN EDWARDS in *Pulpit Digest.*

130. The choicest piece of eloquence . . . that have Abraham Lincoln for theme . . . was a brief tribute delivered by the late Homer Hoch, Chief Justice of the Supreme Court of Kansas, in the national House of Representatives, February 12, 1923: "There is no new thing to be said of Lincoln. There is no new thing to be said of the mountains or of the sea or of the stars. The years go their way, but the same old mountains lift their granite shoulders above the drifting clouds; the same mysterious sea beats upon the shore; and the same silent stars keep holy vigil above a tired world. But to mountains and sea and stars men turn forever in unwearied homage. And thus with Lincoln. For he was mountain in grandeur of soul, he was sea in deep undervoice of mystic loneliness, he was star in steadfast purity of purpose and of service. And he abides."

—EDGAR DEWITT JONES in *Sermons I Love to Preach,* Harper & Bros.

131. In John Drinkwater's *Abraham Lincoln* there is a dramatic scene, with Lincoln alone in his office in the White House. The Union had divided and the awful war was ravaging the nation. The President stands, gazing at a map hanging on the wall: a map of the United States of America. As he gazes upon it, he lifts his arms as if to take to his heart all of the states, North, South, East and West, in affectionate embrace. The gesture was symbolic. The Union he could save, himself he could not save.

—EDGAR DEWITT JONES in *Sermons I Love to Preach,* Harper & Bros.

132. No single brief utterance of Lincoln is more portentous than the line he wrote to a federal authority in Louisiana. "I shall do nothing in malice, for what I deal with is too vast for malicious dealing."
—Carl Sandburg in *This I Believe.* Copyright, 1954, by Help, Inc. Reprinted by permission of Simon and Schuster, Inc.

133. Irving Stone in *Love Is Eternal* concludes his narrative account of Mary Todd and Abraham Lincoln with an interview between Mrs. Lincoln and Parker, the President's guard:

"Parker entered, a heavy-faced man with half-closed lips. He trembled. 'Why were you not at the door to keep the assassin out?' she asked fiercely. Parker hung his head. 'I have bitterly repented it. But I did not believe that anyone would try to kill so good a man in such a public place. The belief made me careless. I was attracted by the play, and did not see the assassin enter the box.' 'You should have seen him. You had no business to be careless.' She fell back on the pillow, covered her face with her hands. 'Go now. It's not you I can't forgive, it's the assassin.' 'If Pa had lived,' said Tad, 'he would have forgiven the man who shot him. Pa forgave everybody.' "
—Copyright 1954 by Irving Stone, reprinted by permission of Doubleday & Company, Inc.

134. When people talked about Lincoln, it was nearly always about one or more of these five things: (1) how long, tall, quick, strong, or awkward in looks he was; (2) how he told stories and jokes, how he was comical or pleasant or kindly; (3) how he could be silent, melancholy, sad; (4) how he was ready to learn and looking for chances to learn; (5) how he was ready to help a friend, a stranger, or even a dumb animal in distress.
—Carl Sandburg in *Abraham Lincoln: The Prairie Years.* Copyright, 1954, by Carl Sandburg. Reprinted by permission of Harcourt, Brace and Company, Inc.

135. The least of us can stand for the greatest things. It is not difficult to see the operation of [this] principle in those capacious personalities that have bestridden the world. One sees it plainly, for example, in a character like [Abraham] Lincoln. Abstract from Lincoln the things he came to stand for and we have a queer remainder. For Lincoln, taken by himself, was unprepossessing and ungainly, came from lowly origins and small opportunities, had no superficial graces that cover inward lack. Rather, like a very plain wire grown incandescent, Lincoln shone with what he came to stand for. He achieved a personal suggestiveness that is one of the marvels of our history. Think of him and see how inevitably you are reminded of magnanimity, patience, steadfastness under strain, devotion to the nation's unity, love of liberty, deepening faith, and spiritual life! He came to stand for those things which man must love or else perish.
—Harry Emerson Fosdick in *The Secret of Victorious Living,* Harper & Bros.

136. Did you ever see that little cabin down in Kentucky where Abraham Lincoln was born? There is a marble building around it now but inside there is that little house that once held so much of greatness. It doesn't seem possible that such a little cabin could be home to such a man. But it was. And it was there that, according to the story, Tom Lincoln talked to his wife about the little boy. He was a fine chap, said the proud

father, but there was one thing lacking. "He can't sing. He can't sing," said Tom. And then his wife answered, "No, Tom, he can't sing, but he will make the whole world sing." I hope that story is true. If that mother didn't say those words, I know she meant them, for that's just the way a mother would talk.
—CHARLES RAY GOFF in *A Better Hope,* Fleming H. Revell Co.

137. Recently in Washington I stood befor the Lincoln Memorial and [saw] again that noble figure seated there, and read on the carved stone the immortal words of the Gettysburg Address. A newspaper editor in Harrisburg, thirty-five miles away from Gettysburg, heard Lincoln's Gettysburg Address. Fall for that kind of stuff? Not he! He was no sucker! He was a hard-headed realist. So he wrote this in his paper: "We pass over the silly remarks of the President; for the credit of the nation, we are willing that the veil of oblivion shall be dropped over them and that they shall no more be repeated or thought of." Ah, you fool, you stood in the presence of greatness, and you disbelieved! It is you who were blind. It is you, the skeptic, at whom the centuries will laugh until the end of time.
—HARRY EMERSON FOSDICK in *Great Preaching Today,* Alton M. Motter, ed., published in 1953 by Harper & Brothers. Used by permission.

138. [Carl Sandburg] took his little daughter to Springfield, Illinois, to visit Lincoln's tomb. The custodian showed them through the building, and then they stood before the tomb itself. A number of other visitors had gathered there, too, and they all stood in silent reverence. Then suddenly his daughter tugged at his coat sleeve and said in a voice loud enough to be heard by all, "Daddy, when are they going to roll the stone away?"
—PRESTON BRADLEY in *Happiness Through Creative Living,* Hanover House.

BROTHERHOOD WEEK

OUR BROTHER'S BROTHER

139. Charles Brown, one of the ablest preachers of the last generation, preached a powerful sermon by saying, "No, we are not our brother's keeper, but we are our brother's brother." Today we realize even that answer is outdated. We are far more than our brother's brother, for the life that others live is an extension of our own life and no life today is lived apart.
—Frank A. Court

140. Dostoevski causes one of his characters to [say]: "I am X in an indeterminate equation. I am a sort of phantom in life who has lost all beginning and end, who has forgotten his own name." The affirmation that we find in the Gospel causes us to confront every man with the word, "I know your real name. You are not an X in an indeterminate equation or a phantom in life, you are a child of God, you are a brother of mine in Christ."
—Harold A. Bosley in *Religion in Life.*

141. One of the British soldiers who passed through the terrible ordeal of Dunkirk was asked by a friend when he got back safe to England, "What did it feel like, out there on that beach at Dunkirk, with the sea in front of you, the German army back of you, and the German bombers over you?" His answer was, "It was a strange feeling I had. I felt that every man on the beach was my brother!"
—Clarence Edward Macartney in *You Can Conquer,* Abingdon Press.

142. Sholem Asch in *One Destiny* writes concerning the persecutions of the Jews during World War II and offers remarkable instances of good will: "It was feared . . . that the sympathies shown to the suffering Jews by the population even in German cities might be transformed into open demonstrations, a thing that actually happened in many European cities. After the inauguration of the ghetto in Amsterdam, members of the Dutch aristocracy left their homes and went to live with the Jews in the ghetto. In Denmark, upon passage of an edict forcing Jews to wear a yellow patch on their sleeves, the Danish king put on the yellow armband marked with the star of David."
—Copyright 1945, G. P. Putnam's Sons.

143. The King of Denmark, when he was urged by the Nazis to institute anti-Jewish legislation, is said to have replied: "But you see, there isn't any Jewish problem here. We do not consider ourselves inferior to them."
—Ernest Fremont Tittle in *First Church Pulpit.*

144. After the conquest of Mount Everest newspapers and magazines told how

the daring adventure was made not by a single man but by a team of men. Similarly the Everest of faith is successfully reached when men join their hearts, wills, and desires in a common endeavor. When a man stumbles and falters, he is steadied and encouraged by the strong rope of life which binds us together.
—A. D. Johnson

145. In *What Men Live By,* Richard Cabot tells about friends who went through the horrors of the San Francisco earthquake nearly half a century ago. They told him their most poignant experience was not one of horror or of pity but an almost miraculous attainment of human brotherhood. Cleavages of class and race were forgotten as all shared a similar plight. They helped one another build rude shelters in the parks, took care of one another's babies around fires built from driftwood gathered from the beach. Everybody was everybody's friend. In helping one another as brothers each helped himself master the desolation of his loss.
—Everett W. Palmer

146. When my daughter died of polio, everybody stretched out a hand to help me, but at first I couldn't seem to bear the touch of anything, even the love of friends; no support seemed strong enough.

While Mary was still sick, I used to go early in the morning to a little church near the hospital to pray. There the working people came quietly to worship. I had been careless with my religion, I had rather cut God out of my life, and I didn't have the nerve at the time to ask him to make my daughter well—I only asked him to help me understand, to let me come in and reach him. I prayed there every morning and I kept looking for a revelation, but nothing happened.

And then, much later, I discovered that it *had* happened, right there in the church. I could recall, vividly, one by one, the people I had seen there—the solemn laborers with tired looks, the old women with gnarled hands. Life had knocked them around, but for a brief moment they were being refreshed by an ennobling experience. It seemed as they prayed their worn faces lighted up and they became the very vessels of God. Here was my revelation. Suddenly I realized I was one of them. In my need I gained strength from the knowledge that they too had needs, and I felt an interdependence with them. I experienced a flood of compassion for people. I was learning the meaning of "Love thy neighbor. . . ."
—Helen Hayes in *This I Believe.* Copyright, 1952, by Help, Inc. Reprinted by permission of Simon and Schuster, Inc.

147. Albert Schweitzer as a boy was very husky and oftentimes wrestled with the other boys in the school in the village. He writes that one day when he had thrown a neighbor boy, he heard that youngster say, "If I could have broth to eat every day like the pastor's son has, I'd be so strong you couldn't throw me." And Schweitzer went home to tell his parents that as long as that neighbor boy could have no broth, he would have none. He discovered that in the wintertime the other boys were wearing old, rough shoes that did not keep their feet warm. He had good shoes, but he told his parents he would not wear good shoes if the other boys could not have them. He was a great problem to the pastor because he would not live up to his social status. To Schweitzer it was

the Christian teaching, as he says, that put him over with every man, every boy. He refused to take advantage of his position. This is Jesus' influence in life, and you can never escape it.
—GERALD KENNEDY

OF ONE BLOOD

148. If we accept the verdict of science and the Christian religion, we must admit that either all men are brothers, or no men are brothers. Either God is the father of all men, or he is the father of none. Either the lives of all children are sacred, or the life of no child is sacred. If the Americans and the English are brothers, then the Americans and the Germans are brothers. If God is the father of the Chinese, he is the father of the Japanese. If the life of the King of England is sacred, then the life of a miner in Wales is sacred. If the life of the President of the United States is of supreme worth, then the life of a Negro mill hand in South Carolina is also of supreme worth. If the life of a multimillionaire is precious, then the life of a sharecropper is precious. If the life of a white child comes from God, then the life of the blackest Negro child also comes from God. Either all or none. It is this philosophy that both creates and resolves tension. But it seeks always to bring people together under the rule of God.
—BENJAMIN E. MAYS in *Missions,* Vol. 150, No. 2, pp. 93-94.

149. The key [of American democracy] is that word "community." Europeans know what teamwork is. They will get together on the football field or in their version of Christian Endeavor or the Knights of Columbus, in a trade union or a political party. But few among them take the final step that we take in our cities and townships and counties, joining together—Christians and Jews, Catholics and Protestants, management and labor, Democrats and Republicans —for the good of all. What characterizes America is this devotion of its citizens to the community as a whole. This is so much a part of our life that we never give it a thought.
—LEWIS GALANTIÈRE in *The Reader's Digest.*

150. We talk about building bridges of brotherhood around the world in answer to the communist pretensions, and that's a splendid vision. But brotherhood begins on a man-to-man basis at home and not on a man-to-man basis across the oceans. Without that footing it is idle talk and an empty vision.
—ERIC JOHNSTON

151. A troop of Boy Scouts, hiking in the country, found to their delight a stretch of unused and rusted railroad tracks. Each Scout tried his skill in walking on the rails. Most of the boys balanced precariously for a few moments and then tried again. But two boys had no such difficulty. They stood opposite each other on the rails, each extending a hand to the other. They balanced without faltering as they walked briskly along the track. That day's lesson will long linger in my mind, for one boy was white and the other colored. I realized that, as we extend a hand to another person, we shall walk more steadily along the road of life.
—W. A. KUNTZLEMAN

152. In one of our large cities a Friends' school for children faced on one street and back of it in the next block was a public school for Negro children. The two play yards joined each other and there was no fence between them. At re-

cess time the five-to-ten-year-olds from each school played games together. Susan's mother had told her she might invite each Saturday for lunch one of her friends from school. The only stipulation was that she must report whether anyone was coming. One Thursday Susan said, "Mother, I've invited a friend for Saturday noon." Knowing the playground situation, the mother replied, "That will be very nice. Is she black or white?" Susan thought for a minute, then answered, "I don't know, but I'll look tomorrow."
—MURIEL H. BROWN in *The Secret Place.*

153. Albert Einstein . . . during a stopover in China on a world tour . . . refused to ride in a rickshaw because it was pulled by a human being. "I will not be a part of making any man a draft animal," he explained.
—DWIGHT E. STEVENSON in *Faith Takes a Name,* Harper & Bros.

154. Professor W. E. Hocking once asked C. F. Andrews the question, "How do you preach the Gospel to a Hindu?" To which Andrews replied, "I don't. I preach the Gospel to a man."
—D. T. NILES in *That They May Have Life,* Harper & Bros.

155. The University of Chicago was begun by the Baptists in 1857. Senator Stephen A. Douglas, who had given ten acres of land for the campus and was president of the board of trustees, was invited to make the main address at the laying of the cornerstone of the first building. This ceremony was to be on the Fourth of July. In his political activities, Douglas had been accused of temporizing on the slave issue. Therefore, when the Reverend Joseph E. Roy, minister of the Plymouth Congregational Church in Chicago, an ardent abolitionist, was asked to offer the prayer, he demurred on the ground that Senator Douglas might be embarrassed. But President Burroughs insisted that Roy go ahead, which he did, closing his prayer thus: "O Lord, on this day of our liberty, we earnestly remember our brethren in bonds and must pray that the day may come when they, too, may rejoice in the Fourth of July." Later Douglas claimed a sore throat and cut short his speech. The next day one of the newspapers reported, "Roy's prayer gave Douglas the bronchitis."
—FRED L. BROWNLEE in *These Rights We Hold,* Friendship Press.

156. A young Mormon student was writing a Ph.D. thesis in the field of Mormon history. His professor said to him one time, "Do you think that you, being a Mormon, can be unprejudiced enough to write this history of the Mormon Church?" And the young man replied, "I think so, if you, being a non-Mormon, think you are unprejudiced enough to judge it."
—GERALD KENNEDY

BROTHERS IN ACTION

157. Earl Grey writes of his father, a former governor general of Canada: "He lit so many fires in cold rooms." That is a beautiful eulogy. There are many who are hungry for lack of food. There are more who are hungry because they do not eat of the bread of life. Many are cold because there is no fuel to heat their homes. But many more are cold because they do not share a sympathetic love with those who care.
—FRED R. CHENAULT

158. Years ago a play appeared entitled *The Man Who Played God.* The title came from the deaf man in the play, who had learned to read people's lips.

He lived on the top floor of a high apartment near Central Park in New York City. From this vantage point with a spyglass he watched people on the park benches and by reading their lips could tell what they were saying. To those in trouble he would send down a servant to tell them that their problem was known and help would be sent. When asked where this mysterious kindness came from, the servant replied, "From the man who plays God."
—Wallace Fridy in *A Lamp Unto My Feet,* Abingdon Press.

159. During the dense fog which enveloped and penetrated the city of London some months ago, a man and his wife came out to a subway exit, wondering which way to start to their home near by. A stranger appeared out of the fog and asked if he could help. When they told him of their predicament, he led them straight home. Thanking him, they asked how he could be so sure of himself. "I'm blind," he said. He had been working happily all day, guiding people in his neighborhood that he knew. . . . Are there not many who are lost in the fog and cannot find the way? Is there a light in us? Is there some sense of direction in us that can lead them, no matter how dense the fog?
—Arnold H. Lowe in *Power for Life's Living,* Harper & Bros.

160. When Gandhi visited England in the late twenties . . . some of the papers in England called attention to the fact that he held no official position in the Indian government and asked, "On whose authority does he come?" Gandhi never missed that kind of opportunity and replied, "I come clothed with authority—the authority of the needs of my people."
—Harold A. Bosley in *Preaching on Controversial Issues,* published in 1953 by Harper & Brothers.

161. When Martin of Tours walked through a village, he saw a beggar who was shivering from the cold. Martin took off the capella he was wearing and, tearing the coat in half, gave one half to the beggar. He was thereafter called a capella lender, and it is from this term that we derive our word "chaplain." A chaplain is "one who will lend his coat." This is what Christ said every Christian must be willing to do, and yet so rare has this selfless love been in our world that an example of it has been recorded in history and given a new word to our vocabulary.
—William Goddard Sherman

162. At a pastor's conference an enthusiastic young preacher announced with obvious sincerity that by the grace of God he had conquered sin and was entirely free from it. An older minister asked him how many suits of clothes he had. He answered: "Three." Whereupon the older minister mused aloud: "Three suits of clothes in a world where millions of people have only rags for a covering."
—Ernest Fremont Tittle in *First Church Pulpit.*

163. Winburn Thomas of Indonesia, a delegate to the Second Assembly of the World Council of Churches, told the Evanston meeting the story of a Mrs. Wang, one of the thousands of women and children who took refuge in a safety zone near Shanghai during the early years of the Sino-Japanese War. Most of the refugees were not Christian. Mrs. Wang was a baptized believer. Every day she stood in line with a bowl to receive rice for herself and her four children. Every day she received

such portions of rice as were available for distribution. One day at the foot of the receiving line a newcomer, who carried a baby and led a child by the hand, took her place behind Mrs. Wang. After Mrs. Wang had received her rations, the newcomer asked for rice and was told that it was all gone. She then turned to Mrs. Wang and asked that she share hers. Mrs. Wang refused, saying she and her children needed it all for themselves, and walked away. But not far. She retraced her steps, helped the hungry woman to her feet, and said: "Sister, can you forgive me? Of course I will share my rice with you. For a moment I had forgotten my Lord."
—LAWRENCE E. FISHER

164. A ragamuffin who didn't have the slightest idea of what "transfusion" meant was told that only a transfusion would save the life of a pal. So the boy went to the doctor's office, rolled up his sleeve when instructed, and lay quietly upon the table. After a time he looked up at the doctor and said, "Doctor, when do I die?" The doctor smiled reassuringly. It was then that the lad learned for the first time that a blood transfusion was not another word for the kind of death necessary to assure the life of his friend.
—HARRY K. ZELLER, JR.

165. Tommy was deeply impressed by the minister's appeal for food for the hungry people of the world who have never had enough to provide for daily needs. On the way home after the church service Tommy said to his father: "That big chemical industrial plant can make almost anything. Why can't they make soil into food?" A while later Tommy and his father were walking through their cornfields. His father said: "These stalks are doing what man has never learned to do. They are turning soil into delicious food." "But we can help, can't we," asked Tommy, "by sending a portion of the golden seed to countries where people are hungry? Our corn will help them to realize the miracle of soil and brotherly love."
—JOHN H. BLOUGH

166. Not as a Stranger by Morton Thompson tells of young Doctor Luke who goes to practice in a little town where a Jewish doctor is ostracized because of his faith. Doctor Luke recognizes in him a skillful doctor and tries to change the attitude of the village. An older doctor tells him that he cannot change it because it is the way of the world. The young doctor blazes out, "Well, if it is the way of the world, you don't need to live in that world!" But it is not as a stranger but as a member of the human race that the young doctor finds himself. Driven by emotions too great for him, caught in his dedication to his medicine, he is a lonely, defeated individual, unhappy with his wife, distrustful of others, and self-sufficient in his own medical skill. Then on a hunting trip with the newspaper editor and some of the other citizens he becomes lost. He hungers for humanity, he senses a new appreciation of the fineness of his wife, he thinks of the other doctors in the community and their struggle for health, and he knows he must live not for himself but for the humanity to which he belongs. When he is found, he returns for the first time really to practice medicine, not as a stranger but with the priceless ingredient of love.
—FRANK A. COURT

LOVE MAKES A DIFFERENCE

167. The secret of brotherhood is found in our capacity to look beneath surface manifestations to the inner purpose, the

spiritual enterprise, and the aspiring heart of those whom we meet. Harlan Miller has written concerning the problems represented by the people on any city street. Each seems bent on some trivial errand, but his look is misleading. In the jostling throng there is one boy headed for the draft board, another for the physician's office to learn the result of a medical examination. One passes a new widow and next to her a woman seeking divorce. He sees a man with an incurable disease and a little girl with a toothache. A couple are hoping to borrow money for a down payment on property, and a family will be soon selecting a casket. Such are the problems masquerading behind the unrevealed faces on any street in any city. Sometimes we have eyes and see not. Like the travelers on the Emmaus road, greatness may be walking at our side and we recognize it not. Jesus had the faculty of seeing more than meets our eyes. In the depth of one's focus the ability to see beyond the face to the heart adds to life the quality of sympathy.
—Charles F. Jacobs

168. Our Maker gave us two hands. One to hold to him, the other to our fellow man. If our hands are full of—or struggling for—possessions, we can hold to neither God nor humanity. If, however, we hold fast to him who gave us life, who is our ever-present Partner, his loving Spirit will flow through us and out to our neighbor. That is the way of joy, love, achievement and inner peace.
—Louis L. Austin in *This I Believe.* Copyright, 1954, by Help, Inc. Reprinted by permission of Simon and Schuster, Inc.

169. Pygmalion labored long and carefully and produced a statue of a perfect woman. He loved the exquisite statue his genius had produced and, embracing it, kissed its cold lips. But he was loving a lifeless thing. Finally he asked Venus, the goddess of love, to give him a living woman as beautiful as the one he had carved. That night when he embraced his statue, the lips were warm with life. The statue according to the Greek myth had become a living thing. There is mighty little life in the stranger we pass on the street or in the enemy beyond our fence; but when divine love enters our hearts, God gives to friend and foe the warmth of human fellowship.
—Dale S. Bringman

170. Love makes a difference. John was the busiest youth in the neighborhood. He was active in church, in Sunday school, in the scout troop. He carried papers and played in the high-school band. He didn't have time or money or energy for anything else. But then Alice moved into the neighborhood. Soon he was waiting to see her pass and hoping that she might smile. He found time to walk with her to the drugstore for a coke and to visit her home. John, who hadn't time or money or energy for any other activity, somehow found time to be with Alice. Love had made the difference. When people really love Jesus Christ, they somehow find time and money and energy for him. Genuine love finds a way.
—Dale S. Bringman

171. David Smith, whose long and varied career within the church brought him into contact with many unpleasant cranks, once said that a crank is a person "in sore need of sympathy and compassion." If we knew all the attending circumstances that have warped the mind of the crank, Smith contended, we would not attack him for that would be like striking a wounded animal who is

desperately in need of solicitous care. The predicament of the folks described by the psychologist Ferenczi may well be the plight of many cranks: "They want to love their neighbors, but they don't know how." Never having received love, they cannot give love. They have become hard and cold, relentless and loveless, in their attitude toward life. This attitude in turn has further isolated them from others. Though they are in the crowd, they are not part of the fellowship. Is there any greater challenge to Christian love than that which the crank offers?
—Karl H. A. Rest

172. I see my neighbor in a special light. For the Creator is trying to do the same kind of business within him as within me. So I have learned to knock on doors expectantly. Sometimes I find the person who opens the door is willing to risk even slackened production to express his basic and often, perhaps, buried instinct for mutuality. I had a friend who constantly gave expression to this instinct, the late colorful, gently human vicar of St. Martin's, Trafalgar Square, London, Dick Sheppard. I found he had a curious habit, whenever he left a hotel room, of praying for the next person who would occupy the room, that he might make a better go of things in life than he himself had. He saw humanity in a special light, as bound together in and under God.
—Elmore McKee in *This I Believe*. Copyright, 1954, by Help, Inc. Reprinted by permission of Simon and Schuster, Inc.

173. The third chapter of Rabbi Liebman's book *Peace of Mind* is titled "Love Thyself Properly." It is a plea to us so to cultivate our lives, so to enrich them and purify them, that the true self becomes something very noble and fine. If we do not love ourselves properly, we cannot love our neighbors properly if we are to love them as we love ourselves. And if we do not have an exalted standard for ourselves, we cannot have a high standard for others. Only the standard of Christ for ourselves makes us ready for the practice of the Golden Rule.
—Charles R. Bell, Jr.

HARDHEARTEDNESS

174. Some folks enjoy putting a man in his place. When I see this being done, I know I am dealing with hardhearted men. When I look down on a man for being the color God made him, I don't reflect on the man; I reflect on God.
—Clovis G. Chappell

175. In *Prince of Players* by Eleanor Ruggles it is recalled that Julia Ward Howe, the author of "The Battle Hymn of the Republic," once gave a large reception for Edwin Booth and his wife. She invited her good friend Senator Charles Sumner to come and said to him, "I do wish you to know Mr. Booth." "I don't know that I care to," said Sumner. "I have outlived my interest in individuals." Mrs. Howe made a rejoinder that leads to the very heart of our Christian faith: "Fortunately, God Almighty has not, by last accounts, got so far."
—Charles L. Seasholes

176. In Belgium . . . we visited the Church of our Lady in Bruges. It is a beautiful, large Gothic structure. Our guide pointed to a little balcony high up on the left side of the nave, fairly close to the high altar. He explained that it had been built by Louis de Grotehuis, whose mansion next to the cathedral was responsible for his name—Louis of the Great House. After chopping a hole through the wall of the

church, he had constructed a concealed, private stairway leading up to this little private box seat which he built for himself and his family. There they could hide behind a screen while they worshiped, without having to mingle with the common people. Evidently Louis of the Great House thought that he and people of his kind constituted the church.
—O. A. GEISEMAN in *The Pulpit.* Copyrighted by the Christian Century Foundation and used by permission.

177. Gertrude Stein, strange as it may seem to those who know her only as the author of the immortal line, "A rose is a rose is a rose," was a wonderfully skillful medical student at Johns Hopkins University Medical School. She was almost awarded a degree because of her great competence in the dissection of corpses. It was denied because she had no interest whatever in the treatment of living patients.
—HALFORD E. LUCCOCK in *Communicating the Gospel,* Harper & Bros.

178. When I saw the pyramids, I marveled at these wonders of ancient architecture; but I remembered, too, that these are colossal monuments to man's oppression of man. When I looked at them, I thought of the countless hours of grueling toil that built them, of the gasping efforts of a million slaves, of the brutal force that compelled their erection. But I also saw how the winds of God had slowly worn them away, how ageless desert sands were leveling them inexorably, how the highest monuments to evil finally yields to God.
—WILLIAM FREDERICK DUNKLE, JR.

179. Carl Sandburg in *Always the Young Strangers* writes of John Standish, president of Lombard College. He resigned in a huff after three years' presidency and later left all of his property to another college. "He may have been wronged by Lombard," records Sandburg. "Somehow I never found the time to really look into what happened. I merely knew that he read a thousand important books in several languages, that he lectured to hundreds of teachers' institutes on how to educate the young, that he traveled three times around the planet Earth, that he loved trees and did a work with trees, for which I am infinitely thankful, that somehow all his travel and reading and love of trees couldn't help him when his heart nursed a hate."
—Harcourt, Brace & Co., Inc.

180. On a farm near Langeloth, Pennsylvania, owned by the same family since the Revolution, brown spots appeared where nothing would grow. Sulphuric acid fumes from a plant at Langeloth had poisoned the soil. Old Elder Lyle of the Cross Creek Presbyterian Church, owner of the farm, said: "This land has just given up trying to be good." Just so with people. Blow the fumes of racial or class prejudice against them long enough, and they too will give up trying to be good.
—HERBERT BEECHER HUDNUT

181. Few lessons in my youth have so long remained in my memory as one which occurred when as a college youth I hitchhiked a ride with a potato-chip salesman. I had accepted a ride although the salesman had said that he would need to make stops at a number of stores along the way. At each store he delivered bags of chips, and at each store he picked up unsold bags. I noticed that the unsold bags at one store were placed at the top of the consignment left at the next store. I asked about this. "I leave

fresh potato chips at each store and take away the unsold and stale chips. But the man at the next store doesn't know that part of his order is not fresh." I wondered at his deceit and determined that at the heart of brotherhood is the need for inner honesty, an honesty which demands righteousness even when we are not observed.
—John Edward Lantz

182. [A] laundry in a small American town . . . had a monopoly on its type of trade. However, two enterprizing Chinese opened a laundry across the street, and, because their work was neat, the price right, and they got it out on time, they were accorded a large measure of business by the thrifty housewives. In order to meet the competition, the original laundry resorted to the device of putting up a sign which read: "100 per cent American. We hate Orientals, Negroes, Jews, and foreigners." And, because there are always a number of "hatriots" per square inch in every community, the Chinese lost out. Finally, however, they devised a counter measure. They painted a much larger sign in their window which read: "200 per cent American. We hate everybody."
—John I. Daniel in *Pulpit Digest.*

183. John Homer Miller tells of a woman who lived unhappily in a New York apartment. She objected to the noise the people above her made. Finally after much effort she was able to get a different apartment in the same building. Before time to move she thought about the joy of getting away from the old place. In her joy she didn't notice the old annoyances. Her mind was already in her new home. Then when the time came to move, she looked at her old apartment and saw its real advantages and concluded that it was better. She looked at it with a fresh mind, and it looked good to her. She stayed. "Why," she exclaimed, "I didn't have to move into a new apartment. All I had to do was to move into a new mind."
—Wallace Fridy in *A Lamp Unto My Feet,* Abingdon Press.

184. Personally the skin is what holds us together. Socially and nationally the skin is what keeps us apart.
—Robert Newell Zearfoss

185. I remember a scene from Amos and Andy. There was a big man who would slap Andy across the chest whenever they met. Finally, Andy got enough of it and said to Amos: "I am fixed for him. I put a stick of dynamite in my vest pocket and the next time he slaps me he is going to get his hand blown off." Andy had not realized that at the same time his own heart would be blown out. The dynamite of hatred may inflict some injury on someone else and also blow out our own heart.
—Charles L. Allen in *God's Psychiatry,* Fleming H. Revell Co.

THE NARCISSUS COMPLEX

186. Oscar Wilde once said, "To love one's self is the beginning of a lifelong romance." How many have indulged themselves in just such an affection! In Greek mythology there is a story of an inordinate self-love. Narcissus, a handsome youth, looking one day into the quiet waters of a pool saw the reflection of himself. He gradually pined away as he looked longingly at his own reflection. Psychologists refer to inordinate self-love as a narcissus complex. Those who love themselves to the exclusion of all others do not think of themselves soberly but live in a vacuum of self-indulgence.

187. A superintendent of a mental hospital was once asked whether his patients could be described as "beside themselves." He replied: "No, they are very much themselves. They are pickled in themselves. That's why they are here."
—Edward W. Stimson

188. The disease we all have and that we have to fight against all our lives is, of course, the disease of self. I am pretty sure that writing may be a way of life in itself. It can be that, because it continually forces us away from self toward others. Let any man, or woman, look too much upon his own life, and everything becomes a mess. I think the whole glory of writing lies in the fact that it forces us out of ourselves and into the lives of others. In the end the real writer becomes a lover.
—Sherwood Anderson in *Letters of Sherwood Anderson,* Howard Mumford Jones, ed., Atlantic Monthly Press and Little, Brown & Co.

189. The creed of the Squire in John Galsworthy's novel *The Country House* fits more people than we like to admit: "I believe in my father, and his father, and his father's father, the makers and keepers of my estate, and I believe in myself and my son and my son's son. And I believe that we have made the country, and shall keep the country what it is. And I believe in the Public Schools [equivalent in America to a private preparatory school], and especially the Public School that I was at. And I believe in my social equals and the country house, and in things as they are, for ever and ever. Amen."
—Chas. Scribner's Sons.

190. A prominent man was being interviewed by a newspaper reporter. The reporter said, "I understand, sir, that you are a self-made man." The man turned to the reporter and said slowly, "Yes, I guess I am what you would call a self-made man." Then he added ruefully, "But if I had it to do over again I think I'd call in a little help."
—Charles B. Templeton in *Life Looks Up,* Harper & Bros.

LENT AND EASTER

THE SUPREMACY OF CHRIST

191. A story is told of Arturo Toscanini and his rehearsal of the New York Philharmonic Orchestra in Beethoven's Ninth Symphony. If it is apocryphal it deserves to be true. . . . When the maestro judged that all were ready, he had them play the entire work without interruption. . . . When the finale reached its stirring close, there was silence. . . . "Who am I?" he asked. "Who is Toscanini? I am nobody. . . . It is Beethoven—he is everything!" In the realm of music it is true. To a Christian, a similar question comes: Who am I? Who are you? We are nobody. Christ is everything!
—David A. MacLennan in *Joyous Adventure,* published in 1952 by Harper & Brothers.

192. Jesus Christ is still the one absolutely unique and perfect Man in human history. No man ever spoke as he did, and no man ever lived as he did. After twenty centuries he still towers head and shoulders above the rest of us, and is without peer in the realm of human character and influence.

But how could this be? The only adequate answer to that question that has ever been given is that he is the answer to our age old question, What is Man? He is God's revelation to us of ourselves. He is the perfect pattern that we must follow, the only sure guide through time, the final and absolute authority for all the sons of men.
—A. Ian Burnett in *Lord of All Life,* Rinehart & Co., Inc.

193. Only a handful received him. True enough he had a short-lived surge of popularity which never won his confidence, but his following was limited throughout to a small and insignificant group; not because he was ignored by all, but because he was rejected by many. Yet through the centuries this Person has claimed more attention than any other. He has been the object of more study, the center of more controversy, the inspiration of more self-sacrifice, the prime loyalty of hundreds of millions. He was not a philosopher; not a builder of systems. More than this he has become the object of philosophizing and system-building. In this regard he stands abreast of Nature and history; not just a thinker, but One about whom the world thinks.
—J. Donald Butler in *Four Philosophies,* Harper & Bros.

194. A little less than two thousand years ago, there came into our world among the Jewish people and to it a personage who gave substance to the illusion perceived by our fathers in their dream. Just as water fills up the hollowness of the ocean, so did he fill the empty world with the spirit of the one living God. No one before him and no one after him has bound our world with the fetters of law, of justice, and of love, and brought it to the feet of the one living Almighty God as effectively as did this personage who came to an Israelite house in Nazareth of Galilee—and this he did, not by the might of the sword, of fire and steel, like the lawgivers of other nations, but by the power of his mighty spirit and of his teachings. He, as no one else before him, raised our world from "the void and nothingness" in which it kept losing its way and bound it with strong ties of faith to the known goal, the predetermined commandment of an almighty throne so as to become a part of the great, complete, everlasting scheme of things. He, as no other, raised men from his probationary state as a beast, from his dumb, blind, and senseless existence, gave him a goal and a purpose and made him a part of the divine. He, as no other, works in the human consciousness like a second, higher nature and leaves man to rest in his animal state, wakens him, calls him, raises him, and inspires him to the noblest deeds and sacrifices. He, as no other, stands before our eyes as an example and a warning—both in his divine form and in his human one—and demands of us, harries us, prods us to follow his example and carry out his teachings. Through his heroic life, he casts us down like dust before his feet. No one but he sheds about himself such an aura of moral power, which, with a divine touch, has molded our world and our character; and no one's strength but his own has reached into our time, being the most potent influence in our everyday lives, inspiring us to goodness and exalted things, being the measure and scale for our deeds at every hour and every minute.

—SHOLEM ASCH in *One Destiny*. Copyright 1945, G. P. Putnam's Sons.

195. Alexander the Great, who lived three and a half centuries before Jesus, conquered the world and created a colossal empire. He and Jesus had some things in common. Both began their careers very young, and both ended them at the untimely age of thirty-three. Alexander was born in a mansion—Jesus in a manger. Alexander was the son of a king—Jesus, the Son of a carpenter. Alexander died a worshiped king on a throne; Jesus died a mocked King on a Cross. Alexander's life seemed like a great success; Jesus' life appeared as a dismal failure. Alexander shed the blood of millions for his own gain; Jesus shed his own blood for the salvation of millions. Alexander died in Babylon in splendor; Jesus died on Calvary in shame. Alexander conquered every throne; Jesus conquered every grave. Alexander enslaved all men; Jesus made all men free. Alexander made history; Jesus transformed it. The person of Jesus stands among men unequaled and unsurpassed. He is unique.

—RUSSELL V. DELONG in *The Pulpit*. Copyrighted by the Christian Century Foundation and used by permission.

196. In the town of Rimini in Italy there stands near the banks of the Rubicon a wind-bitten column. It marks the spot where Julius Caesar crossed the Rubicon and changed the destiny of his world. In his day and generation Caesar bestrode the world like a Colossus. But how few he influences today! Who cares about the Gallic wars? the Aedui? the Sequani? or Vercingetorix? Save for the schoolboys who wearily work their way through his sentences, to whom does Caesar speak? But Christ and his words are alive forevermore. As long as the

heart has passions, as long as life has woes, as long as man's life is haunted by the thought of the infinite, as long as sin and death inflict their fearful wounds, the words of Christ will live. His gospel is an everlasting gospel.
—CLARENCE EDWARD MACARTNEY

197. Charles Reynolds Brown tells of a conversation between Auguste Comte, the French philosopher, and Thomas Carlyle, the Scottish essayist. Comte declared his intention of starting a new religion which would supplant entirely the religion of Christ. It was to have no mysteries, but was to be as plain as the multiplication table and its name was to be "Positivism." "Very good, Mr. Comte," Carlyle replied, "very good! All you will need to do will be to speak as never man spoke, and live as never man lived, and be crucified, and rise again the third day, and get the world to believe that you are still alive. Then your religion will have a chance to get on."
—JAMES P. WESBERRY in *The Pulpit.*

THE MASTER TEACHER

198. Christianity is unique in possessing a teacher who lived what he taught. "Words," wrote Harnack, "effect nothing; it is the power of the personality that stands behind them. He himself stands behind everything that he said."
—ROBERT J. MCCRACKEN in *Questions People Ask,* Harper & Bros.

199. In his famous book *Ecce Homo,* Sir John R. Seeley pointed out that Jesus never lived up to his teachings—he lived them. What a splendid distinction. Jesus' goodness did not smell of perspiration. It came logically and easily from a great resource within his soul, and as the effortless beauty of the lily surpasses the effortless beauty of Solomon, so the beauty of Christ's goodness surpasses that of all the perfectionists and ascetics. They tried too hard; he was good without trying—if I may put it that way. They succeeded in pounding out a counterfeit virtue; he produced the genuine article. Theirs was a manufactured little thing tainted with body odor; his was a pure living fruit with a rich fragrance.
—ANGUS J. MCQUEEN in *The Upper Room Pulpit.*

200. His aim, as the Great Teacher of men, was, and ever is, not to relieve the reason and conscience of mankind, not to lighten the burden of thought and study; but rather to increase that burden, to make men more conscientious, more eager, more active in mind and moral sense. That is to say, he came not to answer questions, but to ask them; not to settle men's souls, but to provoke them; not to save men from problems, but to save them from their indolence; not to make life easier, but to make it more educative. We are quite in error when we think of Christ as coming to give us a key to life's difficult text-book. He came to give us a finer text-book, calling for keener study, and deeper devotion, and more intelligent and persistent reasoning.
—WILLIAM P. MERRILL in *Christian Internationalism.* Copyright 1919 and used by permission of The Macmillan Co.

201. Arnold J. Toynbee in his reflections upon history observed that the source of creative action in any society is never the society itself. Always social action springs directly from the life and work of a given individual. Leaders who dominate their age are always a very small minority, and yet their creative genius is such that it expresses itself in tangible effects through its influence upon the lives and actions of their followers. Whether the leader plays the part of a conqueror and responds to a challenge in such a way that he achieves a victory or whether he accepts the role of a saviour and rescues an enterprise from failure and final collapse depends of course upon the condition of the society in which he operates, whether it is in a state of growth or of disintegration.

Jesus of Nazareth as leader fills both these roles. He is at once a conqueror and a saviour; for against the challenge of an order of life built around the selfish interests of unregenerate humanity he leads to victory the armies of the Kingdom of God, while in opposition to those same disruptive and disintegrating forces expressing themselves within the new society which he has created he champions the cause of the individual man and insures his best interests in the world.

—WILLIAM R. CANNON in *The Redeemer,* Abingdon Press.

202. We learn in Paul Wellman's *The Chain* that it was not Little Robbie, the pious and amiable comforter, but his successor, Father John Carlisle, who saved the members of St. Alban's parish from their annihilating complacency and prejudices. For Father Carlisle, like the Master whom he served, was not afraid to go into the slums and to be found associating with sinners. The gospel he preached and the deeds he performed disturbed the people, and in the end this was the salvation of his parish. Great religious leaders have the faculty of disturbing their followers. It was said of Jesus, "He stirs up the people."

—CHARLES F. JACOBS

203. [Jesus] gives in the realm of character the four great helps which every man requires. He gives man a sense of duty to the highest; he gives him an ideal of what the highest is; he gives him a sense of shame that he is not realizing the highest in his own life; and he is in him the power . . . I will not say to achieve, but to strive to achieve, until at last at the end of the upward calling men come to the perfect fulfilling of their lives in him.

—ROBERT E. SPEER in *Colgate-Rochester Divinity School Bulletin.*

THE ETERNAL PRESENCE

204. A primary child stood proudly to say his Bible verse. His voice was clear, his words plain, his message powerful: "Jesus said, *'Glow,* I am with you always.' "

—JUANITA B. ANDERSON in *Missions,* Vol. 150, No. 4, p. 236.

205. If you are writing a poem and the rhymes won't come or the lines won't fit you may cry, "Oh, William Shakespeare, help me!" and nothing whatever happens. If you're feeling jittery you may think of some hero of the past, like Nelson, and say, "Oh, Horatio Nelson, help me!" But again there isn't the slightest response. But if you're trying to lead a Christian life and realize you're coming to the end of your own moral strength and you cry, "Oh, Christ, help me!" something does happen, at once, just like that. There is a living Spirit immediately available, and millions have proved his existence.

—J. B. PHILLIPS in *Plain Christianity.* Copyright 1954. Used by permission of The Macmillan Co.

206. Sixteen years ago I saw a picture I shall never forget. It was done by a young French soldier named Herbert de Mareau. He painted his picture in 1914. Four years later he was killed in

the battle of Château-Thierry. He called his painting *Never Alone.* It shows a young soldier wounded and lying in the marshes of Flanders, his helmet fallen off, his rifle at his side. Alone he lies, not another human being in sight. Yet not alone, for by his side, with arms outstretched, stands a figure, compassion in his eyes, courage in the touch of his hands.
—John A. Redhead in *The Upper Room Pulpit.*

207. In *The Robe* by Lloyd C. Douglas, Marcellus asked Justus: "Where do you think [Jesus] went?" "I don't know. . . . I only know that he is alive—and I am always expecting to see him. Sometimes I feel aware of him, as if he were close by. . . . It keeps you honest. . . . You have no temptation to cheat anyone, or lie to anyone, or hurt anyone—when, for all you know, Jesus is standing beside you." "I'm afraid I should feel very uncomfortable," remarked Marcellus, "being perpetually watched by some invisible presence." "Not if that presence helped you defend yourself against yourself, Marcellus. It is a great satisfaction to have someone standing by—to keep you at your best."
—Houghton Mifflin Co.

208. To live day by day in the companionship of the present Christ; to know that, great as have been his gifts to us in the past, he holds still better things in store for the future; to be united through him in understanding and sympathy with men and women of other names and creeds from whom apart from him we had remained eternally separate, this is to experience the peace of Christ which passeth understanding.
—William Adams Brown in *How to Think of Christ,* Chas. Scribner's Sons.

209. Dr. William P. Merrill, when he was pastor of the Brick Presbyterian Church in New York, was once asked by a parishioner, "Dr. Merrill, when do you think Christ is coming again?" "Why," exclaimed Dr. Merrill, "I didn't know he had been away."
—J. Carter Swaim in *Do You Understand the Bible?* Copyright, 1954, by W. L. Jenkins, The Westminster Press. Used by permission.

210. A woman in Brooklyn bequeathed her eyes to the eye bank for sight restoration. Upon her death in 1948 in the Methodist Hospital her eyes were flown to Baltimore where the corneas were transplanted. Today someone else is seeing through the eyes of Harriet Hubbard. This is a parable of something more wonderful even than new corneas in the eyes of our bodies: to see the world with the eyes of Christ, the eyes of our hearts and minds made new. Millions of folk have done that. Think of the pages and pages that have been added to the gospel on account of what men have done seeing life with the eyes of Christ.
—Robert E. Luccock in *If God Be For Us,* Harper & Bros.

211. Jesus is like a portent moving through two thousand years of history. No two minds form the same impression of him. Each man's "experience" of him is personal. Every epoch expresses in its own way and with its own words what "eye hath not seen, nor ear heard . . . the things which God hath prepared for them that love him . . ." the things that Jesus came to announce: the Kingdom of God on earth.
—From *Why Jesus Died* by Pierre van Paassen. Reprinted by permission of The Dial Press, Inc. Copyright 1949 by Pierre van Paassen.

212. Willa Cather made a true observation on literature when she wrote that the peculiar quality of a first-rate writer can never be defined but only experienced. That truth reaches out from literature into the Christian religion. Christ can never be completely defined. The Son of man hath not where to lay his head in any neatly defined scheme of thought. He can only be experienced.
—Halford E. Luccock in *Communicating the Gospel,* Harper & Bros.

213. "Consolation in Christ" (Phil. 2:1) is a phrase which has warmed and comforted the hearts of millions of men. The word "consolation," at least as commonly used nowadays, implies solace, "an easing of grief, loneliness, discomfort." Goodspeed renders the phrase "relation to Christ," and the Revised Standard Version reads "encouragement in Christ." Moffatt translates as follows: "the stimulus of Christ." Consolation, relation, encouragement, and stimulus are all translations of the original word; and each is suggestive in its own way. Christ is consoler and encourager; he is also the stimulator. The word "stimulus" is derived from a Latin word meaning "a goad, sting, torment, pang, spur, incentive." The English meaning is "to rouse to action or increased action."

214. Jesus was not a social reformer. Jesus lived under a despotic totalitarianism and never attacked it. He never suggested the freeing of slaves, he never attacked drinking or gambling, nor did he speak about international relations. He was a specialist in religion, not in sociology, interested in man's relation to God. But social change has flowed as a result from his great religious passion and will continue to flow. But it is a result, and will cease if its source is cut off.
—W. Aiken Smart

215. Christ helps us to keep our balance and self-control by high thinking. When one is climbing a mountain cliff, it is better to look up rather than down. When I stand at the edge of Niagara Falls and let my eye follow the line of the falling water, I feel a tendency to grip the rail to steady myself. But one day on a flight from Detroit to New York the pilot carried us over that mighty cataract. As we swept over it and then circled back again, I felt no dizziness. We were high enough to be cut off from the spell which fastens on me when I stand at the edge of the falls. Similarly Christ gets our minds up into the altitude of high thought and high tastes where we do not feel the downward drag of the vicious and the vulgar.
—Ralph W. Sockman

216. I well remember those times when as a theological student at the University of Chicago I paused to listen as the chapel's great carillon played a medley of vesper hymns. One needed to concentrate or the street noises would drown out the music of faith. In much the same way the voice of Jesus is lost in the babble of the world's confusing tongues if we do not pause to concentrate on his words. Yet when we listen, his voice sounds clearly above the tumult.
—John B. Schlarb

THE MIND OF CHRIST

217. The apostle Paul wrote, "We have the mind of Christ" (I Cor. 2:16 R.S.V.). Moffatt's translation reads: "Our thoughts are Christ's thoughts." Thinking as Christ thought—this is the Christian's privilege and obligation. But Paul warns that only the spiritually-minded man will know the mind of Christ. To others Christ's thoughts are meaningless.

218. The noblest and best men and women of every age and every clime have acknowledged Christ's moral and spiritual grandeur as the leader and guide of mankind. The selfless Francis of Assisi prayed that he might be as selfless as Christ; Brother Lawrence, performing the lowliest duties in a monastery kitchen, prayed that he might be as humble as Christ; David Livingstone, during the perils of darkest Africa, prayed that he might be as adventurous as Christ; the virtuous Catherine of Siena prayed that she might be as pure as Christ; the fearless General Gordon prayed that he might be as courageous as Christ; and the gentle Mahatma Gandhi prayed that he might be as kind as Christ. Not only does Jesus stand unchallenged and unchallengeable as the revealer of God, but also as the supreme example in human history of life as God intended it to be lived.

—John Sutherland Bonnell

219. Before Igor Gorin sang "A Merry Fiddler" by Revutzki some time ago, he told us that the number was an old folk song of Ukraine. The fiddler had a battered, hard-used instrument with only one string, but he would stand in the markets of the city and play his music. When anyone would make fun of his fiddle and point out that he had only one string on it, he would reply: "Yes, but I have lots of strings in my heart. I am the merry fiddler who wishes a happy life to all." I expect that is life's secret. If you have music in your heart, you will discover a way to bring it forth in the market place of life.

—Frank A. Court

220. Albert Schweitzer took for his life attitude the philosophy "reverence for life," in other words an attitude of love for every living thing. At the hotel in Estes Park, Colorado, a large St. Bernard dog was the object of attention from visitors. He spurned their attentions by silent disregard. But when Schweitzer came, the dog of its own accord made its way through the crowd and deliberately put up its paw to him. The dog then came to the dining hall and lay down by Schweitzer's table. Love lets down the barriers of fear between persons and persons and between persons and animals. There is no fear in love.

—E. Stanley Jones in *Growing Spiritually,* Abingdon Press.

221. Jesus went to the simple folk for his disciples and his adherents. He did not seek the rich men and the politicians who were entrenched in nefarious practice at the expense of the common man. Any successful general follows the same method. He mingles and breaks bread with the G.I.'s who do the fighting and the dying on the battlefield. It is they who make or break a battle or a campaign.

After V.E. Day I came home with General Eisenhower. We landed in the Azores for breakfast. The general walked around the island, shook many hands, signed many autographs. He boarded the plane and was ready to leave. Suddenly a young soldier about 18 years of age ran up to us and called out, almost in tears: "I have missed General Eisenhower! I must see him and shake his hand!" I said to Ike, "A friend of yours is outside." Ike got off the plane, put his arm around the kid's shoulder, shook hands, and signed an autograph. The young soldier said to me later: "You

have made me the happiest man in the world."
—ROBERT M. LITTLEJOHN in *This I Believe About Jesus Christ,* John Clover Monsma, ed., Fleming H. Revell Co.

222. Love. We are early taught to say it. I love you. We are trained to the thought of it as if there were nothing else, or nothing else worth having which it could not bring with it. Love is taught, always by precept, sometimes by example. Then hate, which no one meant to teach us, comes of itself. It is true that if we say I love you, it may be received with doubt, for there are times when it is hard to believe. Say I hate you, and the one spoken to believes it instantly, once for all. Say I love you a thousand times to that person afterward and mean it every time, and still it does not change the fact that once we said I hate you, and meant that too. It leaves a mark on that surface love had worn so smooth with its eternal caresses. Love must be learned again and again; there is no end to it. Hate needs no instruction, but waits only to be provoked.
—KATHERINE ANNE PORTER in *The Days Before,* Harcourt, Brace & Co., Inc.

223. When I was in New York City, I became lost in the labyrinth of canyoned streets. I asked a man on the street for directions; but he replied, "I'm a stranger here myself." Then I said to myself, "I've been foolish. In a city there is one person who always knows the way." So I found a policeman, who quickly directed me. Then he added, half humorously: "If you wish to save time, call a cab. The cab drivers always know locations." The first cabby I hailed not only saved me time and effort but also promptly delivered me to the right location. Along the road of life we are not without One who can show us the right road to travel. "Commit thy way unto the Lord; trust also in him." (Ps. 37:5.)
—CHARLES L. ALLEN

224. A poignant little story comes out of those dire days following World War II. One relief worker tells of going into a war area and holding a glass of milk before a child whose eyes seemed so much bigger because of the gauntness of his little face. Reflecting the days past when many had to drink out of one cup, the child asked, "How deep shall I drink, ma'am?" And she, deeply moved by so simple and revealing a question, answered huskily, "Drink as deep as you can, son, as deep as you can." It is one thing to ask how deep I shall go in my faith; but because of the grace of God which knows neither exhaustion nor limit the answer is clear, "Drink as deep as you can, as deep as you can," for "my grace is sufficient for thee." (II Cor. 12:9.)
—GENE E. BARTLETT

225. An old lady was receiving congratulations on her birthday. Someone said to her, "My, you are beautiful." Without a moment's hesitation or embarrassment she replied: "I ought to be. I'm 74." Such beauty is not decorative. It is structural.
—OSCAR F. BLACKWELDER in *The Pulpit.* Copyrighted by the Christian Century Foundation and used by permission.

226. The word "gossip" originally meant godparent. A word now used to describe a person who spreads evil talk and who tattles idly formerly identified a person who assumed at baptism the responsibility for inspiring and counseling a youth. In much the same way a noble and constructive person may degenerate into a ignoble and destructive evildoer

if he doesn't refreshen and re-create his mind with that which is worthy and beautiful. Christ is the fountain wherein a man who drinks deeply may find the refreshment needed to keep the soul pure and the heart cleansed.

FOLLOWING CHRIST

227. When Holman Hunt told his artist friends . . . that he was going to paint Christ, they pointed out the absurdity of the undertaking. "You can paint only what you can *see,*" they insisted, as the principle of their school of painting. "You will only waste your time trying to do the impossible." "But I am going to *see* Him," Hunt replied. "I will work by His side in the carpenter shop. I will walk with Him over the hills of Galilee. I will go with Him among the poor, the blind, the lame and the leprous. I will go to Gethsemane with Him. I will travel with Him to Calvary and climb the Cross with Him, until I *see* Him, and then I will paint Him." Those of us who have stood with moved hearts as we have looked at Holman Hunt's "Light of the World," knocking at the closed door, feel convinced that the great painter did live with Christ until he *saw* Him with eyes of joy and wonder. But it was not a dead Christ that he saw, but the living Christ trying to find entrance into the human heart.

—Rufus M. Jones in *New Eyes for Invisibles.* Copyright 1943. Used by permission of The Macmillan Co.

228. "If men do not keep step with their age," said Thoreau, "perhaps it is because they hear a distant drummer." The staying power of the Christian saint, carrying him through opposition and through the unheroic commonplace, is his response to the drumbeat of eternity.

—Dwight E. Stevenson in *Faith Takes a Name,* Harper & Bros.

229. On his seventieth birthday F. M. Meyer said of Christ: "I knew him as a boy. I trusted him because of the testimony of my parents and my minister. Since then I have wintered and summered with him, and spent days and nights with him. I know what he can be when a man sins and fails, and when the heart is hard and loveless. I now know him whom once I simply believed, and on my seventieth birthday this is my assurance—that he is able to keep that which I have committed to him. You cannot wear him out nor tire him. Your sin is no barrier against his love."

—Armin C. Oldsen

230. The mother of Jesus in *Mary* by Sholem Asch says to the brothers of her eldest Son: "Your qualities, however noble they may be, are the qualities of thirst. But your brother is the libation. Your ways are the ways of the quest, of groping in darkness. His is the way of the unerring guide. Go out therefore and cleave to him and your search shall be gloriously ended. For as all rivers tend toward the sea, so every road to God must meet in him. He is the bread of God for those that hunger after it."

—Copyright 1949, G. P. Putnam's Sons.

231. The grand business of being a Christian is seldom a bed of roses, although it brings exalted experiences that are more precious than the so-called prizes of life. Christ summons us to a crusade. "We are called to build temples, not to whittle sticks." It is not enough to admire Jesus, however extravagantly, or to worship him, however devoutly;

we must follow him, which is more heroic.
—Edgar DeWitt Jones in *Today Is Mine,* T. C. Clark, ed., Harper & Bros.

232. The Scottish mother in Ian Maclaren's *Beside the Bonnie Brier Bush* says to her son: "Ye 'ill follow Christ, and gin He offers ye His cross ye'll no refuse it, for He aye carries the heavy end Himsel.' He's guided yir mother a' thae years, and been as gude as a husband since yir father's death, and He 'ill hold me fast tae the end. He'll keep ye too, and, John, I'll be watchin' for ye. Ye 'ill no fail me."

233. A cowboy was converted in one of Bud Robinson's meetings. Out of habit a few days later he dismounted in front of the town saloon and started to tie his horse to the hitching post. Just then Robinson came along and gave this advice, "If you are going to follow Jesus, you had better find a new hitching rail."
—Wallace Fridy in *A Lamp Unto My Feet,* Abingdon Press.

234. A man who had arrived by train in a strange city late one night found no transportation to the hotel. En route he met a policeman who cautioned him that holdups were not uncommon along the poorly lighted streets. "Always keep a margin between yourself and dark alleys and shadowed entrances to buildings," the policeman suggested. That is sensible advice for all life. Allowing a margin of safety between one's self and the dangers of evil offers protection to those who are following Christ.
—Stuart R. Oglesby

THE WAY OF DISCIPLESHIP

235. Down through the centuries men and women, even as you and I, have been aware of being controlled and molded by a dynamic Presence. You may recall Tolstoy's tribute to Lincoln on hearing of the great emancipator's death: "He was a Christ in miniature." That is what we are to become—Christs in miniature.
—David A. MacLennan in *Joyous Adventure,* published in 1952 by Harper & Brothers.

236. Archibald Rutledge has written . . . of the widow of a Negro preacher who was always doing something for the poor, and who seeemd to rear all the orphans and illegitimate children in the community. He was so impressed by the quality of her life that he built her an immaculate little home in his own backyard. He completely equipped it with new furniture and moved her in. To his horror, the first thing she did was to invite into her new, shining home the most disreputable Negro woman in the county. "How," he remonstrated, "could you have invited that creature into your pretty new home?" The soft answer was: "Jesus would."
—Albert E. Day in *An Autobiography of Prayer,* published in 1952 by Harper & Brothers.

237. At Princeton in the Graduate College they have in their lovely Proctor Hall a very unusual west window. The Liberal Arts are depicted in stained glass, with a figure representing each one of these Arts. In the center of the group is the figure of the Christ Child. By the art of the designer, this figure has been so made that when the evening sun dies away in the west, the face of the Christ Child is the last to be illumined in the huge window. There in this magnificent dining hall, students talking together over their coffee cups after the evening meal is over, or perhaps musing in

quietness, are wont to watch while the great window slowly loses its glory as the sun disappears. Last of all remains always the face of the Christ. Under that window in Latin is written a line which every Christian, as well as those striving for a Master's degree, will do well to remember: *"Nec vocamini magistri: quia Magister unus est Christus."* "And be ye not called masters; for the one Master is Christ."

—NOLAN B. HARMON in *Religion in Life.*

238. It takes confidence to beget confidence, belief to establish belief, faith to kindle faith. A man selling bulletproof vests can deluge a police department with illustrated brochures showing the merits of his product. He can give long and learned talks about its effectiveness. All of that means very little until he is willing to go out to the pistol range, put it on, and say, "Go ahead, shoot!" It takes such utter belief in Jesus Christ to convey belief. We cannot expect to do much toward encouraging anyone else to put his life into the keeping of Jesus Christ until first we do.

—EVERETT W. PALMER

239. A few years ago a college girl, greatly troubled, turned to me in her anxiety. For some months we talked and wrote, and then one day I knew that she had come onto solid ground. For this was what she said in a letter to me: "I see now that God does not save me on the *outside.* It is this way: when you are safe on the *inside,* you are safe on every side." She had found the only security that really counts.

—BOYNTON MERRILL in *The Upper Room Pulpit.*

240. Will, speaking at Mr. O'Hara's funeral in *Gone with the Wind* by Margaret Mitchell, says: "There warn't nothin' that come to him *from the outside* that could lick him. . . . There ain't nothin' *from the outside* can lick any of us. But he had our failin's too, 'cause he could be licked from the inside. I mean to say that what the whole world couldn't do, his own heart could. . . . And I want to say this—folks whose mainsprings are busted are better dead."

—Copyright 1936. Used by permission of The Macmillan Co.

241. A prominent layman, in speaking of the late Dr. Ernest Fremont Tittle, once said, "I disagree with him on many things and that makes me very uncomfortable, for it leaves me with the impression that I am really disagreeing with God."

—ROY L. SMITH in *New Light from Old Lamps,* Abingdon Press.

242. A young Presbyterian minister was in charge of a large church in a great industrial city. The most active and generous person of the church was a woman. She was married to one of the most prominent and wealthy men of the community. He never came to church, he did nothing for it, he gave nothing to it. And as the years went on, that man was on the conscience of the young minister. And he said to himself, "I have got to do something about that man." So, after long deliberation, he finally made an appointment with him. He was an older man, austere, sitting behind a great desk in his office. The young man sat in front of him and proceeded with his story. In very simple terms he set before him the Christian proposition and he said, "I think you ought to do something about this one way or the other." And when he finished, there was dead silence. The man never spoke, never moved. So the young man gathered himself together and went over his story again, amplifying it a little. When he finished, still there was silence. At that point he wished he had never undertaken that particular mission, but he drew himself up once again and rehearsed his story. And when he finished, there was not a sound and finally, while he wished for a way out of the room, the man reached for a pad and wrote something on it. He passed it to the young man and this was what he had written: "I am so deeply moved that I cannot speak." It was the first time that an adult, in a frank, straightforward way, had ever set before him the Christian gospel, and he became a member of the church and one of the great Christian leaders in that city.

—THEODORE P. FERRIS in *The Interpreter's Bible,* Vol. 9, Abingdon Press.

243. Some time ago while visiting in one of our church homes—a home in which the mother was a member of our church, but in which the father was not—we talked about other things until little by little the conversation moved toward spiritual matters. Then rather suddenly the young husband said, "While it is true that I have never accepted Christ as my Savior, it is also true that I have never rejected him, because," he explained, "actually no one has ever *asked* me to accept him." I waited a moment and then said, "I wonder if you will accept him now?" He said, "I certainly will."

—EDWARD HUGHES PRUDEN in *Interpreters Needed.* Copyright, 1951, by the Judson Press. Used by permission.

244. Three of America's famous physicians were together in Philadelphia in friendly conversation. All were active Christians. The conversation turned to religion. One of them asked, "What is to you the strongest argument for the existence of God?" As the discussion went on for some time the youngest of the three sat in thoughtful silence. Then one of the others said, "Now let us hear what the young doctor has to say." "Well, to me," he said, "the strongest reason I have for believing in God is that I am personally acquainted with him."

—ALBERT CASSEL WIEAND in *The Gospel of Prayer,* Wm. B. Eerdmans Publishing Co.

245. When our division was sent to the California coast to do amphibious training, late one evening I was walking along the deck of a large army transport chatting with a Jewish medical officer. On his own initiative he started to talk about religion. He had just read Sholem Asch's book, *The Nazarene.* "You know," he said, "I admire the man whom that book describes more than any other man of whom I know. And I have tried to put into my life some of the principles he taught. But sometimes I'm puzzled. As I look around me I find persons who call themselves Christian who, it seems to me, deny the principles this man taught. I wonder sometimes, if I am not more Christian than they are, even if I am a Jew."

—EDWIN T. SETTLE in *Religion in Life.*

246. There was once a scholarly young man who ardently hoped to win the esteem of a certain young woman. But, alas, she remained singularly unimpressed. What is more, she never permitted the occasions of privacy he deemed necessary to advance his cause. One day while driving past a lake he observed another couple getting into a sailboat. The girl, after seating herself gracefully in the stern, placed a picnic basket at her feet. The man skillfully

hoisted the sail. In a few minutes they were off, white sail against the blue sky. The heart of the eager and studious youth leaped with hope as he watched. Being a young man of scholarly habits and having great confidence in the wisdom conveyed by books, he went to the library to study the art of sailing. He learned all that books and pictures could teach. At last came the bright day when he in turn took his beloved to the lake. She got in the sailboat, seated herself daintily, and placed the picnic basket at her feet. He hoisted the sail with manly competence, and off they went. But at that time a speedboat roared past with a mighty wake. This happened to coincide with an unexpected gust of wind. And, alas, the long anticipated occasion was lost, for the young man instantly learned that there is a vast difference between reading about sailing and actually sailing. His experience should remind us of people who spend all their time merely reading, talking, arguing, wishing, and yearning about religion. They get nowhere because they do not relate their desire to action.
—EVERETT W. PALMER

247. Saving faith is that which rests unequivocally on the Word of God, upon God's simple say-so. Napoleon, who was small in stature, was fond of large and powerfully built horses. One day when he was mounted on a spirited charger and was reviewing his troops, his horse became frightened and reared back on his hind legs. Napoleon was in immediate physical peril. A private in the line instantly ran forward, seized the reins, and pulled the powerful horse down. The emperor saluted briskly to his benefactor and said, "Thank you, Captain!" The private replied, "Of what regiment, Sir?" "Of the emperor's guards," was the answer. The soldier tossed his rifle back toward the line from which he had stepped and said, "Let him have it who will." Then he joyfully took his place with the officers of Napoleon's bodyguard.
—STEPHEN W. PAINE

TESTINGS AND GROWTH

248. A character in one of George Macdonald's stories cries out in frustration, "I do not see why God ever made me"; to which her friend replies: "God hasn't made you yet. He is making you and you don't like it."
—HUGH THOMSON KERR in *Design for Christian Living.* Copyright, 1953, by W. L. Jenkins, The Westminster Press. Used by permission.

249. Said Otto Dibelius, a Christian leader in the East Zone of Berlin: "Christ has not made life easy for me. On the contrary. It would have been more comfortable to be without him than to live with him. He puts burdens on the soul which one would rather let pass by unheeded."
—DAVID A. MACLENNAN in *Pastoral Preaching.* Copyright, 1955, by W. L. Jenkins, The Westminster Press. Used by permission.

250. A young lad sailing his little boat on a pond began to cry when the boat got beyond his reach. A big boy who had been watching began to throw rocks in the direction of the boat. The little boy cried all the louder until he realized that the rocks were not sinking the boat but gently bringing it toward him. The rocks hit the water a little beyond the boat, and each ripple moved it closer to shore. Most of us cry out when stones are thrown our way; but if we are patient, we can realize that each trial may contain possibilities for good. God's

purpose may not be apparent at the time of testing, but "we know that in everything God works for good with those who love him, who are called according to his purpose." When we draw upon his resources, God can turn the hour of tragedy into triumph.
—Gordon H. Schroeder

251. During the construction of the Empire State Building in New York City I had the opportunity of inspecting that great edifice under the guidance of the architect who had created it. By means of several different elevators we finally arrived at the skeleton steel structure which was to be the tower on top. I noticed that the steelwork did not fit snugly at the joints, and I remarked about it. "Ah, so you have noticed that," said the guide. "Well, that is one of the most important things in the whole building. Those joints were left somewhat loose so that the building will be flexible. You see this tower sways back and forth in the wind; and if the building were not flexible, it might crack, crumple, and break." So it is with the whole structure of our civilization. Human personality must be tempered like steel that it may be flexible, be capable of adjusting to the winds of turmoil that assail human life. And when God tempers the human soul, he does it with trouble and mercy.
—Ensworth Reisner

252. "The love of Christ constraineth us," Paul wrote in II Cor. 5:14. "Constraineth," which means to hold back or to draw tight by force, is one of the most expressive words in the New Testament. It is what the banks do for a river by keeping the flood waters from rampaging implacably across the landscape and uprooting trees, destroying crops, scattering destruction in a helter-skelter fashion. Paul declared that God had laid hold of him and constrained him. God holds the rampaging river of life to well-directed channels.
—Harry K. Zeller, Jr.

253. The steps of discipleship are suggested by the synonyms of the word "faithful" in *Webster's New Collegiate Dictionary*: "Faithful" implies unswerving adherence to the person or thing to which one is bound by love, allegiance, and so on; "loyal" adds to faithful an implication of unwillingness to be tempted from that adherence; "constant" stresses firmness of devotion or attachment; "stanch," from its earlier sense of watertight, suggests an inherent imperviousness to all influences that would weaken one's loyalty; "steadfast" implies a steady and unwavering course not only in love, allegiance, and so on, but more widely, as in quality or character; "resolute" implies steadfast determination, especially in adhering to a person, a cause, an end, or the like.

254. Year after year we had added new rooms to our one-room summer cabin. One summer we were surprised to find that millions of termites had burrowed into the boards of the original structure, but they had left the new sections untouched. Christ said: "No man also seweth a piece of new cloth on an old garment: else the new piece that filled it up taketh away from the old, and the rent is made worse" (Mark 2:21). Moral termites may eat away at the heart of our lives, leaving only our bright and shining exterior, if we allow evil thoughts and motives to remain in our minds and souls.
—Carlton Van Ornum

255. One day in a Boston hospital I was surprised to find a ward filled with

patients who were radiant with cheer and hope. In a few moments I discovered why that ward was different. In one bed was a miserably sick woman who refused to be discouraged. Her bed was her pulpit, and her Christian courage and faith were influencing all her fellow sufferers.
—Aaron N. Meckel

256. I shall always remember a popcorn wagon in my home town of Atchison, Kansas. Adversity had come to the delightful old couple who ran the wagon. One day I went down to get popcorn with my preacher father, and he made some comment on their constant cheeriness. The husband made this reply: "Well, Chris, when we were having all our troubles, you preached a sermon in which you said that frost turns turnips but sweetens parsnips. We're just learning how to be parsnips."
—Ensworth Reisner

257. To me it sometimes seems that our moralists would do well to cease their upbraidings and apply themselves to the interesting problem—"How is goodness to be made the object of passionate desire, as attractive as fame, success, or even adventure?" If they could excite in men and an enthusiasm for virtue, as the poets, musicians and artists excite in them enthusiasm for beauty, and the men of science for truth; they could devise a morality that has power to charm, they would win all hearts. "To be virtuous," said Aristotle, "is to take pleasure in noble actions."
—W. Macneile Dixon in *The Human Situation,* St. Martin's Press.

258. The world answers back to our faith. It trusts when we trust it. It responds to our confidence. It says to the farmer, "Sow your seed"; to the aviator, "Spread your wings"; to the miner, "Sink your shaft"; to the sailor, "Hoist your sail"; to the engineer, "Swing your bridge"; to the scientist, "Trust your hypothesis"; to the financier, "Make your investment"; to the explorer, "Follow the gleam." Faith is man's highest venture. The poet Whitman puts it thus: "The steps of faith fall on the seeming void and find the rock beneath." It is a "seeming void" on which we set our faith; beneath us, however, is the unseen reality, and faith gives it substance.
—Hugh Thomson Kerr in *Design for Christian Living.* Copyright, 1953, by W. L. Jenkins, The Westminster Press. Used by permission.

259. We define religion as the assumption that life has meaning. Religion, or lack of it, is shown not in some intellectual or verbal formulations but in one's total orientation to life. Religion is whatever the individual takes to be his ultimate concern. One's religious attitude is to be found at that point where he has a conviction that there are values in human existence worth living and dying for.
—Rollo May in *Man's Search for Himself,* W. W. Norton & Co., Inc.

260. Religion is the reaching out of one's whole being—mind, body, spirit, emotions, intuitions, affections, will—for completion, for inner unity, for true relation with those about us, for right relation to the universe in which we live. Religion is *life,* a certain kind of life, life as it should and could be, a life of harmony within and true adjustment without—life, therefore, in harmony with the life of God himself.
—Henry P. Van Dusen in *Life's Meaning,* Association Press.

261. Oliver Wendell Holmes out of ninety years of glorious living said this

of life: "Life is a romantic business. It is painting a picture, not doing a sum; but you have to make the romance, and it will come to the question of how much fire you have in you." Here is the glory of our religious faith. The flame of our life may flicker in the storms of the world. Our hopes may grow dim, and our faith may be overgrown by the defeat of life. But we can bring our life back to God's central altar and central flame. And, once again, the fire within our life can be rekindled in the beauty of truth and great worship.
—Frank A. Court

SPIRITUAL IRRESPONSIBILITY

262. Lives become like the bulletin board of the church, reading, "Sunday at 11:00 A.M., Forward with Christ; Wednesday at 7:30, The Midweek Retreat."
—Gerald Kennedy

263. Phillips Brooks, returning from a trip to the Far East, was asked by a friend about what articles he had brought back with him and what customs duty he had to pay. The friend facetiously asked him too if he had tried to bring back a new religion. Brooks replied that he had not tried to do so; but if he had done so, there would have been no difficulty about customs duties, for America would be glad to import a religion "without any duties."
—Clarence Edward Macartney

264. C. E. Montague's novel *Rough Justice* tells of a young boy who goes to church for the first time and hears the story of Christ presented by his uncle who was the vicar. Brom heard his uncle tell a heart-rending tale of a brave and kind man ferociously hurt a long time ago but who was still being crucified because he desired people to be better, to love and obey God. When they did not, he was crucified anew. Brom wept as he sat in the family pew, but nobody else seemed disturbed. When his uncle had finished, the people rose and sang a hymn. Then instead of rushing out to do something about the Man who still was in pain, they stopped to talk and walked away as if nothing remarkable had happened and as if nothing had to be done. When Brom asked his nurse about it, she said, "We must not take the minister too seriously, or people would think us odd."
—Frank A. Court

265. The Dutch painter Hans Van Meegeren made a fortune by signing his pictures with the names of such eminent masters as Vermeer and de Hooch. His forgeries fooled even experienced art dealers. One day, however, his pictures were hung in a gallery along with those by the masters. Then the forgeries became obvious. Those who halfheartedly profess Christianity may fool even their closest friends, but their inadequate witness will not prove adequate when compared with genuine Christian living.
—J. Calvert Cariss

266. A young Texas minister who had a preaching assignment in the country spent week ends with a rancher who was not a professing Christian. Time and again the youth urged the rancher to give his heart to Christ and join the church. After persistent invitations the rancher finally said, "Henry is a member of your church, isn't he?" "You know he is," the preacher replied. "And Will is a member of the other church, isn't he?" the rancher added. "Yes, he is an officer in that church." "Well," the rancher continued, "Will and Henry are married to sisters, but they have

not spoken to each other in twenty years. If that's all your Christianity can do for them, I want none of it for me."
—ARTHUR V. BOAND

267. Do not be too quick to condemn the man who no longer believes in God; for it is perhaps your own coldness and avarice and mediocrity and materialism and sensuality and selfishness that have killed his faith.
—THOMAS MERTON in *Seeds of Contemplation.* Copyright 1949 by Our Lady of Gethsemani Monastery and published by New Directions.

268. Norman Thomas, perennial Socialist candidate for the presidency of the United States, has the respect of a vast number of men who have never voted for him. He was being introduced one time before a group of distinguished men and the chairman commented on this general respect. Mr. Thomas rose to speak and said: "I would gladly exchange some of this respect for a little support." Christian faith is more than respect for Christ, which he really does not need. It is support of his program and witnessing for his way.
—GERALD KENNEDY in *Go Inquire of the Lord,* Harper & Bros.

269. William Lyon Phelps of Yale University once said that too many people are the slaves of their circumstances, the vassals of time and place. "They are all right at three o'clock in the afternoon," he said, "but look out for them at three o'clock in the morning. They are all right in Poughkeepsie, but look out for them in Paris." It is true that all too many Christians chameleonlike take their color from their environment. They are steadfast when in the company of other Christians, but they falter in any society where the standards of the Master are challenged.
—JOHN SUTHERLAND BONNELL

270. A newspaper advertisement says: "Your spare tire is the most useless and the most important part of your car." Day after day the spare tire is neglected and well-nigh forgotten; but when a flat tire stops the car, a man may well exclaim, "I'm glad I have a spare handy!" Some people's religion is put on a standby basis. It is good to have a preacher at hand for a christening, a marriage, or a funeral; but most of the time their faith is neglected. If a great difficulty or emergency overwhelms a person, he may find that the spiritual strength he needs has been too greatly weakened through neglect to support him.

271. Murmuring and disputing is an indication of unfaith. . . . It is like the little mouse who runs along a plank in the studio of a great artist and looks up at an unfinished painting which is standing there. Seeing the meaningless jumble of color upon color, of highlights and shades, the little mouse pronounces judgment and says, "Well, he certainly made a mess of that one." The insolent little creature is not fitted by his nature to comprehend ultimate good in the realm of art, nor is he willing to allow the talented artist time in which to demonstrate his solution, the denouement of his purpose in this particular artistic situation. Our murmuring demonstrates a lack of faith in a mighty and purposeful God.
—STEPHEN W. PAINE in *Toward the Mark,* Fleming H. Revel Co.

272. A friend of mine while in college went to a distant town to attend a football game. He ate abstemiously at a nearby hamburger stand. But when he

went to pay his bill at the hotel, he discovered that in the same price all his meals in the dining room were included. That is life without love and without God—it is the mere existence of an unfulfilled self when so much more could be included.
—Frank B. Fagerburg

273. The story is told about some boys who broke into a store and swapped price tags on several articles of merchandise. The next morning, when the owner of the store opened for business, he found that nails were twenty dollars each and lawn mowers were eight cents a pound. Electric fans were eighteen dollars each, and coaster wagons were five cents. We are in a world in which the price tags are often mixed up, and we need to get back to God's Word to examine true values.
—Ira H. Peak

274. Alexander Miller, describing to youth the confusion of our world, told of a friend who took a journey through North India. "He saw on a railroad platform there, so he told me, a packing-case ready for dispatch which was labeled, 'This case should be carried bottom upward.' That was bad enough, but it was marked further, 'The *top* is labeled *bottom* to avoid confusion.'"
—*The Intercollegian*

275. E. Stanley Jones has told of seeing in the Malay States grown men sitting on the ridges of the rice fields fishing in a foot of water. Within sight of them the great ocean rolled, but there they sat and fished in the rice fields. Then he added, "I have sat in great conferences and have heard the ponderous debates on trivialities, and involuntarily the thought has forced itself upon me, 'fishing in rice fields,' and all the time the great world problems were roaring in our ears."
—Ira M. Hargett

276. Years ago Peter Taylor Forsyth acutely observed that unless we have within us something that is over us, we succumb to what is around us. Having made man the measure of all things, we have discovered with a rude shock that he is unworthy of so lofty a status. Overwhelmed by the forces which our own ill-guided knowledge has released but which we lack the ethical insight and spiritual power rightly to control, we yield to despair. Our plight convincingly demonstrates the truth of Plato's judgment: "Whenever anyone gives something too big to something too small to carry it, too big sails to too small a ship, too big meals to too small a body, too big powers to too small a soul, the result is bound to be a complete upset."
—S. Paul Schilling in *Religion in Life.*

277. Leslie D. Weatherhead has coined a new Beatitude, "Blessed are they who do not try to make the best of two worlds." These two-world people, says Weatherhead, "are not wicked enough to be happy in wickedness, and they are not disciplined enough to find joy in God. They pass from one world to another without enjoying either. When they are 'enjoying the pleasures of sin for a season,' they feel guiltily unhappy. When they watch the carefree sinners, they suspect them of having a better time than they for all their scruples." This is one of the curses of religion in our day. We have made no decision for one world or another.
—Ensworth Reisner

278. Many ministers have discovered the blessed word "relax," and have com-

pressed the whole Gospel into it, like abbreviating an eighty-eight note piano into one note. . . . They are almost on the verge of rewriting the Scriptures to read, "If any man will come after me, let him relax," or "Go into all the world and keep down your blood pressure." Something is missing. It is the tension of Jesus . . . but we have to remember that Jesus lived a very disturbed and unsuccessful life. He died on a cross.
—HALFORD E. LUCCOCK in *Marching Off the Map,* Harper & Bros.

279. A pastor I was to assist in a revival meeting wrote to ask me what the subject of my opening sermon would be. I told him it would be, "Suppose You Relax." He wrote back and said, "You are either a poor psychologist or your subject has a hidden meaning. My people don't need to be told to relax!"
—C. GORDON BAYLESS in *And Be Ye Saved.* Fleming H. Revell Co.

280. A well-known art critic said: "I regard myself as a Christianity graduate in the sense in which I am a college graduate; I feel toward the church as I do toward the university—the same gratitude, the same affection, the same admiration." Why not graduate from the church the way we graduate from college and leave the things of our childhood behind? But we know that we haven't yet completed the course; we have learned some of the elementals about the worship of God, yet there is a lot more to learn. We have learned a little bit about how to control ourselves and live better lives with our neighbors, but we have much more to learn. Furthermore we don't look forward to completing the course before the time of our earthly life is over. And if that should be possible, most of us, I think, would not want to graduate from the church fellowship. It is not like a university; it is not a place primarily where we come to learn but a place where we come to practice and to live within a context of relationships that are finally knit together in Christ.
—THEODORE P. FERRIS

HE IS DESPISED AND REJECTED

281. Paul Flandrin, the French artist . . . has painted a picture entitled, *Christ Mourns over the City.* But the city on his canvas is not Jerusalem. It has tenements, spurting flame from blast-furnaces, and a pall of smoke. Cathedrals, too, but they seem to be dark as the day dies. Christ stands on a cliff looking down on the city. He seems much greater than the city, and not simply because he is in the bold foreground. He gazes fixedly, motionless, sad, compassionate. "How often would I have gathered thee!" Yes, he could gather that whole city . . . "And ye would not!"
—GEORGE A. BUTTRICK in *The Upper Room Pulpit.*

282. When I was a boy in Glasgow, there hung in our living room a large print of a painting by Sigismund Goetze, entitled *Despised and Rejected.* I know nothing about the artist. I know nothing about the merits of the painting. But, I have never forgotten the picture. In the center was the Christ bound to a Roman imperial altar, overshadowed by an angel with the Gethsemane Cup. On each side of the altar there streamed by a procession of men and women in modern dress. Here was the political agitator and there a common laborer; here a sportsman with the pink edition of the paper, there a scientist with his test tube. A newsboy shouted the latest society scandal and a

woman went by in a widow's weeds. A soldier in uniform and a clergyman replete with clerical collar stalked by in unconscious company. Only one person has any look of surprise or wonder or sympathy for the Christ—a nurse. What is the picture saying? For the artist, Christ is still "despised and rejected" by most folk in the everyday, work-a-day world.
—JAMES T. CLELAND in *The Upper Room Pulpit.*

283. In a new and beautiful church building I noticed that a large picture of Jesus weeping over Jerusalem—a picture which had hung in a prominent position in the old structure—had been relegated to an out-of-the-way closet. I was told that it seemed inappropriate to the new setting. This seems to me to be a parable of our times, for has not Christ's great compassion and suffering been too frequently overshadowed in the teaching of our churches?
—HERSCHEL T. HAMNER

284. Some of us once joined a group of Christians as a part of a procession making its way down the Via Dolorosa. The leader in charge of the ritual found the heat much too oppressive. In order to protect himself he carried an umbrella, using it as he knelt in prayer in Pilate's Court, and along the way. The symbolism of the procession was in strange contrast to the historical incident! Once Jesus found the cross so heavy that he fell beneath it. Now the leader carried an umbrella to protect himself from the heat!
—G. RAY JORDAN in *Beyond Despair*. Copyright 1955. Used by permission of The Macmillan Co.

285. A minister friend tells of going to a large church to preach at a special Good Friday night service. The weather was extremely bad and only a few people came. Apologetically, the pastor said to the visiting minister, "If it had not been for the bad weather we would have had a large crowd to hear you tonight." Jesus died on Good Friday, but his followers did not come to the service because the weather was bad.
—CHARLES L. ALLEN in *God's Psychiatry,* Fleming H. Revell Co.

286. Walter Russell Bowie tells of a minister who had been sent by his home church to the mission fields of Asia and who was on his homeward journey. The airplane in which he was flying came across the deserts to Damascus and then turned southward along the Mediterranean shore. Above all else he had wanted to see Jerusalem, but the pressure of time made it impossible. By his side sat a young aviator who knew every mile of this territory, and when he learned of the minister's desire to see the Holy City, he told him that at a certain point in the Judean hills, if conditions were right, they could get a far distance view of it. As they approached this point, they watched with concentration for the one moment of opportunity. The airplane swept onward; the hills flowed past them. They came to the gap, went past it, but there was no view of the city. "I am sorry," said the aviator. "We have lost our chance." And then in explanation he said what became a parable which the minister would never forget: "If we had been flying a little higher, we should have seen the Holy City."
—WALLACE FRIDY in *A Lamp Unto My Feet,* Abingdon Press.

THE MEANING OF THE CROSS

287. There was a popular monk in the Middle Ages who announced that he would preach one day on the love of

God. On the day appointed the cathedral was filled with eager listeners. He waited till the setting sun caught the stained glass windows, flooding the place with its lovely coloring. Then when the last bit of light had faded from the windows he went to a golden candelabra, took a lighted candle, and walked to a statue of Christ hanging on the cross. He held the candle beside the wounded hands, then the wounded feet, then the open side, and finally the brow which had worn the crown of thorns. The great assemblage, deeply moved, sat still. They had come to hear a sermon on the love of God. They did not find what they had expected, but far more. They saw for themselves the love that bears wrong, and bears it in such a manner that it bears it away. It was something they would never forget.

—JOHN A. REDHEAD in *Getting to Know God,* Abingdon Press.

288. All who think about the Cross seriously can be certain of this: so deadly is sin in the human heart, so enslaving is the fact of guilt, that no victory over sin is possible except through divine initiative. Somewhere in this universe there must be One who can represent the whole race and atone for its evil, so serious is man's sickness unto death, so perverse is man's choice of despair over hope. In the Cross, God descends to bear in his own heart the sins of the world. In Jesus, he atones at unimaginable cost to himself.

—WOODROW A. GEIER in *Religion in Life.*

289. John W. McGarvey, [one-time president of the College of the Bible, Lexington,] was seated in his office when a brokenhearted father, who had lost his only son, broke into the study and in tears and anguish said, "Where was God when my son's life was being snuffed out?" In a moment of inspiration, old Dr. McGarvey looked at him and said, "Right where he was when he gave up his own son!"

—J. CLYDE WHEELER in *The Pulpit.* Copyrighted by the Christian Century Foundation and used by permission.

290. Leslie D. Weatherhead has told of seeing an Italian canvas that portrayed the agony of Christ on the Cross. The body was convulsed with pain. The strong face was drawn taut with the agony it was fighting. On the reverse of the canvas, in dim and mystic tones, there had been painted another figure. The artist apparently drew with reverent restraint, believing it desecration to overstep the bounds that "no man hath seen the face of the Father." Yet it was clear that here was a representation of God himself. The curves of the composition corresponded with those of the suffering Jesus. Then the artist's idea became clear: the Almighty God was suffering, too, with the suffering of the man of Nazareth.

—From *Personal Security Through Faith* by LOWELL RUSSELL DITZEN. Copyright, 1954, by Henry Holt and Company, Inc. Reprinted by permission of the publishers.

291. The Cross of Christ is a spiritual fact, not a physical fact. There is no virtue in the physical fact of Christ's death on a cross. Two rugged beams of wood, blood-stained, that is all. When a man today, out of the depth of his innermost human nature, cries for deliverance from his evil, cries for the energizing of his good, cries for the grace to strive against evil, cries for the harmony of union with the divine, then for him Christ has not died in vain. He has found his way to the cross. The cross is central. It is struck into the middle

of the world, into the middle of time, into the middle of destiny. The cross is struck into the heart of God.
—FREDERICK W. NORWOOD in *Today Is Mine,* T. C. Clark, ed., Harper & Bros.

292. The crucifixion stands for the typical judgment of human beings who refuse to accept the meaning of their own existence in the Way. In time it was a judgment concurred in by some called Jews and some called Romans. But these names are the accidents of time. The crucifixion, in substance, is the judgment still made by every human being who consciously insists he is wiser than the Source of the Way. In submitting to that judgment, as one of the hazards of humanity, the Galilean expressed his primary understanding, that maximum love is the minimum service a whole human being can give, even though that love involve violent death at the hands of those drunk with their own arrogance.
—JEREMY INGALLS in *The Galilean Way,* Longmans, Green & Co., Inc.

293. The obsequious government official's reply to the threat of Rogozhin in Dostoevski's great novel *The Idiot,* though inconsequential in itself, when applied to this supreme act of our Lord's passion is revolutionary. Rogozhin told this newly acquired acquaintance that if he spoke again of Nastasya Filippovna, whom Rogozhin loved, he would thrash him. Then the official replied, "Well, if you thrash me, you won't turn me away: Thrash me, that's just how you will keep me." In crucifying Jesus the world did not drive him away; and the Cross, the sign of shame, as by a miracle, became the instrument of its deliverance and therefore its glory and its prize.
—WILLIAM R. CANNON in *The Redeemer,* Abingdon Press.

WORD FROM THE CROSS

294. *The forgiveness of God,* in my opinion, is the most powerful therapeutic idea in the world. Thousands of people are ill through repressed guilt; and to analyze the repression and make it conscious, then to say only, "Don't do it again," or, "Other people have done far worse things," is not to give a person the help to which he has a right. What a wonderful ministry the church has in being able to offer the cleansing forgiveness of God!
—LESLIE D. WEATHERHEAD in *Religion in Life.*

295. Clement tells that for the rest of his life Peter fell on his knees whenever he heard a rooster crow and with bitter weeping asked God for forgiveness. I don't believe that story. According to one tradition the cheeks of Peter were marked with furrows down which the tears continued to flow. I don't believe that either. Having been assured of Christ's forgiveness, Peter wiped away his tears and devoted his energy to serving Christ. There is another story to the effect that on one occasion when Peter was preaching to a large multitude—and the sermon was not going too well—he heard a rooster crowing in the distance. He paused for a moment and then preached as he had never preached before. That I can believe.
—ARMIN C. OLDSEN

296. An old French poem tells of an adventuress who enticed a young man from his mother's home. The adventuress, wishing to determine that the youth retained no lingering affection for his mother, said: "As a proof of your devotion to me I want you to murder your mother, tear out her heart, and bring it to me." As the young man returned from his evil mission, he stum-

bled and fell. Then from the heart came his mother's voice, "Are you hurt, my son?" Such was the love of Jesus Christ that from the cross where evil men had raised him came the words, "Father, forgive them."
—ROBERT C. NEWELL

297. William J. Hyde in *Dig or Die, Brother Hyde* recalls the time when he was arraigned before a judge arrested for riding a bicycle on the sidewalk. "'Officers,' [the judge] said in a dignified voice, 'you have done your proper duty. I can only commend you.' His voice had a difficult time remaining serious and finally lost the battle and he gave himself a good laugh. Then he spoke to the men more seriously. 'This man you have arrested is my pastor and the worst of the situation is . . . I presented him with the bicycle myself last night. I happen to be president of the Men's Club. . . . Leave the culprit with me. I'll take care of my friend.' The officers shook hands with me before they left me in the tender care of the judge. I used this experience as the basis of my sermon the next Sunday, employing the text, 'We shall all stand before the judgment seat of Christ.' I told the congregation the story of my arrest and tried to show them what it would mean if when we stand before the Judge of all the earth, Christ himself, we could hear him say, 'This is my friend, I'll care for him.'"
—Harper & Bros.

298. Nothing that is worth doing can be achieved in our lifetime; therefore we must be saved by hope. Nothing which is true or beautiful or good makes complete sense in any immediate context of history; therefore we must be saved by faith. Nothing we do, however virtuous, can be accomplished alone; therefore we are saved by love. No virtuous act is quite as virtuous from the standpoint of our friend or foe as it is from our standpoint. Therefore we must be saved by the final form of love which is forgiveness.
—REINHOLD NIEBUHR in *The Irony of American History,* Chas. Scribner's Sons.

299. "Father, forgive them," were Christ's words—words of sharp contrast to the words of the world. Louis Untermeyer in *Heinrich Heine: Paradox and Poet* describes the spirit of the world: "Forgiving was not Heine's business nor his specialty. 'My nature is the most peaceful in the world,' he wrote with deceptive mildness. 'All I ask is a simple cottage, a decent bed, good food, some flowers in front of my window, and a few trees beside my door. Then, if God wanted to make me completely happy, he would let me enjoy the spectacle of six or seven of my enemies dangling from those trees. I would forgive them all the wrongs they have done me—forgive them from the bottom of my heart, for we must forgive our enemies. But not until they are hanged!'"
—Harcourt Brace & Co., Inc.

THE CROSS BEFORE US

300. Some years ago I was driving through the Swiss Alps. I asked a farmer for directions to my destination. He told me that the road through the valley had been badly washed by heavy rains but that the road up on the ridge, though narrow and difficult, was open. I asked the farmer how I would know the ridge road. He pointed to a wayside crucifix that stood by the road above the first fork. It was a common enough sight because the mountains were speckled with these wayside shrines.

Said the farmer, "*Regardez, la croix en avant.*" "See, the cross before you."
—ENSWORTH REISNER

301. Beside the great cathedral which stands at the heart of London there is a marker at the spot where from 1116 to 1613 was St. Paul's Cross, the outdoor pulpit "whereat amid such scenes of good and evil as make up human affairs the conscience of Church and Nation through five centuries found public utterance."
—WALTER RUSSELL BOWIE in *Preaching*, Abingdon Press.

302. A bugle is blown from Castle Rock in Edinburgh at sundown. Once we heard the bugle through heavy fog. We could not see the rock, still less the sunset. But we knew then that there is a rock and a sun's light. How else to describe Jesus? His life is a bugle blown "from the hid battlements of Eternity." His words are like our words, but they have another accent. His deeds are like our deeds, but they are charged with another power. His death is like many another death on our cruel planet, but it cleanses us age on age: we are awe-struck before a Divine pain. By him we know that, out there above the mist, is the Rock and Sunlight.
—GEORGE ARTHUR BUTTRICK in *So We Believe, So We Pray*, Abingdon Press.

303. In the days of the romantic sailing vessels, the three signal flags, "B.N.C.," meant, "I will not abandon you." This was the most important promise a ship could make as it drew up alongside of its distressed sister. It meant life, help, courage, and the promise that a friend was near. In much the same way, the Cross is God's signal flag to distressed humanity.
—ROBERT R. BROWN in *The Miracle of the Cross*, Fleming H. Revell Co.

304. J. P. Priestley tells of stepping inside bombed-out Coventry Cathedral. The roof was gone, and only the four walls remained. The beautiful stained-glass windows had been shattered, and the sunshine streamed through the open frames. At first he was startled by the light, and then he reflected that perhaps that is the way cathedrals should be—open to the heavens and open to the storms and ravages of life. Walking toward the front where the altar used to be, he saw the charred outline of the cross still above the altar space. At first he rebelled against the ugliness of the half-burned cross, and then he said, "Why, a cross was never supposed to be beautiful! How ugly it was on Calvary's hill when it bore the life of the Master." So he found himself inwardly singing the old hymn "Above the hills of time the cross is gleaming."
—FRANK A. COURT

THE POWER OF THE CROSS

305. Two summers ago I preached in London's St. Andrew's Church. Following the service the senior Elder, well in his eighties, told me of the bombings in the last war. He said that, on one of the worst nights, he saw from a distance the whole center of London aflame. As I wrote them down immediately afterward, these are his words: "It seemed all was lost, the war, England, the values of our civilization. As I saw the docks and the center of London all burning I wept like a child. But then a gust of wind cleared the smoke for a moment, and I saw the gold cross of Christ still standing on the dome of St. Paul's. I stopped crying because then I knew there was a power stronger than the swastika—a power that would carry us through and which would live on."
—LOWELL R. DITZEN in *Best Sermons*,

1951-52. Copyright 1952. Used by permission of the Macmillan Co.

306. Some kinds of power cannot be destroyed. This is a problem which faces workers in atomic research, for waste products are created which cannot be disposed of. They cannot be burned nor discarded. They cannot even be buried in the ocean, for they remain radioactive and will be lethally dangerous for more than twenty thousand years. On the hill of Calvary another kind of power, the power of eternal love, was released. Men have for centuries tried to destroy the power of the cross. But it cannot be discarded, ignored, nor forgotten. Not for twenty thousand years but for eternity this power will continue to manifest the immeasurable love of God. Radioactive waste products may destroy for a space of time, but the positive power of love will give strength eternally.
—William Goddard Sherman

307. Some years ago a well-meaning individual hit upon what he felt would be a sure-fire solution to the problems of the world. He said he would like to gather all the people of the world, the more than two billion of them, into a vast amphitheater; and there he would have the most capable person in the world read to that tremendous audience in dramatic and forceful manner Christ's parable of the good Samaritan. Then he would say to the people of the world, "Go and do thou likewise," that is, be kind to one another. And with that he would send them home. I doubt that it would do much good. I question that the mere telling of the story of a man who helped his neighbor ages ago, excellent story that it is, would in itself do much to ennoble the heart of him who hears it. I fervently wish it were possible to gather all the people of the world together into one place: around the cross of Christ on Calvary. I would devoutly pray that, while they were there, they might all be unforgettably impressed with the horror of the sin of humanity and with the boundless love of God in Christ.
—Armin C. Oldsen

308. A newspaper editor went to see the Passion Play at Oberammergau, and came away saying to himself: "This is the story which has transformed the world"; and he seemed to hear an echo from the Bavarian mountains: "Yes, and will transform it."
—Reprinted from *Communion Through Preaching* by Henry Sloane Coffin. Copyright 1952 by Charles Scribner's Sons; used by permission of the publishers.

309. Explain it as we may, the magnetism of the Cross endures and grows. By some quirk of history, or some providence, or some inward law, the death-gallows of that Galilean Peasant in a remote and inconsequential corner of the earth, has cast a healing shadow over every land. The world may not like it. The world may say it darkens life with stern demands. . . . A gallows dismissed by Pilate with a gesture and hated by the Jews as a badge of deepest shame, now comes to strange life, now etched against the skyline of every city, now carried at the forefront of every human march as though, somehow, the issues of life and death are in it.
—George A. Buttrick in *Living Joyously* by Kirby Page, Rinehart & Co., Inc.

310. A legend says of a statue on the Nile that music came from it at every new dawn to lift the hearts of all in that wide valley. The would-be conqueror smashed the statue thinking thus to break the spirit of the Nile people.

But all in vain: the music still came from the ruins of the statue. Try to break Christ, call him only one more man making one more guess: his music is not silenced. Had any other died on his Cross it would have been still a gallows. He dies there—a man can partly carry his brother's burden, but only God can carry the weary load of mankind—he dies there, and the Cross becomes a shrine.
—George A. Buttrick in *Great Preaching Today,* Alton M. Motter, ed., published in 1953 by Harper & Bros. Used by permission.

OUR CROSSES

311. In the days when the Japanese government was determined to wipe out Christianity, a test was made. A crucifix was laid on the ground, and when one suspected of being a Christian was brought up, he was told to walk upon the cross. Those who refused were killed; those who did it were freed. One of these crucifixes has been dug up from a ruin, and the face of Christ has been worn down by those stepping on it. Today that face of Christ, walked upon then, is looking with tender compassion on a people who are standing amid the ruin of their civilization, seeking for guidance.
—E. Stanley Jones in *How to Be a Transformed Person,* Abingdon Press.

312. Franz Werfel's *The Forty Days of Musa Dagh* . . . is the story of Christian heroism that defends something more precious than heart or home. At the end of the book Bagradian remains on the besieged land after his countrymen are evacuated. Not long after the ships sail away beyond the horizon he is shot from ambush while standing on his son's grave. In falling he clings to the wooden cross, tearing it down with him, and lies in death with his son's cross upon his heart. Is that a symbol that no life ever comes to its Christian triumph until we lie with someone's cross upon our heart? Does that mean that no church, no society, no nation can ever live in triumph until it takes upon its very heart the cross of God's whole world? Does it suggest, even more, that once for all times God took his Son's cross upon his own heart, not in dying but in living? I am altogether persuaded that it does mean these things.
—Robert E. Luccock in *If God Be For Us,* Harper & Bros.

313. The Cross is essentially a fact to be known, which demands participation, in which—metaphorically speaking—the self is crucified and, in that crucifixion, is redeemed. The righteousness of Christ, to be sure, we can but follow afar off. But faith's *nevertheless* may repeat his words after him. . . . This, then, is our cross: that we lay down our unrighteousness, and that easy righteousness which is our deepest sin, that the righteousness of the Kingdom of God may rule in us; that we lay down all pride and prejudice that the brotherhood of the Kingdom may encompass us; that we lay down our fear, which is so basically selfish, that the redemptive power of the Kingdom may be seen in us; in short, that in the fiery purgation of history we should die to ourselves and rise again, the people of a faith greater than we. This is our cross: our total surrender, in faith, to the Kingdom of God. It is also our victory, for the Cross and the victory are *one.*
—John Bright in *The Kingdom of God,* Abingdon Press.

314. When I look at a cross, I imagine that the crossarms are not there. I see only the upright. And what I see then is a capital "I." Here is the symbol of my own problem and the problem of my world. Here is the visible sign of my egotism and the collective egotism of economic and social groups, of races and nations. Here is the root cause of anxiety and misery in every situation everywhere down through all the ages of human history. . . . When I look at the Cross seriously, I have to look at myself and see myself in my self-concern and its tragic consequences. Then the crossbar is replaced, and I see the "I" canceled. It is not annulled. It is not suppressed. This is not the denial of individuality. This is not the forcing of persons into a common mold in which the "I" has no meaning at all. . . . As I recognize myself in the "I" without the crossarms, so now I can see what it means to be a "We." But without the cancellation of the "I" in this sense of the crucifixion of my own egotism there can be no "We."

—Charles Duell Kean in *Making Sense Out of Life*. Copyright, 1954, by W. L. Jenkins, The Westminster Press. Used by permission.

315. Recently I witnessed the drama *Unto These Hills* presented by the Cherokee Historical Association and depicting that time in the 1830's when the white men secured through deception the lands of the Cherokees. Tsali, an Indian leader, in anger killed a white soldier and then fled to the hills with thousands of his people. General Scott sent word to Tsali that, if he and his kin surrendered, the government would grant his people permission to live in the Great Smokies. If he refused, the soldiers would hunt down all the Indians. Tsali and his sons stalked heroically from the bush and were sentenced to death by the military tribunal. His sacrifice gave rise to an Indian reservation for the remnant of his race. As I watched the drama, I thought not only of an Indian farmer but of a Palestinian carpenter who freely gave his life not for his race but for all mankind that it might be safely housed in the heart of God.

—G. Curtis Jones

THE CROSS REJECTED

316. Goethe one time said something that I think is important. He said, "There are four things I hate: first, tobacco smoke; second, lice; third, garlic; and fourth, the cross." A strange combination. But he was speaking truly about a good many people. We hate the cross. But let no man ever accept Christianity without knowing that the very heart and center of its insight is the cross.

—Gerald Kennedy

317. Dostoevski tells us the story of two men looking at the painting of Holbein, "The Taking of Christ from the Cross." One said, "I like looking at that picture." The other said, "Some people's faith has been ruined by that picture." And right he was; that picture would ruin the faith of a materialist, an atheist, a communist, and for all who believe that there is nothing after this life.

—Fulton J. Sheen in *Best Sermons, 1951-52*. Copyright 1952. Used by permission of The Macmillan Co.

318. Not Herod, not Caiaphas, not Pilate, not Judas ever contrived to fasten upon Jesus Christ the reproach of insipidity; that final indignity was left for pious hands to inflict. To make of his story something that could neither startle, nor shock, nor terrify, nor excite, nor inspire a living soul is to crucify the Son of God afresh and put him to

an open shame. . . . Let me tell you, good Christian people, an honest writer would be ashamed to treat a nursery tale as you have treated the greatest drama in history.
—DOROTHY L. SAYERS in *The Man Born to Be King,* Victor Gollancz Ltd., London.

319. At this season Christ comes to the very door of your heart. Will you let him enter? Once Edward VII and his wife took a walk at the end of a day. In the dusk she turned her ankle and could not make it back to the palace. They saw a cottage not too far away and went there for help. The king knocked on the door. The farmer had already gone to bed. He shouted out the window: "Who is there? What do you want?" The king replied: "I am Edward, and I need help for my wife. Let me in." The farmer said: "Go away and let a man sleep. Stop this foolishness." The king did not know what to do but later tried again. His wife had to have some relief. The farmer now came down, determined to throw the man off his porch. When he opened the door, he saw it was his king indeed. At once he took them in and helped bandage the ankle. In coming years the farmer retold the story wherever he could find someone to listen, but he always ended it with these words, "Almost I did not let my king in."
—J. R. BROKHOFF

320. One morning in a religious bookstore I watched a salesgirl unpack a box of books. Next to the shelves where she was placing the new volumes was a table on which were displayed altar furnishings, a beautiful cross, and candlesticks. To sort the books better, the girl pushed the cross to one side and put some of the new books on the table. They all happened to be of the self-help variety, an emphasis in which much current religious enthusiasm is centered. Are we not often tempted to push the cross aside in our preaching and teaching to make room for all manner of psychological gimmicks? Does not the most permanent inner stability and fortitude come through an awareness of Christ's love as expressed in the cross, through the faith that the cross brings to our lives?
—ARTHUR A. WAHMANN

THE KING'S ENTRANCE

321. Palm branches have long been associated with Jesus' triumphal entry into Jerusalem. The palm is the symbol of victory, conquest, and kingship. As a symbol for Jesus, the Prince of Peace and Servant-King, the palm has added significance; for the palm of all trees is the servant tree. It offers shade for the weary. It is the source of food for the hungry. From it man obtains sugar, resin, and oil. Its branches are used for the weaving of baskets and the thatching of roofs. The lofty palm suggests mastery and service.
—EDWARD T. CLAPP

322. In *The Robe* Lloyd C. Douglas tells of a slave called Demetrius who on Palm Sunday pushed his way through the rejoicing crowd surrounding Christ to get a good look at him who was being proclaimed. Later he was discussing his experience with another slave. The other asked: "See him—close up?" Demetrius nodded. "Crazy?" "No." "King?" "No," muttered Demetrius, soberly, "not a king." "What is he, then?" "I don't know," mumbled Demetrius, in a puzzled voice, "but—he is something more important than a king."
—Houghton Mifflin Co.

323. In A.D. 156 Polycarp, a Christian martyr, was put to death in Smyrna, and the small struggling Christian community was terrified by the persecution under the proconsulship of Statius Quadratus, and was heartbroken by its leader's death. The man who wrote the record of it, however, for the centuries to read, boiled down a great truth into a few words when he dated the event. "Statius Quadratus, proconsul," he wrote, "Jesus Christ, king forever." I wonder if he guessed that in the twentieth century we should be reading that. Who was "Statius Quadratus, proconsul"? Long since sunk in oblivion! But still above the world's turmoil the affirmation resounds: "Jesus Christ, king forever!"
—HARRY EMERSON FOSDICK in *A Faith for Tough Times,* Harper & Bros.

324.
While we deliberate, he reigns.
When we decide wisely, he reigns.
When we decide foolishly, he reigns.
When we serve him humbly, loyally, he reigns.
When we serve him self-assertively, he reigns.
When we rebel and seek to withhold our service, he reigns.
—WILLIAM TEMPLE

325. Charles Lamb, looking at Robert Haydon's massive spread of canvas on which he painted the "Triumphal Entry into Jerusalem," made a comment to remember. He said, "The face of Jesus looks remarkably like Haydon." . . . We are all in danger of making our portrait of Christ look suspiciously like ourselves.
—HALFORD E. LUCCOCK in *Communicating the Gospel,* Harper & Bros.

TRAGEDY AND TRIUMPH

326. Miguel de Unamuno y Jugo in *The Tragic Sense of Life* points out that an understanding of life's meaning grows out of a realizing of its tragic nature. Just as drama reaches its highest expression in a tragedy, so also life itself achieves its most sublime expression through coming to grips with tragedy. Thus we have the triumph of Easter in a cosmic drama that cannot be separated from the tragedy of Good Friday.
—EDGAR N. JACKSON

327. The drama *Family Portrait* by Lenore Coffee and William Joyce Cowen is based on the life of Jesus and closes with the Crucifixion. In the final act the friends of Jesus have come together. They are bewildered and troubled. Then Mary Magdalen, standing in the center of the stage, says: "He raised me from the dead. I was blind—and now I see. I was deaf—and now I hear. The world will never be the same because he has lived!" And it hasn't been.
—J. R. BROKHOFF

328. In a church in South America there is a painting of an operating room. It cannot be a very old picture because the doctors are dressed in suits which indicate the late 90's. It is a very strange painting. The patient on the operating table is a crucifix, a dead Christ on a cross on the table. The painting might be called "An Autopsy on a Dead Christ." And thereby hangs the tale. Too many churches miss the great Easter fact. Too many people miss the great Easter fact. "He is not here" was the core of that fact.
—J. MANNING POTTS in *The Upper Room Pulpit.*

329. Edgar Carlson makes the grand observation that not even what man did to God on Good Friday could make God stop loving us, and so God returned on Easter. What minister has not at some time shared the feeling of [James] Denney, who wished that he might take a crucifix into the pulpit, hold it high, and say movingly: "See, that is how God loves you!"
—A. GORDON NASBY in *Pulpit Digest.*

330. There was a Cross before Easter and there have been crosses ever since. That is where so many well-intentioned sentimentalists have gone astray and perverted the real essence of the Christian faith. They have so surrounded the Cross with the Easter lilies that they have hidden for a time the harsh outlines of the unyielding wood beneath. But the flowers will fade and the Cross will be seen again in all its demand and challenge. Even on Easter Day the church reminds us that we must die daily if we are to live. But the end is life not death.
—CORWIN C. ROACH in *Pulpit Digest.*

THE GOOD NEWS OF EASTER

331. J. B. Priestley in *Midnight on the Desert* writes of his last meeting with Arnold Bennett at the close of a concert in Albert Hall, which had concluded with Beethoven's symphony *Eroica.* The two men met in the lobby, and Bennett said, "Well, Priestley, it lifts you up; it lifts you up." Indeed, music does lift one up so that he sees things as he has never seen them before. Easter does that too; "it lifts you up."
—WALLACE FRIDY in *A Light Unto My Path,* Abingdon Press.

332. Easter means . . . the vindication, the triumph, of *Jesus* and all he stands for. Easter invites us to forget ourselves and all our worries or doubts or speculations over personal survival, and to think of him. If Jesus, and what *he* stands for, is the thing that must survive and triumph, if your world is to be rational and your life to be livable in it—then you already have the beginning of a faith in the resurrection, and the most important element in that faith. . . . For from first to last, the New Testament faith is an assurance, a conviction of the ultimate triumph—not merely of us, in our tiny private lives, but of God himself and of Christ and of all that Christ stands for in this world.
—FREDERICK C. GRANT in *Christ's Victory and Ours.* Copyright 1950. Used by permission of The Macmillan Co.

333. For the first Christians the paramount miracle was Christ as a present power, not Christ as an admired person in history. I wonder whether we Christians of the twentieth century make it basic today. Do we really understand what it means to believe in the Resurrection of Christ? "Look at the sequence," says James S. Stewart, "risen from the dead, therefore alive for ever; therefore our contemporary; therefore able to confront us face to face." Do we fully realize that in such communion with a contemporary Christ lies the true secret of the Christian life?
—ARCHIBALD M. HUNTER in *Interpreting Paul's Gospel.* Copyright, 1955, by W. L. Jenkins, The Westminster Press. Used by permission.

334. The Easter message tells us that our enemies, sin, the curse and death, are beaten. Ultimately they can no longer start mischief. They still behave as though the game were not decided, the battle not fought; we must still reckon with them, but fundamentally we must cease to fear them any more.

—KARL BARTH in *Dogmatics in Outline,* Philosophical Library, Inc.

335. The Good News of the Resurrection is that Christ is alive here and now. He is here. He left us in the physical body in order that he might not be constrained by the physical body. He could not remain a Jew confined to the narrow limits of Palestine. He must be available now to the man in Hong Kong, Kiev, Sidney, or Omaha—not just to the man in Galilee. "And he departed from our sight," said St. Augustine, "that we might return to our heart, and there find him. For he departed, and behold, he is here."
—WOODROW A. GEIER in *Religion in Life.*

336. Resurrection does not mean escape from this tough earth into a more favorable realm. Such a flight would have been for Jesus loss of the battle into which he had thrown his all. Resurrection means return in power, despite death and burial, and going on with divine force in and through his church, his Body. Easter is the festival of the trustworthiness of God for those who confide in him.
—Reprinted from *Communion Through Preaching* by HENRY SLOANE COFFIN. Copyright 1952 by Charles Scribner's Sons; used by permission of the publishers.

337. On Easter Monday, in 1945, Martin Niemöller was still a prisoner in Dachau prison in Germany. In a sermon to eight fellow prisoners he said: "The resurrection of Jesus, in contradistinction to his passion and death, is not what we designate as a 'historical event.' No unbelieving eye has seen the Risen One, no critical observer has discerned him, and so it is simply excluded that proof be given that the resurrection of the Lord is a fact. It can only be certified through testimony, and thus we may admit it by faith or deny it by unbelief." Here is the heart of the Christian belief: faith in the risen, ever-living Christ.
—RUSSELL Q. CHILCOTE in *The Upper Room Pulpit.*

338. The whole history of the Christian life is a series of resurrections. Every time a man bethinks himself that he is not walking in the light, that he has been forgetting himself, and must repent; that he has been asleep and must awake; that he has been letting his garments trail, and must gird up the loins of his mind; every time this takes place there is a resurrection in the world. Yes, every time a man finds his heart is troubled, that he is not rejoicing in God, a resurrection must follow; a resurrection out of the night of troubled thought into the gladness of the truth. For the truth is, and ever was, and ever must be, gladness, however much the souls on which it shines may be obscured by the clouds of sorrow, troubled by fears, or shot through with the lightnings of pain.
—GEORGE MACDONALD

LIFE IS ETERNAL

339. What an amazing difference there is in the men of the New Testament! They are certain of immortal life. Time is merely a deceiver. Life went on, and it was gain to be without a body and away from earth and uncramped by time. There was no such thing as loss of life. There cannot be loss of life. Life goes on in another room. There is only a passing from one room to another, or perhaps it is more like going out of a stuffy room into the open air of the moors and mountains. . . . Time cannot steal anything vital, cannot hurt or destroy. It is an opportunity to be used, a room to be lived in, a university from

which to graduate; but the spirit of man belongs to another category, and his life is in the eternal.
—LESLIE D. WEATHERHEAD in *The Significance of Silence,* Abingdon Press.

340. There was a famous king in history who appointed a man to live in his royal presence and to say every day to him, "Philip, remember thou art mortal," lest he forget his kinship with the earth. But doesn't every person need another daily whisper in his ears, "Remember, thou art *immortal,*" lest he forget his kinship with eternity?
—J. WALLACE HAMILTON in *Horns and Halos in Human Nature,* Fleming H. Revell Co.

341. Another minister is reported once to have said to Horace Bushnell, "When Christ sees you nearing the gate, Dr. Bushnell, I am sure he will say, 'There comes a man I know.' " With flashing eyes the great theologian replied, "And I shall be able to say I know him—too."
—ARTHUR W. PRESTON

342. Once on a visit to Scotland I came to the Isle of Whithorn, one of the cradles of British Christianity. In the kirkyard are many ancient tombstones, centuries old. One interested me more than others. Almost swallowed by the earth, the marker's inscription at the top remained legible. It was this: "You think I'm forgot. But I'm not!" . . . . He was not a silly egotist, for he and his loved ones knew that "in Christ" a man is loved and known forever.
—DAVID A. MACLENNAN in *Joyous Adventure,* published in 1952 by Harper & Brothers.

343. A colored minister once said: "When an African native is dying, the witch doctors put into his hands as his passport into the other world a dead bone. When the Christian dies, he does not grasp a dead bone, but the living hand of the living Christ."
—ROBERT A. LAPSLEY, JR., in *On Vesper Hill,* John Knox Press.

BEYOND THE SHADOW

344. My mother once said that she thought it was surprising that ministers did not more often preach on the text, "Even though I walk through the valley of the shadow of death," and emphasize the word "through." The valley of the shadow of death itself is not a place that men are going to walk into and stay in its darkness and gloom, but a place they are going to walk through. And having walked through it, with bated breath perhaps, and with pain and grief, they shall come through to that which is beyond, where there is . . . light.
—JACK FINEGAN in *Clear of the Brooding Cloud,* Abingdon Press.

345. After the death of his wife Arthur John Gossip preached, "You people in the sunshine may believe the faith, but we in the shadow must believe it. We have nothing else."
—ROBERT J. MCCRACKEN

346. Reuben K. Youngdahl tells of leaving a home early one morning where death had just taken a young husband. As he was going down the walk, he was met by a young woman who was herself a widow of only a few weeks. As she came toward him, she said, "Pastor, has she got it?" Instinctively he knew what she meant. She wondered if this bereaved one had the awareness of God's presence and the comfort of his love.
—FREDERICK ANDREW ROBLEE

347. The old Conference Minutes of the Methodist Church set down their information by way of question and an-

swer. In the *Minutes* for 1791, I discovered this interesting item:

> Question 10. Who have died this year? Answer: Wyatt Andrews, who died full of faith and the Holy Ghost. As long as he could ride, he travelled; and while he had breath he praised God.

And that is all I know about Wyatt Andrews, but it is enough to make me look forward to meeting him in heaven. I could ask for no finer epitaph for myself than a testimony that as long as I lived I was traveling somewhere.
—GERALD KENNEDY in *Go Inquire of the Lord,* Harper & Bros.

348. I once heard a man say who was very sure of his love for Christ and who was busy at the honorable works of the world: "Heaven is most certainly my home, but at this point I am not homesick." Maybe not homesick, but ready, if conditions demand, to turn homeward, assured that "eye hath not seen, ear hath not heard" what things the Lord has in store for His own.
—JAMES A. JONES in *The Pulpit in the South,* Frank S. Mead, ed., Fleming H. Revell Co.

349. John Baillie relates how a man in his last illness asked his doctor what the future life would be like. Just then the physician heard his dog, which had followed him to the house, scratching at the door. So he told the man that his dog knew nothing of what was happening behind the door but merely wanted to be with his master. "Is it not the same with you?" he asked. "You do not know what lies behind the door, but you know your Master is there."
—J. HAROLD GWYNNE in *The Upper Room Pulpit.*

350. Says Antoninus to Longinus in Robert R. Brown's Good Friday narrative *The Miracle of the Cross:* "It would be a wonderful thing, sir . . . to know when one's work on earth is done and the tribulations of life are over that there will be a song and a smile in a life to come; to believe that we are two-world beings who even while our feet are planted firmly on this earth possess hearts which are tuned to the stars; to be confident that all the inner voices which whisper to our hopeful nature are true and that there is an eternal peace for us in a world to come—such faith would give purpose to mortal life beyond any historic causes and dignify the death even of such criminals as these."
—Fleming H. Revell Co.

351. On the tomb of a minister buried a few blocks from my study I recently saw this inscription:

> I preached as never sure to preach again,
> And as a dying man to dying men.

When I asked one of my friends about this minister, a person who had known him well, he told me this story: "Yes, that inscription well describes him. He died in 1886 at the age of twenty-eight years. On his pulpit he kept that quotation; it was the motivation of his living as well as his preaching. He lived every moment with great intensity, as though it might be the last—and also the best—moment of his life."
—THOMAS S. KEPLER in *And Peace at the Last,* Copyright, 1953, by W. L. Jenkins, The Westminster Press. Used by permission.

352. Someone once said to Robert Browning, "Robert, you'll die in a dress suit." The late William Lyon Phelps, of Yale University, in speaking about Browning, and this comment, observed: "But he didn't. He died in bed like a Christian."
—RUSSELL L. DICKS in *And Peace at the*

Last, Copyright, 1953, by W. L. Jenkins, The Westminster Press. Used by permission.

353. When President Harper, of the University of Chicago, was lying at the point of death, he called into his room a few of his closest friends and asked them to pray with him. "Now let us talk with God," he said; "let us not be formal; let us be simple." After they had prayed with him, he prayed himself and the burden of his prayer was this: "And may there be work to do, tasks to accomplish; and this I ask for Jesus' sake."
—HUGH THOMSON KERR in *Design for Christian Living,* Copyright, 1953, by W. L. Jenkins, The Westminster Press. Used by permission.

354. Ian Maclaren wrote: "Heaven is not a Trappist monastery; neither is it retirement on a pension. No, it is a land of continual progress." One translation of the words of Jesus, "In my Father's house are many mansions" renders them, "In my Father's house are many *stations,*" because Jesus implies that heaven will afford opportunity for endless adventurous and abundant living. "What an encouragement," one exclaims, "to all those who have never 'arrived' on earth, to all who were cut off before the song was sung, or the picture painted, or the vision realized."
—JOSEPH MARTIN DAWSON in *The Pulpit.*

355. During the First World War some church folks in London gave an entertainment for a company of soldiers who were on their way to the front. When it was over, the colonel asked a young officer who had the gift of ready speech to express the thanks of the men to the people. The young officer rose, and in some well-chosen words of wit and charm, he expressed the soldiers' thanks. And then, as if seeking some words with which to close, he said, "We're leaving now for France, the trenches, and maybe to die." He didn't mean to say that. Looking around embarrassedly, he said, "Can anybody tell us how to die?" There was an awkward pause as though he had said the wrong thing, and a period of strange silence in which nobody said anything. Then someone walked quietly to the piano and began to sing the aria from "Elijah"—"O Rest in the Lord." In the quiet that followed, as deep called unto deep, every man's soul was making its way back to some half-remembered thing to which he always had belonged.
—J. WALLACE HAMILTON in *Horns and Halos in Human Nature,* Fleming H. Revell Co.

356. In the book by James Jones entitled *From Here to Eternity* . . . a bugler, a sergeant, and a philosophical rebel are talking. The philosophically minded soldier says: "In our world . . . there is only one way a man may have freedom, and that is to die for it, and after he's died for it, it doesn't do him any good. That's the whole problem in a nutshell." That is a problem—unless one realizes that if one must die for freedom, it does do him good. After death he may enter into a freedom, sweeter, more inclusive than any to be had this side of the grave. When a man realizes that, he is free here—free from fear—free from the power of the tyrant—free to play the man.
—ALBERT E. DAY in *An Autobiography of Prayer,* published in 1952 by Harper & Brothers. Quotation published by Chas. Scribner's Sons.

LOVE'S NECESSITY

357. "Do you believe in a future life?" asks Pierre Bezúkhov in Tolstoy's *War and Peace.* He adds: "I feel that I cannot vanish, since nothing vanishes in

this world, but that I shall always exist and always have existed. I feel that beyond me and above me there are spirits, and that in this world there is truth." To this Andrew Bolkónski responds: "Yes, that is Herder's theory, . . . but it is not that which can convince me, dear friend—life and death are what convince. What convinces is when one sees a being dear to one, bound up with one's own life, before whom one was to blame and had hoped to make it right, . . . and suddenly that being is seized with pain, suffers, and ceases to exist. Why? It cannot be that there is no answer. And I believe there is. That's what convinces, that is what has convinced me."
—Simon & Schuster, Inc.

358. When Dr. W. R. Matthews, dean of St. Paul's Cathedral in London, broadcast four talks on immortality, he received from interested listeners some 1,900 letters. About them he commented: "If there is any lesson to be learned from the letters I have had, it is that love is the main source of the desire for life beyond death."
—Robert J. McCracken in *Missions*, Vol. 151, No. 4, p. 27.

359. The poet Cowper in the realization and appreciation of great friendship wrote to Heskith: "You must know that I should not love you half so much did I not know that you would be my friend for all eternity. There is not room for friendship to unfold itself in such a little nook of life as this."
—Roy A. Burkhart

360. "What a heroic battle Johnny fought!" said Dr. Wilder Penfield in *Death Be Not Proud* by John Gunther. "A gallant spirit like his cannot be destroyed by a mechanical defect in the body which was given him. Knowing him and thinking of his stubborn refusal to accept defeat makes me believe that that spirit will live on. For such there must be an immortality which we who tinker at the body may guess at but not understand."
—Harper & Bros. Copyright, 1949, by John Gunther.

361. One night a young girl was taking a walk with her father. For some time she said nothing, and her father finally asked what she was thinking about. "I was just thinking," she said, "if heaven with its stars is so beautiful wrong side out, how wonderful it must be on the right side." Your loved ones who died in faith are enjoying this blessedness. This makes it possible to smile through your tears and to be genuinely happy that they have passed on.
—J. R. Brokhoff

362. An inscription in the crypt of Allegheny Observatory, University of Pittsburgh, reads: "We have loved the stars too fondly to be fearful of the night."
—*Stories on Stone,* Oxford University Press.

363. The final, and, in the writer's opinion, most fundamental argument for immortality is the character of God. If God be good, then somehow human persons must be immortal. To promise so much, only to destroy us; to raise such hopes, and then to frustrate them; to endow us with such capacities that are never to be fully used; to instill in us a love for others, all of whom are to be annihilated, is unworthy of God. Faith in immortality thus rests on faith in God. If there be a God, man's immortality is certain; if not, immortality would not be worth having.
—From *An Introduction to Philosophy* by Edgar S. Brightman. Copyright, 1925, 1951, by Henry Holt & Company, Inc. Reprinted by permission of the publishers.

FESTIVAL OF THE CHRISTIAN HOME

FOUNDATIONS OF THE HOME

364. It is . . . in the home that the foundations of the kind of world in which we live are laid and in this sense it will always remain true that the hand that rocks the cradle is the hand that rules the world. And it is in this sense that women must assume the job of making men who will know how to make a world fit for human beings to live in.
—ASHLEY MONTAGU in *The Saturday Review.*

365. Shortly after a British jet plane crossed and recrossed the Atlantic Ocean in about eight hours, a Low cartoon was reprinted in *The New York Times.* It pictured a jet plane traveling at fantastic speed. The plane was labeled "man's scientific progress." On the ground was a huge turtle moving slowly and ponderously. The turtle was labeled "man's moral progress." In a vivid way this cartoon symbolizes what could be the tragedy of the modern age, and what is without doubt one of the most compelling reasons for greater attention to moral and spiritual values in our homes and in our schools.
—WILLIAM RUSSELL in *Vital Speeches.*

366. Every home is a cell. It is a cell in the penological sense, or it is a cell in the biological sense. It is a prison, or it is a unit of growth. It is a jail, or it is a living body. A prison is a place where people are denied their freedom, and a jail an instrument of cramping and hurting. But when you speak of cells as plants and animals and human beings have them, then all the mystery of life is bound up in them. Cells like that have vigor and vitality. They have movement and development. They have freedom and hope.
—ROY M. PEARSON in *Here's a Faith for You,* Abingdon Press.

367. John Buchan, describing qualities which seem "to flourish more lustily in the United States than elsewhere," wrote: "First I would select what, for want of a better word, I should call homeliness. It is significant that the ordinary dwelling, though it be only a shack in the woods, is called not a house, but a home. This means that the family, the ultimate social unit, is given its proper status as the foundation of society. Even among the richer classes I seem to find a certain pleasing domesticity. English people of the same rank are separated by layers of servants from the basic work of the household, and know very little about it. In America the kitchen is not too far away from the drawing-room, and it is recognised, as Heraclitus said, that the gods may dwell there. But I am thinking chiefly of the ordinary folk, especially those of narrow means. It is often said that Americans are a nomad race, and it is true that they are very ready to shift their camp; but the camp, however bare, is always a home. The cohesion of the family is close, even when its members are scattered."

—*Pilgrim's Way,* Houghton Mifflin Co. Used by permission of Tweedsmuir Trustees. Published as *Memory Hold-the-Door* by Hodder & Stoughton, Ltd.

368. The home is a place where we can begin to remake our culture. If our culture has slipped into unsound habits of irresponsibility and egocentricity, the home is a place where we can begin to mitigate these habits. If our culture has slipped into carelessness regarding human values, the home is a place where these values can be cherished and made to grow in influence. If our culture has learned to put a disastrously high premium on competition, the home is a place where the cooperative arts can be a strength and a delight. Nowhere in our culture is there an institution that can, more variously and deeply, serve the needs of our maturing than can the home.

—HARRY OVERSTREET in *The Mature Mind,* W. W. Norton & Co., Inc.

369. Of all social institutions the good family has possibly been the most effective agency of altruism. . . . More successfully than any other group it has transformed its members into a single entity, with a common fund of values, with common joys and sorrows, spontaneous co-operation and willing sacrifice. . . . Viewed from this standpoint, the contemporary Western family leaves much to be desired. It has increasingly failed in its main task; has increasingly generated the forces of egoism and demoralization. . . . Each ego seeks to preserve its freedom and independence. They remain intact in their bargaining, calculating, pleasure-seeking and utility-hunting. And the pleasures and utilities themselves tend, in accordance with the sensate nature of our culture, to grow more and more physiological, materialistic, and hedonistic.

—PITIRIM A. SOROKIN in *The Reconstruction of Humanity,* Beacon Press.

370. Gilbert Keith Chesterton has said [that] he would like sometime to enter his home in a totally different way from what was his usual custom. He went on to suggest that he might get a ladder and enter like a burglar in the night, through one of the rear upper windows of his home; and so obtain a new thrill, a new experience, a new point of view of his own home. From this point of view things would look different. . . . He is expressing the wish that he could have new eyes to see the meaning and value, and perhaps the defects, of the things that were most familiar to him.

—HUGH THOMSON KERR in *Design for Christian Living.* Copyright, 1953, by W. L. Jenkins, The Westminster Press. Used by permission.

371. One day while making a pastoral call, a mother said to me: "Will you read this letter? It's from Bob." I sat down and read the letter. When I had gotten half way through, I knew why she wanted me to read it. Bob was away in the service. This is what he said: "You know I have a feeling that I am coming home all right. I don't know why but I feel that God is taking care of that. What I want to say is: When I do get home, I hope that, when we have finished dinner at night and we're all there at the table, we will just stay there and look at one another and realize for just a little while nothing else but the fact that we are there together. That's all I want."

—HAZEN G. WERNER in *Pulpit Digest.*

HOUSEHOLD OF FAITH

372. I am most of all thankful for my birthplace and early nurture in the warm atmosphere of a spiritually-minded home, with a manifest touch of saintliness in it; thankful indeed that from the cradle I was saturated with the Bible and immersed in an environment of religion of experience and reality. It was a peculiar grace that I was born into that great inheritance of spiritual wisdom and faith, accumulated through generations of devotion and sacrificial love. I never can be grateful enough for what was done for me by my progenitors before I came on the scene. They produced the spiritual atmosphere of my youth. I became heir of a vast invisible inheritance. There is nothing I would exchange for that.
—RUFUS M. JONES in *The Recovery of Family Life* by Elton and Pauline Trueblood, Harper & Bros.

373. My earliest memories have a definitely religious atmosphere. . . . I cannot recall a time when I did not already feel, in some dim way, that I was "not my own" to do with as I pleased, but was claimed by a higher power which had authority over me. . . . For, as far back as I can remember anything, I was somehow aware that my parents lived under the same kind of authority as that which, through them, was communicated to me. They too behaved as though they, even they, were not their own.
—JOHN BAILLIE in *Our Knowledge of God,* Chas. Scribner's Sons and Oxford University Press.

374. How can we ever be true children of God unless we begin by being faithful sons and daughters within our own homes? Home, to quote W. E. Channing, is "the nursery of the infinite." "Home interprets heaven," says another. "Home is heaven for beginners." Loyalty to home is the first loyalty of life, and submission to its discipline is the first steps that any of us can take towards the fuller life of the sons and daughters of God. To be God's child, we must begin by proving ourselves faithful children of our earthly homes. That is the way our Lord took, and it remains the way of life for all who would follow him.
—A. IAN BURNETT in *Lord of All Life,* Rinehart & Co., Inc.

375. Some time ago . . . a quarter-page advertisement of a commercial company . . . showed a family in a church pew. They were singing a hymn, with the exception of the six-year-old boy who, unseen by his parents, was leaning forward to yank the braid of the little girl's hair in the next pew. The caption under the picture read: "What makes a family secure?" The answer was given in this fashion: "A lot of things go to make it up. Things like a cool hand at night on a child's hot forehead. . . . Little private jokes that wouldn't mean much outside the family. Affectionate teasing . . . closeness, warmth, a sense of sharing . . . the deep, underlying knowledge that you *belong.*"
—From *Personal Security Through Faith* by LOWELL RUSSELL DITZEN. Copyright, 1954, by Henry Holt and Company, Inc., Reprinted by permission of the publishers.

376. Here . . . are two spiritual fellowships: the Church and the family. But we are not to think of them as existing side by side. They are not to be considered as standing in or functioning in a parallel relationship, for this would mean that they never meet. It is incorrect to imagine that they can exist independently. They are never to be viewed separately. . . . For the fellowship that is imbued with Christ's Spirit as found

in the true Church and in the true family is a single fellowship. It is one, though it is operating in two phases on the human scene.
—WESNER FALLAW in *Toward Spiritual Security*. Copyright, 1952, by W. L. Jenkins, The Westminster Press. Used by permission.

WHERE LOVE IS

377. Gilbert Laue is a free-lance writer, and his wife is a successful lawyer. They decide that he will do his writing at home and look after their son. In his book *So Much to Learn* he tells how as a father he tries to do what every mother does so skillfully—change diapers, dry tears, and teach the child the joy of living. "I have tried to tell the story of love—its tremendous importance to all of us, especially to the young. I have tried to look into what love means and demands twenty-four hours a day—at breakfast and dinner and lunch, at bath time and nap time and play time." We discover about Christianity in our homes not as we try to write about love but as each one of us tries to live it to the height of his ability.
—FRANK A. COURT. Quotation published by Henry Holt & Co., Inc.

378. We receive love—from our children as well as others—not in proportion to our demands or sacrifices or needs, but roughly in proportion to our own capacity to love. And our capacity to love depends, in turn, upon our prior capacity to be persons in our own right. To love means, essentially, to give; and to give requires a maturity of self-feeling. Love is shown in the statement of Spinoza's . . . that truly loving God does not involve a demand for love in return. It is the attitude referred to by the artist Joseph Bender: "To produce art requires that the artist be able to love—that is to give without thought of being rewarded."
—ROLLO MAY, in *Man's Search for Himself*, W. W. Norton & Co., Inc.

379. Some time ago there was a tragic accident. In the night a husband heard a prowler downstairs. He got up, and in the darkness he fired a gun. Instead of a prowler it was his wife. On their way to the hospital in the ambulance she said to him, "My dear, do something." He replied with all the desperation of a husband at his wit's end, "What can I do?" She said to him, "You can pray." Later when I visited her, she said to me, "I had never heard my husband pray before, and it was worth all this pain just to share that with him, knowing now that our love has become one with the greater love of God."
—ROBERT W. BURNS

380. Newell W. Edson of the American Social Hygiene Association has listed the following signs as indicative of true love: (1.) A genuine interest in the other person and all that he or she says and does. (2.) A community of tastes, ideals, and standards with no serious clashes. (3.) A greater happiness in being with the one person than with any other. (4.) A real unhappiness when the other person is absent. (5.) A great feeling of comradeship. (6.) A willingness to give and take. (7.) A pride in the other person when comparisons are made.

Mr. Edson doesn't mention what I would call the greatest sign of true love, and that is the eagerness to make sacrifices for the beloved, to give and not to count the cost.
—J. BURTON THOMAS in *For Better, For Worse.*

381. Once a boy went out of his home to do something that his parents felt was wrong. He was involved in an accident

and lost both legs. It was a terrible blow, but the father told me one of the most beautiful stories I have ever heard. He said, "When his mother and I saw him in the hospital cot lying there aware that he had lost both legs, he said, 'Will you forgive me?'" They both ran up and hugged him and said, "Of course, we have already forgiven you." And he answered, "Then I can live without my legs."
—Roy A. Burkhart

HOUSES AND HOMES

382. Because of the housing shortage near the military base where he was stationed, a young doctor and his wife and three children had to live in cramped quarters in a hotel. A friend said to the doctor's six-year-old daughter, "Isn't it too bad that you don't have a home?" "Oh, we have a home," the youngster replied quickly. "We just don't have a house to put it in."
—M. Elizabeth Lynch in *The Reader's Digest.*

383. A friend of mine some time back said, "I want you to ride out and see the beautiful new home I have bought." Knowing him very well, I said, "Bud, you don't buy a home. You buy a house and then you build the home."
—From: *Spiritual Revolution,* by Pierce Harris. Copyright 1952 by Pierce Harris, reprinted by permission of Doubleday & Company, Inc.

384. Bess Streeter Aldrich in *A Lantern in Her Hand* tells of Abbie Deal, who dreams about her new home on the Nebraska prairies. She desires a picket fence around the yard, a nice fence, painted white, with red hollyhocks and blue lockspur alongside it. "You're quite a dreamer, Abbie-girl," says her husband, Will. Abbie does not laugh. She is suddenly sober. "You have to, Will." She says it a little vehemently. "You *have* to dream things out. It keeps a kind of an ideal before you. You see it first in your mind and then you set about to try to make it like the ideal. If you want a garden—why, I guess you've got to *dream* a garden."
—Grosset & Dunlap, Inc.

385. The family is that relationship of parents and children, initiated and fostered by creative interaction, which generates, individualizes, and integrates personality, on the one hand, and promotes the growth of culture in the community, on the other hand. God is the Creativity of life which speaks to us through this creative interaction. God is this creative love that promotes growth. Of what are we aware, then, when we are aware of God? We are aware of that Creativity which sustains all our living and which yields quality and meaning in our experiences. Religion is that way of living which gives God the most important place in all situations.
—Regina H. Westcott in *The Family Lives Its Religion,* Harper & Bros.

386. We all know what "home" means. Home is not necessarily a place fixed in geography. It can be moved, provided the old proven values which made it home and lacking which it cannot be home, are taken along too. It does not necessarily mean or demand physical ease, least of all, never in fact, physical security for the spirit, for love and fidelity to have peace and security in which to love and be faithful, for the devotion and sacrifice. Home means not just today, but tomorrow and tomorrow, and then again tomorrow and tomorrow. It means someone to offer the love and fidelity and respect to who is worthy of it, someone to be compatible with, whose dreams and hopes are your dreams and

hopes, who wants and will work and sacrifice also that the thing which the two of you have together shall last forever; someone whom you not only love but like too, which is more, since it must outlast what when we are young, we mean by love because without the liking and the respect, the love itself will not last.
—WILLIAM FAULKNER in *The Atlantic Monthly.*

387. In *The Crime of Sylvestre Bonnard* by Anatole France the hero tells a much-traveled lady that he has lived in the same house for thirty years. The lady is distressed. He says: "It is only a very small corner of the world, but honestly, Madame, where is there a more glorious spot?"

THE BONDS OF MARRIAGE

388. André Maurois has suggested that this vow be made a part of every marriage ceremony: "I bind myself for life! I have chosen; from now on my aim will be, not to search for someone who may please me, but to please the one I have chosen." To this he adds: "This decision can alone produce a successful marriage, and if the vow is not sincere the couple's chances for happiness are very slim, for it will run the risk of disruption when the first obstacles and the inevitable difficulties of life in common are encountered."
—*The Art of Living,* Harper & Bros.

389. Love is the passionate and abiding desire on the part of two people . . . to produce the conditions under which each can be and spontaneously express his real self; to produce together an intellectual soil and an emotional climate in which can flourish, far superior to what each could achieve alone.
—ALEXANDER MAGOUN in *Love and Marriage,* Harper & Bros.

390. At a wedding reception I heard a guest say to the bride, "I am so happy for you and Tom. Yours should be an unusually happy marriage, one of those fifty-fifty marriages which are so rare these days. You and Tom seem to have the real knack of meeting each other halfway." The bride's reply I shall never forget. She said, "You are very kind to say that, but the truth is that Tom and I have vowed to make ours a hundred-hundred marriage. By that we mean each of us will go not only halfway but all the way, one hundred per cent of the way, to make our marriage a genuine success."
—JAMES S. KEMPER

391. The true nature of marriage is only disclosed to faith. It is not presumptuous and it is not dogmatic to speak of Christian marriage as the truest form of marriage not only in the sense that marriage is most perfectly realized within the sphere of Christianity, but also in the sense that here both its significance and its nature have been more clearly perceived. And this connection with the Christian faith is more necessary than ever today—for arid rationalism is entirely unable to perceive the meaning of marriage, or of itself, to solve the problems of marriage.
—EMIL BRUNNER in *The Divine Imperative.* Copyright, 1947, by W. L. Jenkins, The Westminster Press. Used by permission.

392. In the *Autobiography of Calvin Coolidge* the former president wrote in these words concerning Grace Goodhue: "From our being together we seemed naturally to come to care for each other. We became engaged in the early summer of 1905 and were married . . . on October fourth of that year. I have seen so much fiction written on this subject

that I may be pardoned for relating the plain facts. We thought we were made for each other. For almost a quarter of a century she has borne with my infirmities, and I have rejoiced in her graces."
—Rinehart & Co., Inc.

393. *The Immortal Lovers* is the title of Frances Winwar's story of Elizabeth Barrett and Robert Browning. When asked if she regretted her elopement: " 'It has made the happiness and honour of my life,' she answered, 'and every unkindness received from my house makes me press nearer to the tenderest and noblest of human hearts. . . . Husband, lover, nurse—not one of these has Robert been to me, but all three together. I neither regret the marriage . . . nor the manner of it.' She had never forgotten how, when they had been together scarcely a fortnight, Robert had said to her with earnest tenderness: 'I kissed your feet, my Ba, before I married you. But now I would kiss the ground under your feet, I love you with so much greater love.' That love, incredible as it had seemed to them, overwhelmed as they were by its tremendous impact, had continued growing like the living thing it was, searching profounder depths, expanding in spiritual light."
—Harper & Bros. Copyright, 1950, by Frances Winwar.

394. I once heard a Negro bishop introduce his wife in the most beautiful introduction of a wife I have ever heard: "This is the gracious lady. Thirty years ago I looked into the limpid depths of her eyes and I've never gotten over the spell of it."
—E. Stanley Jones in *How to Be a Transformed Person,* Abingdon Press.

395. On the occasion of his retirement from Riverside Church [Harry Emerson Fosdick said] he had been puzzled all his life . . . by the fact that, on the whole, women have not accomplished as much in a public way as has been accomplished by men. Why is this true? Obviously the brains of women are as good and perhaps better than the brains of men. Yet the sober truth is that there have been relatively few women in the list of composers, artists, scientists and statesmen. "At last," said Dr. Fosdick, "I know the answer. No woman ever had a *wife!*"
—Elton and Pauline Trueblood in *The Recovery of Family Life,* Harper & Bros.

396. A dramatist named Alfred Sutro once wrote a fine, if forgotten, play called *A Maker of Men,* in which a bank clerk returns home, after missing promotion, and says, "I see other men getting on; what have *I* done?" His wife answers: "You have made a woman love you. You have given me respect for you, and admiration, and loyalty, and devotion—everything a man can give his wife, except luxury, and that I don't need. Still you call yourself a failure, who within these four walls are the greatest success?"
—Channing Pollock in *Guideposts in Chaos,* Thomas Y. Crowell Co.

397. Go to your homes from here by bus, train, automobile—that is new. Go up to your apartment in an elevator —that is new. See the gadgets with which our modern homes are furnished —they are new. But if you chance to have a copy of Homer's *Odyssey* handy, read this: "There is nothing mightier or nobler than when man and wife are of one heart and mind in a house." Wherever in the universe there may be homes, that is true.
—Harry Emerson Fosdick in *A Faith for Tough Times,* Harper & Bros.

WHY THE WALLS CRUMBLE

398. Marriages sometimes break up not because a husband and wife may have nothing in common but because of those feelings which they share in common. A minister, called to the home of a woman whose marriage was cracking, asked, "Do you two have anything in common?" "Yes," the woman replied, "neither of us can stand the other."
—MERVIN C. HELFRICH

399. Lloyds of London will insure almost anything under the sun—including the weather!—but even Lloyds will not insure the success of a marriage. They will insure a ship on a twenty-five thousand mile trip around the world. They will not insure a marriage over a twelvemonth journey. The richest values of life are never mathematical, they are moral ventures.
—HALFORD E. LUCCOCK in *Sermons I Have Preached to Young People,* edited by Sidney A. Weston. Copyright, The Pilgrim Press. Used by permission.

400. A man once said about his sick wife, "There is nothing I would not do for her." One of the neighbors replied, "That is just the trouble, you have been doing nothing for her for forty years."
—CHARLES L. ALLEN in *In Quest of God's Power,* Fleming H. Revell Co.

401. Thornton Wilder in *The Bridge of San Luis Rey* tells how the old Marquesa longed for the love of her daughter with a selfish and possessive yearning. She sought it as a tribute to herself. When her daughter's love was withheld, the Marquesa became cynical. She believed in the goodness of no one. Said the author, "She saw that the people of this world moved about in an armor of egotism, drunk with self-gazing, athirst for compliments, hearing little of what was said to them, unmoved by the accidents that befell their closest friends, in dread of all appeals that might interrupt their long communion with their own desires."
—CHARLES M. CROWE in *Sermons from the Mount,* Abingdon Press. Quotation published by Albert & Charles Boni, Inc.

402. In his *Picturesque Notes of Edinburgh,* Robert Louis Stevenson told of two spinster sisters who had a falling out; and thenceforth no word was ever spoken between them. A chalk line on the floor separated their two domains. "It bisected the doorway and the fireplace, so that each could go out and in, and do her cooking, without violating the territory of the other's." So through the years they were separated within the four walls of that home.
—CLARENCE EDWARD MACARTNEY

403. Richard Baker writes: "The family is a unique human institution. It is the one community that is able to maintain itself without sacrificing the individuals who make it up." But why does a family bind individuals together without fettering their spirits? Because the family is activated by Christ's principles of love, fellow feeling, and united effort. When these stop, the family starts to fail.
—RALPH W. SOCKMAN

404. A famous Negro pastor of other days told of visiting the home of a parishioner, a teamster whose house was on the boulevard. The pastor found the front door of the house closed, so he walked around to the open back door. With an exclamation of disgust he walked into the house, closed the back door, and threw the front door open. Turning to the family he said, "You have the back door open to the filth and dirt, but the front door that opens on the flowers and beauty is closed."
—FRANK A. COURT

MOTHER'S DAY

A MOTHER'S INFLUENCE

405. One wife wisely says, "The wife and mother usually hoists the sails of the family ship every day. We determine whether those sails shall catch the breezes of God's love and understanding, or the winds of bickering and discord." This gracious wife and mother adds, "When a man succeeds, he does so by climbing a ladder steadied by a woman who believes in him."
—E. STANLEY JONES in *Growing Spiritually,* Abingdon Press.

406. A woman who runs her house well is both its queen and its subject. She is the one who makes work possible for her husband and children; she protects them from worries, feeds them and cares for them. She is Minister of Finance, and, thanks to her, the household budget is balanced. She is Minister of Fine Arts, and it is to her doing if the house or apartment has charm. She is Minister of Family Education and responsible for the boys' entry into school and college and the girls' cleverness and cultivation. A woman should be as proud of her success in making her house into a perfect little world as the greatest statesman of his in organizing a nation's affairs.
—ANDRÉ MAUROIS in *The Art of Living,* Harper & Bros.

407. If a woman can come to see her work in the guidance of a home as a ministry, a way in which she can fulfill the intention of God for her, she may be able to glorify her life *in her own eyes* and that is what is needed first. Motherhood is not merely a biological phenomenon; it is not merely dull domestic work; it is not merely a job; it is a holy calling. "Behold your calling" is the heartening admonition to the tired mother, who envies her husband his interesting public work, as it is to the factory worker who envies the lot of the white collar worker.
—ELTON TRUEBLOOD in *Your Other Vocation,* Harper & Bros.

408. Somebody has pointed out that of the sixty-nine kings of France only three were really loved by their subjects and that these three were the only ones reared by their mothers instead of by tutors or guardians. Whatever ability most of us have to make others love us is largely due to the love our mothers put in and around our lives.
—WILLIAM FREDERICK DUNKLE, JR.

409. To be a mother of men, a woman must make men of her boys. She demands their best, not because it belongs to her, but because it is due them. For that which is due children is not ease and luxury but hardening of muscles, the habit of work, a sense of honor, and a self-respect born of integrity.
—Quoted by ADELINE BULLOCK. Reprinted from *This Week* Magazine. Copy-

right 1946 by the United Newspapers Magazine Corporation.

410. Perhaps it is no wonder that the women were first at the Cradle and last at the Cross. They had never known a man like this Man—there never has been such another. A prophet and teacher who never nagged at them, never flattered or coaxed or patronized; who never made arch jokes about them; never treated them either as "The women, God help us!" or "The ladies, God bless them!" who rebuked without querulousness and praised without condescension; who took their questions and arguments seriously; who never mapped out their sphere for them; never urged them to be feminine or jeered at them for being female; who had no axe to grind and no uneasy male dignity to defend; who took them as he found them and was completely un–self-conscious.

—DOROTHY L. SAYERS from *Unpopular Opinions*. Copyright 1947 by Dorothy L. Sayers.

A MOTHER'S PRAYER

411. A young minister I know never took Christianity seriously until he was in the Air Corps stationed in India during World War II. There he was converted and decided to offer himself for the ministry. When the war was over and he came home, he told his mother and father of what had taken place and of his desire to prepare for the ministry. He told me his mother looked upon him as only a mother can and said, "Son, since you were a baby in my arms, I prayed that you might become a minister." Not every mother's prayers can be answered in this respect, but I venture that of every 1,000 men in the ministry today at least 998 of them are there in large part as an answer to the earnest, fervent prayers of godly mothers.

—EVERETT W. PALMER

412. Many years ago when Grover Cleveland was sitting alone after his election as Governor of New York, he began to think of his early life, his apparent successes, and the future. He was writing a letter to his brother, and in it he said, "Do you know, if Mother were alive I would feel so much safer." There are men and women today who would feel safer if their mothers were alive. She would steady the hand and the heart and the step, and put inspiration and renewed ideals into the hearts of her grown sons and daughters.

—HUGH THOMSON KERR in *Design for Christian Living*. Copyright, 1953, by W. L. Jenkins, The Westminster Press. Used by permission.

413. I used to ask the busy mother of six young children, "Don't you get awfully tired and find that you need to rest in the afternoon?" Because her work was the expression of her deep love, and because she had an inner rest so many of us know not of—"In him I live and move and have our being"—she could answer, "Oh, I keep going, and I get my second wind."

—JOSEPHINE MOFFETT BENTON in *Martha and Mary,* Pendle Hill Pamphlets.

414. A woman whose husband suddenly died, leaving her to raise six children of her own, adopted twelve others. Such an unusual woman warranted a newspaper feature, and a girl reporter was sent to interview her. During the course of the interview the reporter asked the widow how she managed to raise all those children and to do it so gracefully. "It's very simple," the widow answered. "You see, I'm in a partnership." "A

partnership? I hadn't heard about that. What sort of a partnership?" The woman's face broke into a sunny smile as she replied. "One day a long time ago I said to the Lord: 'Lord, I'll do the work and you do the worrying,' and I haven't had a worry since."
—Harold E. Kohn in *Feeling Low?* Wm. E. Eerdmans Publishing Co.

415. We went past a village in a mountain district in Japan called "the Place to leave your Mother." In the feudal days the old who had reached seventy were brought here to die. A young man carried his mother up the mountain to leave her there. He noticed she was breaking the twigs as she went along. Asked why, she replied: "I don't want you to lose your way in coming back." The young man could not leave his mother after that. . . . Her love changed a custom.
—E. Stanley Jones in *Growing Spiritually,* Abingdon Press.

416. Mary stands at the foot of the Cross in Robert R. Brown's narrative *The Miracle of the Cross.* Longinus says to his companion: "Antoninus, this man and the woman at his feet are, in a sense, a life-giving formula. Crucified of body he may be, crucified of spirit she surely is; yet the two together, son and mother, sustain each other and express the ageless triumph of love by a perfect family relationship."

"It is a thing any man can understand." Antoninus' voice is gentle. "Where there is such love there is victory, even in defeat. In such mutual suffering, each for the other, a mysterious, unconquerable power is miraculously born. One cannot see it here without wanting to play the more obedient son himself."
—Fleming H. Revell Co.

IN TRIBUTE

417. [My mother] was a woman of ordinary intelligence and of high moral nature. She was never sufficiently prized. Speaking broadly, the world is divided into two classes: those who deserve little and get much, and those who deserve much and get little; and it is a source of unceasing regret to me that my mother belonged to the latter class.
—Herbert Spencer

418. I like to think of the sterling character and Spartan courage of Mary Ball, the mother of Washington. Every virtue her son possessed, she passed on to him. She was imperious at times, and had a habit of issuing orders and demanding instant obedience. Punctuality was her creed and woe unto those of her family who did not move by the stroke of her clock. However, in spite of her strength of will and very great nobility of character, she in no wise sought to drive him to decisions in harmony with her own. When he went out against the French, she bitterly opposed it. She mourned: "Oh the fighting and the killing." Then, lifting her eyes to Heaven, she added: "God is our sure trust. To Him, I commend you." When the Revolution broke, she again wept: "Oh, is there to be more fighting, more blood shed? Surely, it will end in the halter."

At the close of the Revolution, when her son returned victorious from Yorktown, he sent his orderly ahead to prepare her so that the shock would not be too great. Touching his three-cornered hat, the orderly said: "Madam, His Excellency will be here within the hour." "His Excellency!" exclaimed the proud old mother. "You tell George I'll be glad to see him." Then, to her maid: "Patsy, I shall need a white apron."

When we see the great chieftain praying at Valley Forge, we need to remem-

ber Mary Ball, who went daily to pray at Meditation Rock, where she now lies buried.
—IVAN H. HAGEDORN in *Pulpit Digest.*

419. One of the most beautiful tributes to a mother is James Barrie's *Margaret Ogilvy*. The first chapter is entitled "How My Mother Got Her Soft Face." The oldest son in the family, who showed great promise as a scholar, was sent away to school. One day the tidings came that he was very ill. The whole family trooped down the brae to the station to see the mother off to get between death and her boy. Just after the train had gone, the father came out of the telegraph office, and said huskily, "He's gone!" Barrie writes: "From that day I knew my mother forever. When she got home the first thing she expressed a wish to see was the christening robe, and she looked long at it and then turned her face to the wall. That is how she got her soft face and her pathetic ways and her large charity, and why other mothers ran to her when they had lost a child. 'Dinna greet, poor Janet,' she would say to them, and they would answer, 'Ah, Margaret, but you're greeting yoursel.' "
—CLARENCE EDWARD MACARTNEY in *You Can Conquer,* Abingdon Press. Quotation published by Chas. Scribner's Sons.

420. When the monument at Wyuka, Nebraska City, Nebraska, to Caroline Morton, wife of J. Sterling Morton, Secretary of Agriculture under President Cleveland, was finished, the father took his four sons to the graveyard and told them that if they should ever do anything to disgrace their mother's name their own names would be removed from the inscription which reads:

Caroline
Wife of J. Sterling Morton
Died at Arbor Lodge
June 29, 1881, aged 47 years.
She was the Mother of
Joy, Paul, Mark and Carol Morton.

All of the names remain.
—*Stories on Stone,* Oxford University Press.

421. On the gravestone to Agnes Howard, died 1857, aged 76, on Ocracoke Island, North Carolina, is written:

She was!
But words are wanting to say what
Think what a wife should be
She was that.

—*Stories on Stone,* Oxford University Press.

MEMORIAL DAY

DAY OF REMEMBRANCE

422. Over the portal of the allied cemetery in North Assam, where lie the bodies of many of our American soldiers who fought in India and Burma during the Second World War, stand these words: "Tell Them That We Gave Our Todays for Their Tomorrows."
—KENNETH IRVING BROWN in *Not Minds Alone,* Harper & Bros.

423. During World War I, Sir Gilbert Murray said that he went around the quadrangles of Oxford with a heavy heart because he was conscious that brave young men were dying for him in France. Every sensitive thoughtful person has some such feeling as he walks amid the securities and advantages of a land like America. Brave men have suffered and died to provide these.
—From: *How to Believe,* by RALPH W. SOCKMAN. Copyright 1953 by Ralph W. Sockman, reprinted by permission of Doubleday & Company, Inc.

424. Christians . . . may well remember what Konstantine Simonov in his *Days and Nights* put upon the lips of a common soldier. In the siege of the city upon which at that moment the fate of many nations hung, one of the desperate defenders, looking out upon the attacking forces, said to the man at his side, "They don't give any date when they will take Stalingrad. . . . What is the reason?" And the man replied, "*We* are the reason." So in reply to the question why God's spiritual purpose for his world shall not be overrun, let individual Christians dare to say, "We are the reason!"
—WALTER RUSSELL BOWIE in *Preaching,* Abingdon Press.

425. Lincoln's most beautiful piece of prose is not the Gettysburg oration, stirring indeed though that was, nor the inspired Second Inaugural, but the closing paragraph of the First Inaugural address. There were no ghost writers then, and public men wrote their own speeches. But the First Inaugural, as Lincoln had written it, came to a blunt and severe ending—"With you, and not with me, is the solemn question of 'Shall it be peace, or a sword?' " When he showed the speech to Seward, Seward told him it was too stern and abrupt a conclusion and wrote out another paragraph which he submitted to him. In this paragraph Seward employed the metaphor of the chords of memory proceeding from the battlefields of the past and the patriot graves, and how they "will yet again harmonize in their ancient music when breathed upon by the guardian angel of the nation." Lincoln took this paragraph and with the touch of genius transmuted it to pure gold: "We are not enemies, but friends. We must not be enemies. Though passion may have strained, it must not break our bonds of affection.

The mystic chords of memory, stretching from every battlefield, and patriot grave, to every living heart and hearthstone, all over this broad land, will yet swell the chorus of the Union, when again touched, as surely they will be, by the better angels of our nature."
—CLARENCE EDWARD MACARTNEY

426. On Wisconsin's monument to the memory of its 378 young men who perished at the terrible stockade at Andersonville on the red hills of Georgia are inscribed these lines by Thomas Campbell:

And is he dead, whose glorious mind
Lifts thine on high?
To live in hearts we leave behind
Is not to die.

—CLARENCE EDWARD MACARTNEY

427. William Tyler Page, one-time clerk of the House of Representatives and author of *The American's Creed,* wrote this tribute for the Tomb of the Unknown Revolutionary Soldier in Presbyterian Meeting House churchyard, Alexandria, Virginia:

Here lies a soldier of
The Revolution whose identity
Is known but to God.
His was an idealism
That recognized a Supreme
Being, that planted
Religious liberty on our
Shores, that overthrew
Despotism, that established
A people's government,
That wrote a Constitution
Setting metes and bounds
Of delegated authority,
That fixed a standard of
Value upon men above
Gold and lifted high the
Torch of civil liberty
Along the pathway of
Mankind.
In ourselves his soul
Exists as part of ours,
His memory's mansion.

—*Stories on Stone,* Oxford University Press.

428. Foretelling the future good will between the English and Americans is this inscription on a stone built into the retaining wall of a garden on North Main Street, Ridgefield, Connecticut:

In Defence of American Independence
At the Battle of Ridgefield
April 27, 1777
Died
Eight Patriots
Who Were Laid in These Grounds
Companioned by
Sixteen British Soldiers
Living Their Enemies, Dying Their Guests.
"In Honor of Service and Sacrifice
This Memorial Is Placed
For the Strengthening of Hearts."

—*Stories on Stone,* Oxford University Press.

429. In the town of Lany, twenty-five miles outside the city of Prague, there are four unmarked graves. They are the resting places of the three Masaryks and Eduard Benes. A friend who was there stated that, some months before his death, Dr. Benes visited the cemetery. He expressed a desire to be buried alongside his friends and compatriots. It was also his desire that the graves should go unmarked. "For," said he, "if the people love me, I shall live in their hearts and they will never forget the place of my grave; hence an identification is unnecessary. If they do not love me, I shall be forgotten in their hearts; and the most elaborate tombstone will make no difference."

—HOWARD THURMAN in *Deep is the Hunger*, Harper & Bros.

TESTIMONY OF DEVOTION

430. A three-and-a-half-year-old boy named Tommy stood in front of a store-window Memorial Day display. He gazed eagerly at a field of small crosses and exclaimed, "Look, Daddy, at all the t's! Do they all stand for Tommy?" The father replied, "Those t's are crosses, and each one represents the loving devotion of a soldier for Tommy and his family and his nation."

—G. THOMAS FATTARUSO

431. If a soldier dies merely through the hazards of war, that is one thing. But if he dies for a cause to which his country has linked its destiny, such as human freedom or the maintenance of justice, he has linked himself to a cause which is great and glorious. If that cause is eternal, an eternal significance is given to his dying. But if not, his attachment to it gives him the distinction of a patriot and a hero, but not necessarily that of a saint. To die for justice, for freedom, links a man to something different from mere devotion to a flag. Justice is not temporal, it is eternal. In dying for it, one gives significance to his final act. If a man will link himself to the will of God and the reign of God over all human affairs; if he lives for it, dies for it, his life and death are merged in the life and purpose of God and therefore he is indestructible.

—JOHN GARDNER in *Letters to "Bill" on Faith and Prayer,* Fleming H. Revell Co.

432. So long as the English tongue survives, the word Dunkerque will be spoken with reverence. For in that harbor, in such a hell as never blazed on earth before, at the end of a lost battle, the rags and blemishes that have hidden the soul of democracy fell away. There, beaten but unconquered, in shining splendor, she faced the enemy. They sent away the wounded first. Men died so that others could escape. It was not so simple a thing as courage, which the Nazis had in plenty. It was not so simple a thing as discipline, which can be hammered into men by a drill sergeant. It was not the result of careful planning, for there could have been little. It was the common man of the free countries, rising in all his glory out of the mill, office, factory, mine, farm and ship, applying to war the lessons learned when he went down the shaft to bring out trapped comrades, when he hurled the lifeboat through the surf, when he endured poverty and hard work for his children's sake. This shining thing in the souls of free men Hitler cannot command or attain or conquer. He has crushed it, where he could, from German hearts. It is the great tradition of democracy. It is the future. It is victory.

—*The New York Times*

433. On his TV program Groucho Marx asked a high-school teacher and coach who had been a famous college athlete why he had not gone into pro football instead of teaching. The answer was, "Well, you see, there was a war on about the time I graduated from college; and out on an island in the Pacific a bullet caught me in the thigh. They amputated my leg, and you can't very well play pro football with a wooden leg." When Marx asked, "How does it affect your life to be thus handicapped?" the teacher replied, "What do you mean—handicapped? I have a wife, and we have four fine boys. I'm doing what I want to do. I teach a class or two in

high school and have a great group of boys to work with. I live in the greatest country in the world. I don't make much money at teaching, but we have enough to get along with, and we are happy. Just what do you mean that I am handicapped because I gave a leg to my country?"
—Frank A. Court

434. I read recently of a boy who applied for a job as an usher in a theater, and the manager asked him, "What would you do in case of a fire?" "Oh, don't worry about me," said the boy, "I'd get out all right." Well, that self is in all of us. But not so long since I read about a boy in Korea, who was given the Congressional Medal posthumously. Once when he was ambushed he exposed himself and drew the fire of the enemy so that his buddies would escape, and that self too is in all of us. One self asks, "What is there in it for me? Nobody, nothing matters, just so my own self-centered, self-seeking wishes are satisfied." And the other self says, "Greater love hath no man than this, that a man lay down his life for his friend."
—Harold Cooke Phillips in *Great Preaching Today,* Alton M. Motter, editor, published in 1953 by Harper & Bros. Used by permission.

435. A visitor to a veterans' hospital tried to sympathize with a solder who had lost his leg, saying, "I am sorry you lost your leg." The lad replied: "I didn't lose it. I bought a clean conscience with it."
—Hugh Thomson Kerr in *Design for Christian Living.* Copyright, 1953, by W. L. Jenkins, The Westminster Press. Used by permission.

436. "Why do you commiserate with me?" asked an English mother when friends sympathized with her over the son she had lost in the Battle of Britain. "He lived for twenty happy, clean years and then he died for England. What better could he have done than that?"
—Robert J. McCracken in *Questions People Ask,* Harper & Bros.

437. In the bitter civil war of the seventeenth century, a son of the Duke of Ormonde laid down his life in what both his father and he believed the cause of right. Someone commiserated the older man on his sore loss, and got the reply: "I would not give my dead son for the best living son in Christendom."
—Henry Sloane Coffin in *Here Is My Method,* Fleming H. Revell Co.

438. It has been said that "society is a great and silent compact between the dead, the living and the unborn." The Flag is the visible evidence of this compact. It ties the generations together. It gives continuity to civilization.
—Edward F. Hutton in *Vital Speeches.*

PENTECOST

WORK OF THE SPIRIT

439. The Quakers lay great stress on the illumination of the Holy Spirit and the voice of God which speaks within our conscience, the Inner Light. In the early days of the Friends one of their number, as he was retiring for the night, heard what seemed to him a voice which bade him to go to a meetinghouse forty miles away and that, when he reached there, he would be given a message for the people. It was a dark, dismal night; but obedient to the Light, he mounted his horse and rode all through the night to this distant village, arriving just as the Friends were going into their meetinghouse. After a half hour of silence he arose and, somewhat troubled and perplexed, said, "I do not understand what is happening. I thought last night that I heard the voice of the Lord telling me to come here and meet with you; and now that I have come, I find that I have no message." Then he sat down, and there was another half hour of silence. After a time the elders arose and, as their custom was, shook hands with one another. But one of them, when he shook hands with the visitor, said to him: "Perhaps our brother had a message to deliver after all. Perhaps that message was, 'Mind the Light.' "
—CLARENCE EDWARD MACARTNEY

440. If we are to receive through the Holy Spirit the factors which make for growth in Christ we must put ourselves in contact with them. When Anatole France set out to write a book, he changed the decorations of his home, creating an atmosphere expressive of the period which was currently engaging his thoughts. When, for instance, he was writing *Thaïs,* he surrounded himself with the art of ancient Greece. For his work on Joan of Arc, he hung on his walls beautiful tapestries of fifteenth-century France.
—From *How to Believe,* by RALPH W. SOCKMAN. Copyright 1953 by Ralph W. Sockman, reprinted by permission of Doubleday & Co., Inc.

441. A young lady came to me one night at a youth camp. She had a list of questions she wanted to ask. In the service that night the Holy Spirit worked mightily in the souls of the youth. At the close of the service the young lady said: "Pastor, I do not need to discuss these questions with you now. I was the problem. Christ is the answer for my life."
—IRA H. PEAK

442. New York City, so far as it lies on Manhattan Island, is kept reasonably clean by two rivers, into which at the east and the west end of each street a sewer discharges its filth, which is swept down the Bay and out into the Atlantic. The Holy Spirit is ours, corporately and individually, in the Church, in the nation, in our particular community, to achieve a similar "putting away," if we will only *let* him.

—Reprinted from *Communion Through Preaching* by HENRY SLOANE COFFIN. Copyright 1952 by Charles Scribner's Sons; used by permission of the publishers.

443. Alexander Irvine offers a tender and beautiful tribute to his mother in *My Lady of the Chimney Corner*. She was one of those understanding souls to whom individuals turn in time of need. So when Eliza lost her boy, she sought out Anna. Anna asked Eliza to pray that God would lay his hand on her tired head and bless her. With a start Eliza replied: "He's done it, Anna, He's done it, glory be t' God, He's done it! . . . There was a nice feelin' went down through me, Anna, an' th' han' was jist like yours!" "The han' was mine," said the Lady, "but it was God's too. . . . God takes a han' wherever He can find it and jist diz what He likes wi' it. Sometimes He takes a bishop's and lays it on a child's head in benediction, then He takes the han' of a dochter t' relieve pains, th' han' of a mother t' guide her chile, an' sometimes He take th' han' of an aul craither like me t' give a bit of comfort to a neighbor. But they're all han's touch't be His Spirit, an' His Spirit is everywhere lukin' fur han's to use."

CHILDREN OF THE SPIRIT

444. There is no greater drama in human record than the sight of a few Christians, scorned or oppressed by a succession of emperors, bearing all trials with a fierce tenacity, multiplying quietly, building order while their enemies generated chaos, fighting the sword with the word, brutality with hope, and at last defeating the strongest state that history has known. Caesar and Christ had met in the arena, and Christ had won.

—WILL DURANT in *Caesar and Christ*, Simon & Schuster, Inc.

445. Early Christians did not so much speak of a person going to church, but more often thought of the church as being present with each person at his place of daily employment. To the degree that his work represented the Spirit's call and the Spirit's response, to that extent the Church was actively fulfilling its mission through him. In his chores were embodied its repentance and forgiveness, its struggle with temptation, its victory. In his inward thoughts and outward activities were manifested its faith, its prayers, its hopes. His faithfulness in love helped to knit the Body together. Thus early Christians located the frontier of God's war along the line of human associations and decisions encountered in their day-to-day living.

—PAUL S. MINEAR in *Work and Vocation*, Harper & Bros.

446. When the early church fathers came together, they talked about their powers; but when modern churchmen come together, they talk about their problems.

—ARTHUR J. MOORE

447. If a man travels far enough away from Christianity he is always in danger of seeing it in perspective and deciding that it is true. It is much safer, from Satan's point of view, to vaccinate a man with a mild case of Christianity, so as to protect him from the real thing.

—CHAD WALSH in *Early Christians of the 21st Century*, Harper & Bros.

448. Hope S. Johansen, writing of the restoration of St. Stephen's Cathedral in Vienna after World War II, said that it was discovered that soot had been smeared on the walls and pillars to create an atmosphere of mourning for royal

funerals centuries ago. This had contributed to the darkness within the cathedral. During the restoration the walls were cleaned until they sparkled. When the life of a church becomes clouded by difficulties, despair, and doubts, it is necessary to turn to the story of the early Church for renewed inspiration and vitality.

449. A good stained-glass window is made up of thousands of tiny pieces of colored glass held together with lead. The result is a figure. Clare Boothe Luce has written, "The portrait of a saint is only a fragment of a great and still uncompleted mosaic—the portrait of Jesus." Each saint is like a piece of colored glass in a total picture depicting Christ. The Church, the communion of saints, is the body of Christ. The lead holding the saints together is the Holy Spirit.
—J. R. Brokhoff

450. George A. Buttrick lists six essential things which early Christians possessed which are possessed by few members of the modern Church: (1) A tranforming, communicable experience of the living Christ. (2) A passion to pass it on. (3) An unbreakable fellowship with the other members of the converted group. (4) A love for men which was not dependent on being loved, or liked, or flattered; a love not in terms of sentimental feeling, but of unbreakable good will and high desire. (5) An inward security or peace not dependent on the number of things there are to do in a day. (6) A deep sense of joy not dependent on being happy; for joy is not the opposite of unhappiness, but the opposite of unbelief, and the word "joy" is too great and grand to be confused with the superficial thing we call happiness. It was joy and peace which Jesus said he left men in his will.
—*Living Joyously* by Kirby Page, Rinehart & Co., Inc.

451. "Demas hath forsaken me," wrote Paul, "having loved this present world." (II Tim. 4:10.) What was it that turned the fellow worker of Mark and Luke from the gospel mission? Did he become discouraged when he compared the poverty and struggle of the apostle with the wealth, luxury, and splendor of imperial Rome? Did such pleasure resorts as the one uncovered at Canopus, Egypt, with its red granite temple and two dozen luxurious bathing pools beckon? If only he could have known how the Mediterranean sand dunes would cover up the resorts of the world. If only he could have seen the Church Paul loved sweep on mightily in a great mission to save our world.
—Roger J. Squire

452. A group of Boy Scouts were amazed when they saw the deep-red and blazing rocks long after the wood in their campfire had been consumed. Their scoutmaster told them of a Colorado pioneer who built a rock cabin. After he had completed the house, he started a fire in the fireplace. The whole cabin became a burning holocaust, for the rocks were oil shale and were impregnated with oil. Lives of men, created in the divine image, have within them light and heat which break forth in a great brilliance when they are set on fire by the spirit of God.
—John H. Blough

CHURCH OF OUR FATHERS

453. H. R. L. "Dick" Sheppard was once showing a group of visitors through Canterbury Cathedral. When they came to those famous chancel steps, the desti-

nation of so many thousands of pilgrim journeys, Sheppard took one man and pressed his knee to the step saying, "Kneel here; it is a great thing to kneel where faithful pilgrims have knelt in days ahead of you." We do that in the communion of the Church. We kneel where others have knelt and then risen to go out victors over the destructive power of alcohol, sex, temper, hate, weakness, fear because they found at the heart of the Church One in whose grip they could handle these things.
—ROBERT E. LUCCOCK in *If God Be For Us,* Harper & Bros.

454. The way of God has been charted, mapped and marked by countless millions of men who have lived and died, most of them nameless. They have posted the road, at first but a part of the road, for the mountain peak of death loomed up too lofty, too forbidding for them to surmount, until there came One who calling himself the Way, marked the highway from start to finish.
—CORWIN C. ROACH in *Preaching Values in the Bible,* Cloister Press.

455. On the frontispiece of a book by Stephen Graham is a picture of a lighted candle. Underneath are the words: "May I waste so that I show the face of Christ." The symbol and the inscription portray the devotion and sacrifice of twenty centuries of Christian discipleship.

456. A medieval philosopher wrote of the earlier thinkers: "We are like dwarfs seated on the shoulders of giants. We see more things than the ancients and things more distant, but it is due neither to the sharpness of our sight nor the greatness of our stature; it is simply because they have lent us their own."
—HAROLD A. BOSLEY

457. We need, said Burke, in his stately language, to auspicate all our proceedings with the old warning of the Church, "*Sursum corda*—Lift up your hearts." But how, from the levels of our ordinary lives, our average minds, can we raise ourselves, if only for a space, to heights beyond our own capacity, even beyond our normal vision? The answer is that we can raise ourselves on the shoulders of those who have walked on higher levels. What unaided we could not do we can do by their help.

Religion is the greatest instrument for so raising us. It is amazing that a person not intellectually bright, perhaps not even educated, is capable of grasping, and living by, something so advanced as the principles of Christianity. Yet that is a common phenomenon.
—RICHARD LIVINGSTONE in *The Atlantic Monthly.*

458. Charles Samuel Braden, in *War, Communism and World Religions* comments on his interviews with many Chinese Christians and concludes: "I had the distinct feeling as I talked with person after person, Protestant and Catholic, priest and lay worker, that I was living once again in the first century of the Christian Church. Christian heroism is no monopoly of the early Church, or the medieval Church. It is being practiced today. Right now men and women are suffering, even to martyrdom, for the faith they cherish, in more than one area of the world—nowhere more than in China. Faced with a spirit such as these people exhibit, it is not hard to believe that Communism must ultimately lose in its struggle for the control of men's minds and spirits."
—Harper & Bros.

459. In one of his little books, Elton Trueblood writes of "The Fellowship of

the Unashamed." Paul must have originated fellowship, for, in a day when it was dangerous to be known as a Christian—when the label *Christian* had about the same connotation as the term *criminal*—Paul was so enthusiastic about his religion that he eagerly declared to the world, "I am not ashamed." This note of pride in his faith differs broadly from the attitude of too many modern disciples who want the quiet respectability of church membership but carefully avoid the social embarrassment of becoming vigorously Christian.
—EUGENE PEACOCK in *The Pulpit*. Copyrighted by the Christian Century Foundation and used by permission.

460. When New England villages were first built, they used to have a custom of what was called "centering the town." The boundaries of the village would be determined; then lines drawn from the four farthermost corners to bisect in the middle; and where the lines crossed, there the town was to be "centered." There at the exact center the earliest colonists built their church.
—HARRY H. KRUENER in *The Intercollegian*.

461. In her book *Meetinghouse Hill*, Ola Elizabeth Winslow tells the story of the meetinghouses of early New England and of their relevance to the life of the people. The significance of the meetinghouse "to later times, as to its own, is that somehow it embodied fundamental loyalties and created a state of mind in which these loyalties took on reality. In some way, not easy to understand perhaps, it stood for 'the good of the whole,' the 'mind of the town' and 'holy walking.' In some way it teased the thought of village men and women beyond village boundaries and the Here and Now of their lives. It stood for the eternal against the transient. . . . It is the story of convictions and purposes, of a protest plus an experience of living, of intangibles such as are not often sowed and reaped in one generation or in many generations. Moreover, as the seeds of its earlier plantings and reapings have been widely blown, they have sometimes yielded unpredictable fruit."
—Copyright 1952. Used by permission of The Macmillan Co.

462. The Boston and Maine Railroad timetable in 1850 listed a Sunday train but solemnly warned Sunday riders: "Persons purchasing tickets will be required to sign a pledge that they will use the ticket for no other purpose than attending church." We laugh at this today because our world has become so secular that the Sabbath has become one of golf, not God, one for folks to work in the garden, mowing the lawn, take a trip, or sleep past church hour.
—J. R. BROKHOFF

463. Moshe Wolfe in *East River* by Sholem Asch says: "When a man labors not for a livelihood but to accumulate wealth, then he is a slave. Therefore it is that God granted us the Sabbath. For it is by the Sabbath that we know we are not work animals, born to eat and to labor; we are men. It is the Sabbath which is man's goal—not labor, but the rest which he earns from his labor. It was because the Jews made the Sabbath holy to God that they were redeemed from the slavery in Egypt. It was by the Sabbath that they proclaimed that they were not slaves but free men."
—Copyright 1946, G. P. Putnam's Sons.

THE LIVING CHURCH

464. In 1830 Benjamin Constant, the French philosopher, received a message at the hands of his friends in Paris who

were overthrowing the Bourbons. "A terrible game is being played here: our heads are in danger; come and add yours." That was the appeal of Christ to his followers. What we need in the Church now is the same crusading spirit for, to quote Berdyaev, . . . these are times when "Christianity is going back to the state she enjoyed before Constantine; she has to undertake the conquest of the world afresh."
—ROBERT J. MCCRACKEN in *Questions People Ask,* Harper & Bros.

465. To the young people of my generation [Gilbert Keith Chesterton] was a kind of Christian liberator. Like a beneficent bomb, he blew out of the Church a quantity of stained glass of a very poor period, and let in gusts of fresh air, in which the dead leaves of doctrine danced with all the energy of Our Lady's Tumbler. . . . It was . . . stimulating to be told that Christianity was not a dull thing but a gay thing, not a stick-in-the-mud thing but an adventurous thing, not an unintelligent thing but a wise thing, and indeed a shrewd thing—for while it was still frequently admitted to be harmless as the dove, it had almost ceased to be credited with the wisdom of the serpent. Above all it was refreshing to see Christian polemic conducted with offensive rather than defensive weapons.
—From the preface by DOROTHY L. SAYERS of *The Surprise,* by Gilbert K. Chesterton. Copyright, 1953, by Sheed and Ward, Inc., New York.

466. Let God be thanked there is on earth an institution that has a high opinion of man, declaring that he is a son of God, who has divine possibilities; an institution that transcends race, nation and class; an institution which is loyally undertaking to embody the spirit of Christ, and in His name to relieve human suffering, promote human welfare and carry on a ministry of reconciliation among men.
—ERNEST F. TITTLE

467. The church . . . has always been a great centering force for women. Through what ages women have had their quiet hour, free of interruption, to draw themselves together. No wonder woman has been the mainstay of the church. Here were the advantages of the room of her own, the time alone, the quiet, the peace, all rolled into one and sanctioned by the approval of both family and community. Here no one could intrude with a careless call, "Mother," "Wife," "Mistress." Here, finally and more deeply, woman was whole, not split into a thousand functions. She was able to give herself completely in that hour of worship, in prayer, in communion, and be completely accepted. And in that giving and acceptance she was renewed; the springs were refilled.
—ANNE MORROW LINDBERGH in *Gift from the Sea,* Pantheon Books, Inc.

468. When Gutzon Borglum started to carve the Confederate memorial on Stone Mountain in Georgia, he solved his first great problem in a unique way. He needed to throw on the face of the eight hundred foot sheer wall of granite the outline of the figures of marching men to guide him in his work. Many devices were tried without success. Finally he ordered a specially designed and constructed projection machine. The machine weighed a ton. It was anchored eight hundred feet from the mountain and threw a clear picture two hundred feet high from a slide three inches high. It was the only machine like it in the world. With it the stonecutters could work according to scale and plan. It is a

parable of the church at work in the world today. The shining flame of the eternal God projects through the church a pattern of the Kingdom of God on the hard, steep granite face of the world.
—CHARLES M. CROWE in *The Years of Our Lord,* Abingdon Press.

469. Visiting the New Church at Amsterdam, I said to one of the caretakers of this beautiful Gothic structure, "Would you tell me when this New Church was built?" I supposed he would say sometime in the latter part of the nineteenth century. "This church," he replied slowly and with emphasis, "was built in 1408." When I had recovered my equilibrium, I said, "Eighty-four years before the discovery of America yet you call it the 'New Church.'" "Well," he said, "you see the 'Old Kerke' over yonder was built in 1300."
—JOHN SUTHERLAND BONNELL

470. One day in London I talked with a vicar whose church had been bombed in World War II. It was about eleven o'clock at night that the bomb had landed, he said, an incendiary which lodged itself in a corner of the room beyond the reach of ladders, and by midnight the awful blaze had reached its height. "I was seventy-two years old when that happened," the vicar said, "and as I watched the fire burning down my church, I knew the end had come for me." But just as it became surely apparent that no help of man could save the great building from ruin, down from its huge stone tower came the sound of the clock striking twelve. "I am still here!" it seemed to be saying, "I, the church, am still here! And I will be here. I will always be here." "That gave me back my hope," the vicar told me. "I knew then that my church would rise again." And it did.
—ROY M. PEARSON in *Here's a Faith for You,* Abingdon Press.

471. [The Church] has been an institution in time whose very reason for existence was found in its claim to represent sanctions which came from eternity. It has existed in a relative world, and yet it has asserted its foundations in absolute meanings. It has lived its life in an imperfect society, and yet it has declared that it represented the demands of perfection. In the very nature of the case it has shared the limitations of the temporal, and this has affected the adequacy of its witness to the eternal. Inevitably it has taken upon itself qualities of the relative, and this has depleted its power as the representative of the absolute. It has taken to itself qualities of the imperfect society of which it was a part, and this has often compromised and even betrayed its upholding of standards which belong to the world of perfection. Disconcerting and even ugly as these paradoxes are, they inevitably emerge in any institutions in which the temporal and the eternal, the relative and the absolute, the imperfect and the perfect meet.
—LYNN HAROLD HOUGH in *The Christian Criticism of Life,* Abingdon Press.

472. When Robert Murray McCheyne, saint of Scotland, lived in Dundee, his watch always showed the correct time. Whenever he left the city his watch did not tell the exact truth. In Dundee he passed by the church every day and unconsciously regulated his watch by the clock in the tower. Elsewhere he had no standard for telling the time.
—ANDREW W. BLACKWOOD in *Expository Preaching for Today,* Abingdon Press.

473. The Christian church is not a society of integrated personalities, nor of philosophers, nor of mystics, nor even of

good people. It is a society of broken personalities, of men and women with troubled minds, of people who know that they are not good. The Christian church is a society of sinners. It is the only society in the world, membership in which is based upon the single qualification that the candidate shall be unworthy of membership.
—CHARLES CLAYTON MORRISON in *What Is Christianity?* Harper & Bros.

474. When I glance over the long catalogue of sins committed by churchmen and the Church, I am convinced that the most effective argument for the claim that the Church is a divine institution is the fact that it has survived the sins of its members. Most human institutions crumble under this weight in a few years or centuries, but not the Church. Only an institution created and recreated by God could have not only survived but flourished through two thousand years as has the Church.
—HAROLD A. BOSLEY

475. People who refuse to join the church because, as they claim, "there are too many hypocrites in the church" remind me of those times when I played hide-and-seek with my two-year-old daughter. She had not learned that in order to hide behind something you have to be smaller than it is. She would hide behind her little rocking chair or a table leg. The man who rejects Christian responsibility because of the "hypocrites" in the church is hiding behind the hypocrites and shows that he is smaller than they are.
—C. R. FINDLEY

476. Under the most unusual circumstances we can sometimes speak a good word for Jesus Christ. One morning when I was rushing to meet an appointment, a patrolman stopped me. "You are driving thirty-one miles an hour in a thirty-mile zone," he said. I thought this was unjust; but accepting my civic responsibility, I went unhesitatingly to the traffic court. I was surprised when the judge introduced himself as an inactive member of my church. He required that I pay a fine and then said: "I've been wanting to meet you. I have not been in church for some time, but my wife and I are both concerned with the youth of this community." He told me the efforts he was exerting and asked me about the endeavors of the church. The Christian concern was persuasive, and the judge and I locked hands in a common cause. Soon the church treasurer reported that the judge had sent a substantial pledge, and thereafter he became an earnest church worker. The patrolman I later learned had had an argument with his wife on the morning of the arrest and was in a bad humor but through our brusque meeting I was able to help someone to build a home on Christian foundations.
—JOHN EDWARD LANTZ

477. An American writer, seeking a quiet and inspiring setting for his work, built a home in the Blue Ridge Mountains of Virginia. Nestled against the mountainside, it overlooked a glorious valley. One day while on a hike the writer met an old woman, a native of the region. With shy courtesy, but surprising directness, she asked: "Be them y'er lights that shine across the valley? Ye ain't a' goin' to let 'em be shrouded up, 'er ye? Or be ye?" Over the world there are millions of people who, looking across their dark valleys, are saying to the Church: "You aren't going to let your lights be shrouded up, are you?"
—EVERETT W. PALMER

CHALLENGE

478. When Mr. William E. Gladstone was Prime Minister of Great Britain he was asked why he attended church so faithfully. . . . "I go to church," said the Victorian statesman, "because I love England." So you and I might say, "I go to church . . . because I love America, and that 'other country,' the Kingdom of God on earth."
—David A. MacLennan in *Joyous Adventure,* published in 1952 by Harper & Brothers.

479. Gandhi's description of a church he attended in South Africa when a young man can be taken and applied clause by clause to many a congregation in this country. He had come into contact with a family who invited him to accompany them to their place of worship. "At their suggestion," he says, "I attended church every Sunday. The church did not make a favorable impression on me. The sermons seemed to me to be uninspiring. The congregation did not strike me as being particularly religious. They were not an assembly of devout souls; they appeared to be rather worldly-minded, going to church in conformity to custom. Here at times I would involuntarily doze. I was ashamed, but some of my neighbors who were in no better a case lightened the shame. I could not go on like this and soon gave up attending the service." One wonders how often that has been the identical experience of young people in America.
—Robert J. McCracken

480. Frederick B. Speakman tells of a little old lady who visited Westminster Abbey. "She glanced at every stone and symbol and inscription with the steady eyes of hungry interest, yet silently conveyed the idea that she wasn't about to be impressed. And when at last she spoke, it was to break into [the guide's comments] with a question that left the guide slack-jawed and puzzled. With one quick gesture she swept Westminster Abbey, that citadel of church tradition, that rich storehouse of historic Christian greatness, and said, 'Young man, young man, stop your chatter and tell me, has anyone been saved here lately?' "
—*The Salty Tang,* Fleming H. Revell Co.

481. A chaplain who served in World War II reported that after each enemy bombing raid the attendance at his chapel services increased. It was so obvious that when the attendance dropped the men would joke, "Chaplain, we need another raid." We have often belittled this tendency to become religious in time of suffering or danger, and yet it is deep in the hearts of all of us.
—Russell L. Dicks in *And Peace at the Last.* Copyright, 1953, by W. L. Jenkins, The Westminster Press. Used by permission.

482. There is a beautiful and accurate simile of Brunner's "The Church exists by mission, as fire exists by burning." When the fire dies it is no longer a church. It meets the fate that has overtaken Salem, Illinois, called "The town that became a museum." So there can be a church that becomes a museum. We can go on a conducted tour around it. There is the creed in a glass case; there are the records in the safe. There are the mummies, once alive. And there will be no communication.
—Halford E. Luccock in *Communicating the Gospel,* Harper & Bros.

483. In the state of Oregon, an old, abandoned church was put up for sale. There had been no services in it for many years and the denominational heads decided it would be wisest to dis-

pose of the property. But a storm of protest arose and the local paper was full of letters written by irate citizens objecting to the sale of a historical landmark. The man who had one time been its pastor remarked that, if people had shown that much interest in it while it was still alive, it would not have been abandoned. So it is with men and their concern for salvation. Not until the very last minute, when they have lost everything, do they ask with real intensity: "From whence shall my help come?"
—GERALD KENNEDY in *Go Inquire of the Lord,* Harper & Bros.

484. One of the maladies of many church members is "excusitis." It is a disease of the mind and heart. Its symptoms are irresponsibility, indifference, uncertainty, and laziness. When asked to render a useful service in the church, the person parades a list of "good" excuses. They may be "good" reasons, but they are not "real" reasons. The indifferent and irresponsible person manufactures flimsy curtains of pretense. "Good" excuses usually lay bare the conflict between what we are and (1) what we wish we were, (2) what we know we should be, and (3) what we wish others to think we are. Psychologists describe this sickness as "rationalizing" or attributing one's actions to rational and creditable motives without adequate analysis of the true motives.

485. Meeting a member who had been absent from the church services, I said, "Good morning, I have greatly missed you of late." He answered, "We have moved, and I have found that it is just too far for me to attend regularly." I inquired where he was employed, and when he answered, I called his attention to the fact that it was farther to his place of business than to the church. He merely replied, "Well, that's different."
—ROSS H. STOVER in *The Upper Room Pulpit.*

486. Warwick Deeping in a famous old novel, *Sorrell and Son,* causes one of his genial pagans to describe the experience of actually going to church this way: "It always makes me feel queer. . . . As though I had fallen suddenly through a trap door into another world. Not our world." You hardly know whether to laugh or cry over one who feels so strange in the church. He would not understand Jesus' feeling at home in the Temple or anyone's feeling at home in the church—and at least half the adult citizens of our country would agree with him.
—HAROLD A. BOSLEY

487. If a person is a socialist or a Communist, I will know it in twenty-four hours; if he is a member of a labor union, I will know it within a few days; but if he is a member of a Christian church, it may be years before I will ever learn of it.
—HUGHES WAGNER

488. A young clergyman was in conference with the managing editor of a great metropolitan newspaper—a man who had a reputation for being a skilled craftsman in his field, a courageous crusader, and a political leader of high principles. He could not, however, be called a churchman in any sense of the word. "If I were a Christian," he said, "and if I really believed the things the Christians say they believe, I think I would be desperate. I cannot understand how any man can believe such doctrines as the Church preaches and be complacent in a world like ours."
—ROY L. SMITH in *Stewardship Studies,* Abingdon Press.

489. Perhaps our obsession with the good time is nowhere more strikingly revealed than in American church life. . . . American churches were formerly dedicated to individual salvation, but they have turned out to be institutions dedicated, since the vogue of the social gospel, to maintaining a good time more decorous than that of the country club but not essentially different. The young people's meeting, the ladies' aid, the church supper, the church gymnasium, and even the church dance are characteristic contributions to theology. . . . Why should the devil have all the good tunes? Why drive young people to cabarets and dance halls when the church parlors are available? The argument is irresistible, but it does not conceal the assumption that the promise of a good time is more potent than the promise of relief from sin. . . . Nor is this shift in value confined to the young. Not only do ministers fail to mention hell to ears polite, they fail to mention hell at all. The terrors of death are gone. . . . Heaven has also quietly disappeared . . . because the idea of beatitude is so antithetic to the idea of a good time had by all that an eternity of endless hymns is essentially meaningless.
—HOWARD MUMFORD JONES in *The Pursuit of Happiness,* Harvard University Press.

490. In one of our small mountain towns some time ago, a young preacher made a funeral announcement for which I have great admiration. He knew he was going to move anyway, so he just told the truth. He said: "The funeral of Mr. Ben Brown will be held from this church tomorrow afternoon at three o'clock. And Mr. Brown will be here himself, in person, for the first time in three years."
—PIERCE HARRIS in *The Pulpit in the South,* Frank S. Mead, ed., Fleming H. Revell Co.

491. Churchmen too often have sought shelter and warmth. When Holman Hunt set out to paint his famous "The Light of the World," he spent the major part of three years trying to get the proper atmosphere for depicting Christ at the door. In his effort to paint the wintry light of Christ's lantern, he spent many, many nights out in the wind, his feet wrapped in straw to keep them warm. If it took a great artist three years to catch the spirit of the presence of Christ, how can we expect to possess the "Light of the World" in ease and comfort?
—CHARLES L. ALLEN

492. A character in *Point of No Return* by John P. Marquand is described in these words: "He knew all the little answers, but he missed the large questions."
—Little, Brown & Co.

493. A young minister, trained in Spurgeon's own School of the Prophets, came to see the great preacher in much distress of mind. "I haven't had a conversion, as the result of my ministry, for months," he wailed. "But surely," remarked Spurgeon, "you don't expect conversions every time you preach." "Well, no," answered the young man hesitatingly. "Then that is why you don't get them," was the older man's swift reply.
—JOHN PITTS in *Religion in Life.*

COMMENCEMENT

THE DEDICATION OF LIFE

494. Whatever your career may be, do not let yourselves become tainted by a deprecating and barren skepticism, do not let yourselves be discouraged by the sadness of certain hours which pass over nations. Live in the serene peace of laboratories and libraries. Say to yourselves first, "What have I done for my instruction?" and as you gradually advance, "What have I done for my country?" until the time comes when you may have the immense happiness of thinking that you have contributed in some way to the progress and to the good of humanity. But whether our efforts are, or not, favored by life, let us be able to say, when we come near the great goal, "I have done what I could."
—Louis Pasteur

495. I have always considered life as though it were a piece of solid granite. . . . You take the chisel of your will power and carve the granite. To have a design ready before you start is as essential as it is to have a sharp chisel. It is within you, within the power of all of us, to get both these requirements.
—Jean Sibelius quoted by Lili Foldes in *The Reader's Digest.*

496. Charles Evans Hughes said the well-balanced life "means faith without credulity; conviction without bigotry; charity without condescension; courage with pugnacity; self-respect without vanity; humility without obsequiousness; love of humanity without sentimentality; and meekness with power."
—Reprinted with permission of publishers from *You Can Master Life* by John H. Crowe. Copyright, 1954, by Prentice-Hall, Inc., 70 Fifth Avenue, New York 11, New York.

497. Dr. Robert A. Millikan . . . told the country's leading physicists that a lifetime of scientific research has convinced him that there is a Divinity that is shaping the destiny of man. . . . "Just how we fit into the plans of the Great Architect and how much he has assigned us to do, we do not know, but if we fail in our assignment it is pretty certain that part of the job will be left undone. But fit in we certainly do somehow, else we would not have a sense of our own responsibility. A purely materialistic philosophy is to me the height of unintelligence."
—Fulton Oursler in *Guideposts.* Copyright by Guideposts Associates, Inc. Published at Carmel, N. Y.

498. "I always tell my young people, 'Walk proudly in the light,'" says Mary MacLeod Bethune, Negro educator and founder of Bethune-Cookman College. "Faith ought not to be a puny thing. If we believe, we should believe like giants. I wish this blessing for my students and

for American youth everywhere: 'May God give you not peace but glory!' "
—*The Reader's Digest*

499. Possibly the game [of life] cannot be won; but if it can be won, it will be the players in the game who win it, not the superior people who pride themselves on not knowing the difference between a fair ball and a foul, to say nothing of those in the grandstand or in the bleachers whose contribution is throwing pop bottles at the umpire.
—MAX C. OTTO in *William James, the Man and the Thinker,* University of Wisconsin Press.

500. [A] young painter [was] in a class William Hunt was teaching out by a lake as the sun went down. Hunt noticed this artist was spending his strokes painting an old red barn, and hadn't even gotten to the glories of the evening sky. And this wise teacher standing over his shoulder said finally, quietly: "Son, it won't be light for long. You've got to choose between shingles and sunsets soon. There's time only for one or the other. What is your choice?"
—FREDERICK B. SPEAKMAN in *The Salty Tank,* Fleming H. Revell Co.

501. A story tells of a painting which shows the devil at a chessboard with a young man. The devil has just made his move, and the canvass shows the young man with his queen checkmated. For a time that picture hung; and no one was ever able to make an encouraging comment upon it until one day Paul Morphy, the great chess genius, was brought to see it. He stood there studying the picture and then, as if speaking to the young man who was defeated by the devil, he cried out, "There's your move, young man!" Somehow it would seem to me that might be said today of the millions of people who without realizing it have been trapped by the great adversary in life's game. I would today say to them, "There is your move! That move is to find Christ, who is able to defeat the devil."
—CHARLES R. BELL, JR.

502. The American philosopher, W. P. Montague . . . claims there's one simple question you and I must answer for ourselves before we'll be able to make any sense or any profit at life's strange rates of exchange. This question, "Are the things that matter most finally at the mercy of the things that matter least?"
—FREDERICK B. SPEAKMAN in *Best Sermons, 1951-52.* Copyright 1952. Used by permission of The Macmillan Co.

503. A sixteen-year-old girl had come to her pastor somewhat troubled about the matter of her consecration. "Why do I have to make so many new consecrations?" she inquired, just a bit impatiently. "I did it at the youth camp a year ago, and again this summer, and then tonight in the young people's meeting we were called upon to 'put everything on the altar' again. Why isn't once enough?" "Well, Dottie, it is just a little like Christopher Columbus' voyages to the New World," the preacher replied. "You remember that when he finally arrived at the tiny little island of San Salvador in 1492, he raised the flag of his monarchs, Ferdinand and Isabella, and claimed the land in the name of Spain. Then when he went on to Cuba, he did the same thing again. On each voyage, when he arrived at a new spot, he made a new dedication. Life is a little like that, if we are Christians."
—ROY L. SMITH in *Stewardship Studies,* Abingdon Press.

504. On one occasion Dr. John R. Mott was holding a special mission for stu-

dents at Edinburgh University. He presented the students with the claims of Christ and pressed for an immediate decision. One young student was so profoundly impressed by what he heard that he went to interview Dr. Mott at the close. Dr. Mott spoke to him at some length, and as the student was leaving he said, "Well, Dr. Mott, I will certainly think seriously about what you have said." Mott, with his great knowledge of men, instantly spotted his weakness. Quick as lightning the words flashed back: "Young man, you had better think to a conclusion, and quickly."
—Robert Menzies in *Fight the Good Fight,* Abingdon Press.

505. I came to America to convert and soon found myself converted. First, I was converted to American youth. I expected to find a blasé, fed-up, sophisticated group of young people, but instead I found the finest raw human material that this country has ever produced—frank, upstanding, prepared, but confused, and, when you get to it, wistful and hungry. They are far finer and more open than the students of ten years ago. But one thing they do not have—they have no cause. They are all dressed up and do not know where to go. Nothing grips them supremely. And the tragedy is that they do not see it.
—E. Stanley Jones in *The Christian Century.*

FINDING ONE'S PURPOSE

506. No one, I am convinced, can be happy who lives only for himself. The joy of living comes from immersion in something . . . that we know to be bigger, better, more enduring and worthier than we are. People; ideas; causes; above all, continuities—these offer the one possible escape not merely from selfishness but from the hungers of solitude and the sorrows of aimlessness. . . . The only true happiness comes from squandering ourselves for a purpose.
—John Mason Brown. Reprinted from *This Week* Magazine. Copyright 1947 by the United Newspapers Magazine Corporation.

507. This is the true joy of life, the being used for a purpose recognized by yourself as a mighty one; the being thoroughly worn out before you are thrown on the scrap heap; the being a force of Nature instead of a feverish selfish little clod of ailments and grievances complaining that the world will not devote itself to making you happy.
—George Bernard Shaw in *Man and Superman,* Dodd, Mead & Co.

508. A satisfactory life . . . will ordinarily be clarified in terms of a purpose or aim whose achievement will represent . . . the very meaning of existence. This purpose . . . will lend tonality to all the rest of one's activities. A man like Albert Schweitzer, for example, may live a "life of parts"—as religious leader, philosopher, writer, medical practitioner, and musician; yet each of these parts, satisfying and valuable as it is on its own account, will have additional significance shed upon it by the controlling religious motive by which, in Schweitzer's case, it is woven into its place in the total pattern. Such a life will be the richer because it has both focus and background; it will be the more zestful because it will have the expectations, uncertainties, and surprises of a moving plot; it will be the more satisfying because even its dissonances and asymmetries will be seen in retrospect to contribute to a meaningfully purposive whole.
—Lucius Garvin in *A Modern Introduction to Ethics,* Houghton Mifflin Co.

509. My message has been very simple. To live well we must have a faith fit to live by, a self fit to live with, and a work fit to live for—something to which we can give ourselves, and thus get ourselves off our hands. We cannot tell what may happen to us in the strange medley of life. But we can decide what happens in us—how we take it, what we do with it—and that is what really counts in the end. How to take the raw stuff of life and make it a thing of worth and beauty—that is the test of living. Courage is the first virtue, as kindness is the final joy—to be "a little kinder than is necessary." To take life for granted, grudgingly, is to spoil it; whereas to take it for gratitude, bravely and without fear, is to enjoy it, despite all its aches and ills. To be happy is easy enough if we give ourselves, forgive others, and live with thanksgiving. No self-centered person, no ungrateful soul can ever be happy, much less make anyone else happy. Life is giving, not getting. Life is an adventure of faith, if we are to be victors over it, not victims of it. Faith in the God above us, faith in the little infinite soul within us, faith in life and in our fellow souls—without faith, the plus quality, we cannot really live. To faith must be added a life-wisdom, which may be summed up in six words, the three greatest maxims of the race. Two we owe to Greece, two to Rome, and two to Judea: "Know thyself, control thyself, give thyself." For the rest, hope much, fear not at all, love with all your heart, do your best, seek the best in others; take life and dare it, have a little fun and share it; and put your trust in "the veiled kindness of the Father of men," in whose great hand we stand.

—From *River of Years,* by Joseph Fort Newton. Copyright, 1946, by Joseph Fort Newton. Publ. by J. B. Lippincott Co.

510. The differences in human life depend, for the most part, not on what men *do,* but upon the meaning and purpose of their acts. All are *born,* all *die,* all *lose their loved ones,* nearly all *marry* and nearly all *work,* but the *significance* of these acts may vary enormously. The same physical act may be in one situation vulgar and in another holy. The same work may be elevating or degrading. The major question is not, "What act do I perform?" but "In what frame do I put it?" Wisdom about life consists in taking the inevitable ventures which are the very stuff of common existence, and glorifying them.

—Elton Trueblood in *The Common Ventures of Life,* Harper & Bros.

511. Hear what a student had to say on coming to [Harvard] University after being in World War II: "During my three years' duty aboard an aircraft carrier as communications officer, I saw many men floundering in disordered lives which lacked a central integration: I saw them seek that integration in almost every conceivable form. It was plain to see that only those men with spiritual backbone were the ones who withstood not only the rigors of combat duty, but also—and this was infinitely more difficult—the rigors of moral combat duty which one constantly undergoes in the service. These years in the navy were a profound experience—spiritually, mentally, morally—and it is my sincere desire to use wisely the lessons learned during them."

—Willard L. Sperry in *Sermons Preached at Harvard,* Harper & Bros.

512. John Middleton Murry recently published the letters of his wife, Katherine Mansfield, who died of tuberculosis at the age of thirty-four. Her published short stories and letters promised exceptional creativity as a writer. Like so

many of her contemporaries, she was a reluctant humanist in religion. In the next to the last letter she wrote, there is this searching commentary: "You see, my love, the question is always: '*Who am I?*' and until that is answered, I don't see how one can really direct anything in oneself. '*Is there* a Me?' One must be certain of that before one has a real unshakeable leg to stand on. And I don't believe for one moment these questions can be settled by the head alone." In the same letter (December 26, 1922) she said: "If I were allowed one single cry to God, that cry would be: *I want to be REAL.* Until I am that I don't see why I shouldn't be at the mercy of old Eve in her various manifestations for ever."
—David A. MacLennan in *Pastoral Preaching*. Copyright, 1955, by W. L. Jenkins, The Westminster Press. Used by permission. Quotations by Katherine Mansfield in *Letters to John Middleton Murry,* Alfred A. Knopf, Inc.

513. In one of our colleges, the dean's office discovered that a woman for the last four years had elected the same course in algebra, although she had passed it the first time. The dean, therefore, wrote for an explanation, and the woman replied: "I am so tired of arguing with my neighbors about everything in this world that I wanted to study something I couldn't argue about." Urgent human hunger was speaking there. Wanted: something, even mathematics, that in this perishable world is secure and constant!
—Harry Emerson Fosdick in *A Faith for Tough Times,* Harper & Bros.

514. A few years ago I met a professor who was born in the South Seas, and who has made those islands, their history and their people his life work "What happens," I asked him, "to the men who, 'fed up' with civilization, flee to the solitude of those supposedly idyllic isles?" "They die," he replied. "They die of boredom; they die because life alone is not really life at all; they die because there is nothing to live for."
—Boynton Merrill in *The Upper Room Pulpit.*

515. I remember some years ago standing on a balcony at Warwick Castle in England which overlooks one of the most beautiful scenes it ever has been my privilege to view. There at the base of the castle was the winding river; next to the river were lovely green fields. Next to the fields there were large squares of the beautiful yellow of the mustard plant and stretching off into the distant hills one after the other scenes of breath-taking beauty. Beside me stood one of those tourists who has not added anything to the good name of this country. We looked down at the river, and his sole comment on all that loveliness was, "Isn't it terrible that there is such scum on the river?" He thought he was judging the landscape; he really was judging himself.
—Robert W. Burns

516. Hartley Coleridge, son of the great poet and himself a man of great gifts and capacity, once went back to Oxford, where amid beautiful surroundings and wonderful opportunities he had spent his days in dissipation and folly. Looking on the ancient ivy-covered buildings and the lovely grounds, he exclaimed aloud, "To think that in such a place I lived such a life!"
—Clarence E. Macartney in *Strange Texts but Grand Truths,* Abingdon Press.

517. Once I sat with a man who began as a boy on the farm, worked his way through engineering school, and got a job in a small concern by being able to

repair a small power machine. From that he went on to the making of power machines, then to the building of electric plants for small communities, then to the linking of those communities together until he built up quite a power empire. And now he is discussing the use of atomic power for civilian purposes. His has been a romance of achievement. Yet greater than the electric power which he had developed was the brain power of that former farm boy who could dream and create such material marvels.
—Ralph W. Sockman

518. A newspaper advertisement asked for two drivers to drive cars at forty-five miles per hour for a head-on crash, and those interested could name their price. One asked twenty thousand dollars. A boy from the farm said he thought "twenty bucks" would be enough. How much would you ask for your life?
—J. R. Brokhoff

THE KINDLING OF TALENT

519. "Stir up the gift of God, which is in thee" (II Tim. 1:6). Moffatt translates this verse: "Rekindle the divine gift which you received." Both readings suggest the metaphor of a reawakening of the dying embers of a fire. All of us have "stirred" charred bits of blackened wood in a fireplace. This "rekindling" brings to flame potential fuel which otherwise might be choked for want of air. Paul advises his young friend Timothy to do this with his own life. What gift lies hidden in each of us? What talent have we allowed to wane through disuse or indifference? What skill have we ignored which when rekindled might serve both God and man?

520. More than three centuries ago a handful of pioneers crossed the ocean to Jamestown and Plymouth in search of freedoms they were unable to find in their own countries, the freedoms we still cherish today: freedom from want, freedom from fear, freedom of speech, freedom of religion. Today the descendants of the early settlers, and those who have joined them since, are fighting to protect these freedoms at home and throughout the world. And yet there is a fifth freedom—basic to those four—that we are in danger of losing: the freedom to be one's best. . . . The freedom to be one's best is the chance for the development of each person to his highest power.
—Seymour St. John in *The Saturday Review* and *The Reader's Digest.*

521. Once Dwight Morrow was invited to a conference of students at Amherst, and somebody put this question to him: "What course of study would you recommend for a student who plans to be a banker?" His answer was: "Well, I don't know that I can prescribe any special subjects that could fit you for that particular job, but I can tell you this—if you pick out from the curriculum the hardest subjects you can find, and I don't much care what they are, and on the top of these add the hardest one on the elective list and give to that program for the four years of your college course all the time and efforts you can muster, I won't promise that you will become a banker, but I am sure of one thing: when you are through, there won't be a bank in the country that will not be glad to employ you, and you may end up being its president."
—Fred R. Chenault

522. It doesn't look heavy, a high-school diploma: only a bit of paper (it isn't really sheepskin), a few drops of ink, a bit of colored ribbon from Woolworth's.

It doesn't weigh much; nevertheless, a high-school diploma is heavy. It is heavy with expectations.

There is the expectations of teachers that the diploma bearer will be willing to use the dictionary and the encyclopedia, the expectation that he will think clean and clear and straight and frequently.

There is the expectation of both teachers and parents that he will be teachable, and being teachable is essentially wanting to grow in wisdom and understanding.

There are the citizens who expect him to be a good citizen, informed about the world with its variety of governments but loyal to America.

There are the neighbors who expect him to be dependable, able to carry routine for a succession of days.

And there are those friends who expect him to have a special ability of understanding and caring for people, any people, all people.

The high-school diploma is a heavy bit of luggage when the proud graduate sets out for college.
—KENNETH IRVING BROWN in *Not Minds Alone,* Harper & Bros.

523. "Success," wrote H. G. Wells, "is to be measured not by wealth, power, or fame, but by the ratio between what a man is and what he might be."

524. Success is to be measured not so much by the position that one has reached in life as by the obstacles which he has overcome while trying to succeed.
—From: *Up From Slavery,* by BOOKER T. WASHINGTON. Copyright 1901 by Booker T. Washington, reprinted by permission of Doubleday & Company, Inc.

525. A line from an old Hindu poem . . . says, "Thou hast to churn the milk, O, Disciple, if thou desirest the taste of butter." The line continues by saying, "And it serveth not thy purpose if, sitting in idleness, thou sayest, 'Lo, the butter is in the milk, yea, the butter is in the milk.' "
—HOWARD THURMAN in *Deep Is the Hunger,* Harper & Bros.

526. We are, after all, like lumps of clay.
There are brittle pieces, hard pieces
We have little shape or beauty.
But we need not despair.
If we are clay, let us remember there is a Potter, and His wheel. . . .

We have only to be yielded, that is, willing, surrendered, and
He will do the rest.
He will make us according to the pattern for which, in His love,
He designed us.
And it will be good—for our own good —and for His glory.

—PETER MARSHALL in *Mr. Jones, Meet the Master,* Fleming H. Revell Co.

527. Kierkegaard, the great thinker of Denmark, divided men into two groups. They were the drivers or the drifters. In his book *Either—Or* he said that he wanted to run after every man in the street and ask him the question: Are you alert or inert? A master or a slave? A creator or a creature? A lifter or a leaner? This is Christ's challenge to men. He calls us away from our moral neutrality. He lures us from our earthiness with a lofty vision. He wants us to renounce the evil of mediocre living by making some supreme dedication.
—CHARLES M. CROWE in *Sermons on the Parables of Jesus,* Abingdon Press.

528. When a famous work of art, a painting or a statue, is thrown on the market, directors from many museums

may bid for possession. Suppose that the owner was unable to determine which museum should receive the treasured piece? Would he with a knife cut a canvas into ten equal parts so that ten galleries might share it? Would he with a hammer break a statue into many portions? No, for a work of art must be complete or it is worthless. Yet we distribute the dearest of all treasures, the human soul, among many bidders, and the integrity of the soul is lost. God has said, "Thou shalt have no other gods before me."
—GLENN H. ASQUITH

529. A great violinist stood before an audience and enraptured them with his playing. Suddenly, in the midst of the selection, he paused, took the violin from beneath his chin, raised it in the air, and smashed it into a thousand pieces upon the floor. The audience sat aghast. In the silence the violinist walked to the front of the platform and said quietly, "Don't be alarmed. The violin I smashed was one I purchased for a few dollars in a department store. I shall now play upon the Stradivarius." He took the valuable instrument from the case, tuned it for a moment and began to play. The music was magnificent, but to the majority of those present it was indistinguishable from the earlier selection. When he had concluded, the violinist spoke again. "Friends," he said, "so much has been said about the value of this violin in my hands that I wanted to impress upon you the fact that the music is not in the instrument, *it is in the one who plays upon it."*
—CHARLES B. TEMPLETON in *Life Looks Up,* Harper & Bros.

530. A famous publisher declares, "If you are an articulate person, you utter some thirty thousand words each day." If these words were put in print, they would amount to a fair-sized book a day. These books would, in a lifetime, fill a good-sized college library. All these books are from the same author. All reflect the life and thoughts of the author, in his own words. And not a book can be taken down from the shelves or withdrawn from circulation. The thought is a bit frightening. It emphasizes the fearful responsibility that goes with the gift of speech, and also the glorious privilege that is inherent in "speech seasoned with grace."
—CHARLES W. KOLLER in *Tents Toward the Sunrise.* Copyright, 1953, by The Judson Press. Used by permission.

ON ACCEPTING ONESELF

531. One summer a college friend who had some sort of muscle paralysis decided to sell books, and he began by visiting the home of the college president. The wife of the president informed him that they did not need any books. As he turned to leave, she saw the limp in his walk and said: "Oh, I am so sorry! I did not know you were lame." The young man, who was not seeking pity, bristled all over; and the woman, realizing that she had perhaps said the wrong thing, hastened to add, "I did not mean to imply anything except admiration, but doesn't being lame rather color your life?" "Yes," he replied, "but thank God I can choose the color."
—FRANK A. COURT

532. During [World War II] I happened to have done some psychological reconditioning for the government at Gardner Hospital in Chicago. I dealt with young men and young women who had come home from struggle crippled and maimed as well as with mental problems of various kinds. I came across two people—strangely enough how things

will happen—near whom one and the same shrapnel burst and amputated the right arm of each of these men. One of them said to me as I was making my rounds, "I'll sit back and take it easy and get $107 a month as long as I live; I can sit on the cracker barrel and be a philosopher." The other man heard him and he shook his left arm at me and he said: "Nothing will stop me. I'm going right ahead as if nothing had happened." This leads me to the conclusion . . . : *what happens to us is less significant than what happens within us.*
—Louis L. Mann in *Vital Speeches*.

533. Some years ago a great religious leader came to our state capital to speak at the Y.M.C.A. He had a terrific reputation as an evangelist and, to entertain him, his sponsors called on me and said, "Governor, would you have this man up for dinner before the evening meeting?" I said, "I would be delighted." The time came, but I was late getting home from the office. I rushed in with high expectations to see this dynamic individual who had made such a wonderful record for his God and who was changing people all over the world. And right before me was a gnome-like creature who was not over five feet tall and who looked like something his mother would like to have forgotten. My face registered disappointment, which my guest must have seen. He looked at me and said, "Governor, isn't it wonderful what God can use?" And it was.
—Arthur B. Langlie

534. Men in different professions often acquire insights on people based on their professional relationships. A commercial photographer, for instance, classified his patrons as Pharisees or publicans. The publican, after the suggestion of Luke 18, accepted himself for what he was: but the Pharisee, rejecting the first six or eight proofs, wanted more sittings. "While the pictures are being made," the photographer said, "many customers assume the most outlandish poses and postures. I tell them repeatedly, 'Just be yourself.' They scrutinize the proofs and finally select the most flattering even if it isn't most lifelike. Then they ask to have the hairline lowered a bit, the wrinkles removed, and youthfulness added to the cheeks." After years of professional activity the photographer added: "I long ago discovered that many men will neither accept themselves for what they are nor behave in a manner that is most natural. Why is it that so many of us are always wearing masks of pretense?"

535. A Londoner who lived in the day of Joseph Parker of City Temple said: "I am tremendously fond of Joseph Parker, but I cannot tolerate the little Parkers." Many people fail because they are perpetually trying to be somebody else. All God asks of us is what we have and what we are.
—John Sutherland Bonnell

536. A large crowd of people gathered near an enclosure in the Franklin Park Zoo in Boston as a peacock slowly spread its great tail and displayed its stunning plumage. The great bird stood erect and noble and strutted regally. Just then an old, dun-colored duck waddled slowly from the pond and passed between the proud peacock and the admiring crowd. Enraged, the peacock drove the duck back to the water. In a moment the beautiful bird had become ugly with fierce anger. The plain and awkward duck, having returned to its natural habitat, was no longer unbecoming. In the water it swam and dived gracefully, unaware that many eyes were watching. The peo-

ple who had admired the peacock loved the duck. Each of us was reminded of the dangers of pride and that happiness comes from being just ourselves.
—CARLTON VAN ORNUM

537. Someone has said that the man who boasts of his ancestors is like a field of potatoes in that the best part is underground. A man who traces his lineage back to a signer of the Declaration, to a Mayflower passenger, or to William the Conqueror has reason, of course, to be proud. More important, however, than who his ancestors were is what he is. We must be sure that the farthest branches of the family tree are as strong as the roots. Lincoln put it this way: "I don't know who my grandfather was; I am much more concerned to know what his grandson will be."

538. The convictionless individual fights against the inevitable longing induced by his moments of supreme insight when, for all effort to control it, he experiences a trembling, fearful passion to do some great thing. . . . Arthur Colton has crystallized this experience in his story, "Mr. Smedley's Guest." "Sitting one night by his fireside a man falls asleep and dreams that he has a visitor who strangely does all the things he himself had once dreamed that he would do. He spends an enchanting evening with his guest. Then when the guest is about to leave, he asks, 'Who are you anyway?' and the guest replies, 'The man you might have been.' "
—ROBERT N. DUBOSE in *The Upper Room Pulpit.*

539. [Thoreau] once wrote a deliberately shocking word to a friend, advising him not to worry about his health because "you may be dead already." Such a word from some men would be regarded as an effort to be smart and sophisticated, but coming from Thoreau it simply indicated his simple conviction that most men were not really alive.
—GERALD KENNEDY in *Go Inquire of the Lord,* Harper & Bros.

THE WAY OF WISDOM

540. A sophomore or second-year student, is one whose mind has been alerted to the vast world of knowledge but has not yet grasped all truth. "Sophomore" is derived from two Greek words. *Sophos* means wise as in philosophy, love of wisdom. *Moros* means fool as in moron, one whose mind is not fully developed. The "wise fool" knows enough at least to understand that he does not know everything. Such an attitude is perhaps the beginning of true wisdom.

541. In one of his stories, "The Higher Pragmatism," and in the subtly facetious style of using and misusing the English language which made his writings so popular, O. Henry comments: "Where to go for wisdom has become a question of serious import. The ancients are discredited; Plato is boilerplate; Aristotle is tottering; Marcus Aurelius is reeling; . . . Solomon is too solemn; you couldn't get anything out of Epictetus with a pick." He reminds us that "knowledge comes, but wisdom lingers" and then gives his own sharp distinction between the two: "Wisdom is dew, which . . . soaks into us, refreshes us, and makes us grow. Knowledge is a strong stream of water turned on us through a hose. It disturbs our roots."
—JAMES E. CLARK in *The Presbyterian Tribune.*

542. However Newton may have regarded himself in comparison with other men, he was piously humble in the presence of the mystery of God and the

universe. Just a little while before his death he said: "I do not know what I may appear to the world; but to myself I seem to have been only like a boy, playing on the sea-shore, and diverting myself, in now and then finding a smoother pebble or a prettier shell than ordinary, whilst the great ocean of truth lay all undiscovered before me."
—LOUIS T. MORE in *Isaac Newton,* Chas. Scribner's Sons.

543. Our three-year-old boy came up to us on the beach with his sand bucket full of water. "Here's the ocean, Daddy," he said. That attitude is understandable in a three-year-old, but not so much so when a thirty-year-old comes up with a set of ideas and says, "Here is the truth!" You want to say to him, "That may be your ocean, brother, but there is a lot more where that came from, and it's not in your bucket!"
—HAROLD A. BOSLEY

544. The French critic Vinet once wrote: "Most friends of truth love it as Frederick the Great loved music. It used to be said of him that, strictly speaking, he was not fond of music but of the flute, and not indeed fond of the flute but of his flute." It is a sad and tragic thing when our love of truth is confined to our own flute.
—HAROLD A. BOSLEY

545. When a man is sure that all he wants is happiness, then most grievously he deceives himself. All men desire happiness, but they need something far different, compared to which happiness is trivial, and in the lack of which happiness turns to bitterness in the mouth. There are many names for that which men need—"the one thing needful"—but the simplest is "wholeness."
—JOHN MIDDLETON MURRY in *Son of Women,* Jonathan Cape, Ltd.

546. The average undergraduate has a flat mind and a kind heart. He has not been so much educated as adjusted. That the adjustment is successful is evidenced by his ability to talk with some fluency about soil conservation and the U.N.; he is also vaguely aware that racial prejudice is a bad thing. He admires science without knowing much about it and hopes that science will solve all of our problems. . . . Theoretically a cosmopolite, stretching forth fraternal hands to the Eskimos and the Pakistanis, he is temporally provincial; he has not been asked to shake hands with Socrates or Paul.
—CHAD WALSH in *The Christian Scholar.*

547. There was a certain father who was accosted by a professor who said, "Your son flunked in grammar." The father replied, "I'm sorry, but I want to thank you for something else you have done for my boy; you've given him a great spiritual, altruistic aim and purpose in life. You see, sir, as a father, this is my idea of education: I would rather my boy would come out of your class saying " 'I seed' when he had seen, than to say 'I saw' when he had never seen at all." What good is grammar unless our young people have something to say?
—LOUIS H. EVANS in *Great Preaching Today,* Alton M. Motter, editor, published in 1953 by Harper & Bros. Used by permission.

COUNSEL OF PEERS

548. Queen Mary said to her granddaughter Elizabeth II: "Remember that life is made up of loyalty—loyalty to your friends; loyalty to things beautiful and good; loyalty to the country which you love; and, above all, for this holds all other loyalties together, loyalty to God."

549. When we remember that only a little more than 1500 years ago the ancestors of most of us, many of them painted blue, were roaming the trackless forests of Caledonia, Britain, and Germany, and transalpine Gaul, despised by the civilized citizens of Rome and Antioch, interested, in the intervals of rapine, only in deep drinking and high gaming; savage, barbarous, cruel, and illiterate, we may reflect with awe and expectation on the potentialities of our race. When we remember, too, that it is only a little more than fifty years ago that the "average man" began to have the chance to get an education, we must recognize that it is too early to despair of him.

—Robert Maynard Hutchins in *Education for Freedom,* Louisiana State University Press.

550. To the statistician, the mass-observer, you are one unit in a crowd. To the physicist, you are a mathematical formula, to the chemist a compound of substances, to the biologist a specimen. The behaviourist sees you as an animal modified by conditioned reflexes; the psychologist as a mental type of suffering, to a more or less degree, from morbid variations; the philosopher, as the subject of a conscious experience. You interest the historian as one of the innumerable insects that build up the coral island of human development; the economist, as bee or drone that helps cross-fertilize the cycle of production and consumption. To the postman, you are an address; . . . to the politician, a voter; to the revenue, a taxpayer. . . . So significant you are, so universally relevant. But how, and by what right? Beware of asking; that way lies theology.

—From *Stimuli* by Ronald Knox. Copyright, 1951, Sheed and Ward, Inc., New York.

551. What is the value of life? If a person thinks only of man's physical nature, then his body may be valued at ninety-odd cents. That is the chemical worth of the body of a person of average weight. Someone has judged that there is enough water in a man's body for a small wash, enough fat to make seven cakes of soap, enough iron to make a better than medium-sized nail, enough lime to whitewash a small chicken coop, enough sulphur to kill the fleas on a dog, and enough potassium to fire a toy cannon. Chemically speaking, that is what a man is worth. But Christ never judged man by such a standard. Spiritually speaking, man is a child of God.

552. When the Navy abandoned its search for Amelia Earhart, Walter Lippmann wrote: "The world is a better place to live in because it contains human beings who will give up ease and security and stake their own lives in order to do what they themselves think worth doing. They do the useless, brave, noble, the divinely foolish and the very wisest things that are done by man. And what they prove to themselves and to others is that man is no mere creature of his habits, no mere automaton in his routine, but that in the dust of which he is made there is also fire, lighted now and then by great winds from the sky."

553. What is it that gives dignity to life, lifts it out of mediocrity, saves it from futility and insignificance and makes it in the long run worth living? To get one's eye on the best, even in a bad time, and to stand by that! We are not much as individuals; we can terribly despise ourselves; but there is something that can give even our small lives dignity and significance. To have seen the best in our time, and to have stood by it—that does elevate even the humblest life to dignity and worth. —HARRY EMERSON FOSDICK in *On Being Fit to Live With,* Harper & Bros.

554. Just for the beauty of the language, and the clarity of thought, I should like to read you the "complete" commencement speech in a half-dozen lines. They were written by the great German poet and philosopher, Goethe. "There are nine requisites for contented living: health enough to make work a pleasure; wealth enough to support your needs; strength to battle with difficulties and overcome them; grace enough to confess your sins and forsake them; patience enough to toil until some good is accomplished; charity enough to see some good in your neighbor; love enough to move you to be useful and helpful to others; faith enough to make real the things of God; hope enough to remove all anxious fears concerning the future."
—EDWARD R. MURROW in *The Reader's Digest.*

555. You must learn day by day, year by year, to broaden your horizon. The more things you love, the more you are interested in, the more you enjoy, the more you are indignant about—the more you have left when anything happens. . . . I suppose the greatest thing in the world is loving people and—and wanting to destroy the sin but not the sinner. And not to forget that when life knocks you to your knees, which it always does and always will—well, that's the best position in which to pray, isn't it? On your knees. That's where I learned.
—ETHEL BARRYMORE

556. I believe that there is one story in the world, and only one, that has frightened and inspired us, so that we live in a Pearl White serial of continuing thought and wonder. Humans are caught—in their lives, in their thoughts, in their hungers and ambitions, in their avarice and cruelty, and in their kindness and generosity too—in a net of good and evil. I think this is the only story we have and that it occurs on all levels of feeling and intelligence. Virtue and vice were warp and woof of our first consciousness, and they will be the fabric of our last, and this despite any changes we may impose on field and river and mountain, on economy and manners. There is no other story. A man, after he has brushed off the dust and chips of his life, will have left only the hard, clean questions: Was it good or was it evil? Have I done well —or ill?
—JOHN STEINBECK in *East of Eden,* Viking Press, Inc.

557. Let us be honest with youth and tell them that there is no magic formula of education for war or peace, no fruit of the tree of knowledge which, swiftly eaten, can make us wise as gods, knowing good and evil. Even in these critical days, when educated persons are so desperately needed, the process of education requires time and work and striving. The ability to think straight, some knowledge of the past, some vision of the future, some skill to do useful service, some urge to fit that service into the well-being of the community—these are the most vital things education must try to produce. If we can achieve them in the citizens of our land, then, given the right to knowledge and the free use thereof, we shall have brought to America the wisdom and the courage to match her destiny.
—VIRGINIA C. GILDERSLEEVE in *Many a Good Crusade.* Copyright 1954. Used by permission of The Macmillan Co.

GOD IN EDUCATION

558. One hundred and forty years before the signing of the Declaration of

Independence the motto of Harvard University was given as *In Christi Gloriam* (For the Glory of Christ). The university's founder, John Harvard, was referred to as a "godly gentleman and a man of learning" in the legislative act in 1638 that authorized the founding of this world-famed institution. And, during the administration of the school's first president, Master Dunster, one of the student directives was even more explicit in emphasizing the spiritual values that characterized all phases of early American life. "Let every student be plainly instructed," the directive reads, "and earnestly pressed to consider well, the main end of his life and studies is to know God and Jesus Christ which is eternal life. . . . Christ [is] the only foundation of all sound knowledge and learning."
—James Keller in *You Can Change the World,* Longmans, Green & Co., Inc.

559. All things must speak of God, refer to God, or they are atheistic. History, without God, is a chaos without design or end or aim. Political Economy, without God, would be a selfish teaching about the acquisition of wealth, making the larger portion of mankind animate machines for its production; Physics, without God, would be but a dull enquiry into certain meaningless phenomena; Ethics, without God, would be a varying rule without principle, or substance, or centre, or ruling hand. . . . All sciences . . . will tend to exclude the thought of God if they are not cultivated with reference to him. History will become an account of man's passions and brute strength, instead of the ordering of God's providence for his creatures' good.
—Edward Pusey

560. The theme of religion in education recalls a conversation which Dr. Jacks of Manchester College, Oxford, had with one of the great schoolmasters of England. To the direct question, "Where in your time-table do you teach religion?" the school-man replied:

"We teach it all day long.

We teach it in arithmetic, by accuracy.

We teach it in language, by learning to say what we mean—'yea, yea,' or 'nay, nay.'

We teach it in history, by humanity.

We teach it in geography, by breadth of mind.

We teach it in handicraft, by thoroughness.

We teach it in astronomy, by reverence.

We teach it by good manners to one another, and by truthfulness in all things.

We teach students to build the Church of Christ out of the actual relationships in which they stand to their teachers and to their school-fellows."

—Quoted from *Forward-day-by-day,* January 29, 1936, by permission of Forward Movement Publications.

561. The prior task of education is to inspire, and to give a sense of values and the power of distinguishing what is first-rate from what is not. . . . The ultimate aim and essence of education is the training of character.

—Richard Livingstone in *Ladies' Home Journal.*

562. Ethics without religion has little power to endure. The French Revolution began by striking the idealistic notes of liberty, equality, and fraternity; but it was no deeper than its own idealism. Its power for good was soon exhausted, and it broke loose in uncontrolled violence. When man has nothing more to rely upon than his own spirit, his goodness turns sour. He needs divine support.

He lives most meaningfully when he responds to the gracious overtures of God.
—Karl H. A. Rest

563. Martin Luther once asked, "What does it mean to have a God, or what is God?" To which he gave this answer which is worth remembering: "Whatever thy heart clings to and relies upon, that is properly thy God." . . . The people we call godless are simply the people who have a different god from ours, for every man has something at the center of his life to which his heart clings and upon which he relies.
—Theodore Parker Ferris in *This Is the Day* (Greenwich: The Seabury Press, 1954), p. 52. Used by permission of the publisher.

564. The universal free public school by its very nature is a spiritual enterprise. It concerns itself with all children, regardless of race, creed, or economic condition. It seeks to exemplify good habits and helpful human relations in every study and activity. On a vast scale, it is an expression of the concern which our Judeo-Christian tradition feels for the highest development of all the people. . . . The position of the teacher is unique. He is employed by society for the guidance and improvement of mankind. His obligation is to truth, to humanity, and to God. His task is to help every one who comes under his care to make the most of himself. This is a spiritual enterprise, and only by thinking of it in spiritual terms can the teacher be worthy of his glorious heritage, which includes all the gifted teachers of ages past. . . . We think of the Great Teacher whose exemplification of love as the supreme law of life has inspired, guided, comforted, and lifted humanity for generations.
—Joy Elmer Morgan in *NEA Journal*.

565. Few occupations carry greater responsibility than that of the teacher. The teacher stands in a great and honorable tradition extending from the dawn of history until the present. Teachers, in a singular way, are the guardians of civilization. The Church will ask much of the teachers in the Christian college. They need to believe in themselves, love and respect their students, exercise rare self-discipline, and be able to meet the problems of their students reasonably. *Educare*, the Latin word from which our word education is derived, means "to make a plant grow." S. R. Hole has said: "He who would have beautiful roses in his garden must have beautiful roses in his heart. He must love them well and always. . . . He must have not only the glowing admiration, the enthusiasm, and the passion, but the tenderness, the thoughtfulness, the reverence, the watchfulness of love." This is almost a perfect description of the relationship that should exist between the teacher and his students. The best teacher is one who possesses a feeling of real affection for his students and a deep concern that they shall find out for themselves those things which are of highest value.
—Frank Glenn Lankard in *Vital Speeches*.

566. I feel that most people who enjoy their reading today must owe something, perhaps far more than they realize, to a teacher who could light up a line of poetry or explain just why certain sayings, as well as certain doings, vibrate in the memory. . . . These are the men and women in whose hands our bounteous inheritance of words so largely lies. To them every writer should be grateful, since they determine the quality of his audience. And not writers only. The essence of living is the power of apprecia-

tion, the savoring of thoughts and things. He who does not enjoy does not live.
—Ivor Brown in *I Give My Word and Say the Word,* E. P. Dutton & Co., Inc.

567. During the presidency of Mark Hopkins at Williams College, some village buildings were defaced. When the culprit was caught, he turned out to be the son of a wealthy supporter of the school. Called before the president, he pulled out his pocketbook and said jauntily, "Well, doctor, what's the damage?" Hopkins replied: "Young man, put up your purse. Tomorrow at prayers you will make public acknowledgment of your offense, or you will be expelled." Speaking later of the incident, Hopkins said: "Rich young men come here and take that tone as if they could pay for what they get here. No student can pay for what he gets at Williams College. Can any student pay for the sacrifice of Colonel Williams and our other benefactors? For the heroic sacrifices of half-paid professors who have given their lives that young men might have at the smallest cost a liberal education? Every man here is a charity student."
—Ralph W. Sockman

568. A distinguished industrialist made this statement to an obscure teacher in a Christian college: "The cloth we make wears out, and the marble we finish will eventually disintegrate; the ideal you plant in a human mind lives eternally."
—A. C. Reid in *100 Chapel Talks,* Abingdon Press.

CHILDREN'S DAY

CONCERN FOR THE CHILDREN

569. On the night of the coronation of Queen Elizabeth, Boy Scouts lit a chain of beacons all the way from Lands End to John o'Groat's House. The beacons, each at least ten feet high, were lighted simultaneously and each in sight of the next. Boys and girls, whether Scouts or not, are the beacon lights along the King's highway, the highway of humanity's hope and Christ's kingdom. All who devote themselves to school kids, Sunday-school kids, or just kids, who kindle the fire of idealism in them, are lighting beacons for the King's coronation.
—Charles L. Seasholes

570. A mechanic, after a hard day's work, was seen by a friend of his catching a baseball with his son. The friend stopped and looked over the fence and said, "Bill, aren't you tired?" "Why, yes, I am. Of course, I'm tired." "Well, what under the sun are you doing that for?" "Oh," he said, "I'd rather have the backache now than the heartache later on."
—Herman L. Turner in *The Pulpit.* Copyrighted by the Christian Century Foundation and used by permission.

571. Some time ago a small boy, playing on a wharf in Brisbane harbor, lost his footing and fell between the wharf and an eight-thousand-ton ship. Those who witnessed the accident thought he would surely be crushed to death. Within a few moments two hundred workers had rushed to the spot. Together these men pushed against the ship's side until the boy could be lifted to safety. It is worth the united effort of every member of the Christian Church to save one boy or girl from evil.
—J. Calvert Cariss

572. Gerald Kennedy tells of a city council in a little Nebraska community that divided into different camps concerning the question of planting a hedge or building an iron fence around the cemetery. When the debate was at its highest, an onlooker put out the fires of argument when he said: "What's all this argument about a hedge or a fence around the cemetery? What difference does it make? Nobody in there's going to get out, and nobody that's out wants to get in, so let's take the money and build a playground for our children." Yet many spend most of their time building fences around old cemeteries.
—Frank A. Court

573. We have some freedom to choose our environment as well as our inheritance. Here, too, we cannot control completely the physical features. The boy born in a gashouse district is under a severe handicap. No wishful thinking or pious platitudes about will power can minimize the very real part which material environment plays in shaping youth, and the Christian program must

be dedicated to the cleansing of bad economic conditions. Jane Addams and Al Capone lived in approximately the same kind of slum conditions in Chicago. The fact that Jane Addams became one of our greatest public servants while Al Capone became Public Enemy Number One should not lead to the conclusion that it is the inner spirit rather than the outer environment which counts. Both count. And Jane Addams gave herself to the redemption of the slum areas which are conducive to the Al Capones. Yet we do have to admit that out of the worst social conditions some of the noblest spirits have arisen.
—RALPH W. SOCKMAN in *Now to Live!* Abingdon Press.

574. My deep belief is that all human creatures deserve a happy childhood as a right and as a prerequisite to normal adulthood, and that the first essential to happiness is love. I have observed that if a child does not have a wholehearted love from and for someone before he is five years old he is emotionally stunted perhaps for the rest of his life. That is, he is unable to love anyone wholeheartedly and is to that extent deprived of a full life. . . . It has to be real love. The professional coddling that a trained nurse or attendant gives a baby in a foundling home or hospital does not fool even the baby. It takes more than a clock-watching employee to make a child feel secure. . . . Love is the sunshine of his growing soul, and when there is no sun, the soul stops and body and mind begin to lag.
—From *My Several Worlds* by PEARL S. BUCK. Copyright, 1954, by Pearl S. Buck. Published by The John Day Company, Inc.

575. A little girl sat in her rocking chair hugging a beautiful doll. She alternately kissed the doll, fondled it, and spoke words of endearment. Occasionally she glanced at her mother working at a desk on the other side of the room. As soon as she put down her pen, the child ran to her, climbed on her lap, and said: "I'm so glad you're through—I wanted to love you so much." "Did you, darling?" the mother asked. "I'm so glad; but I thought you were having a good time with your doll." "I was, Mommie," the little girl explained, "but I get tired of loving her because she never loves me back."
—GWYNN MCLENDON DAY in *Path of the Dawning Light,* Broadman Press.

576. A small child was gazing lovingly at a new dress her mother had purchased for her. She looked curiously at the price tag and then said, "I'm expensive, aren't I, mother?" Of course children are expensive. There is not only the monetary expense but also the cost in time and effort and patience and nerves. So great an expense not only endears a child to his parents but makes the child priceless above all possessions.

577. Desperately every child craves the family life he was meant to enjoy. It is expressed well by Frankie Addams in the play, *The Member of the Wedding.* "All people belong to a 'we' except me," Frankie complains. "Not to belong to a 'we' makes you too lonesome." Seldom has the tragic loneliness of unhappy childhood been so well stated.
—JOHN CHARLES WYNN in *How Christian Parents Face Family Problems.* Copyright, 1955, by W. L. Jenkins, The Westminster Press. Quotation copyright 1951 by Carson McCullers and published by New Directions.

578. A small boy rose to his feet to ask his teacher a question; she was annoyed and told him to sit down. He balked and then flatly refused. Whereupon she said,

"If you don't sit down, I'll put you down." He did not budge, so the teacher, ten times stronger then he, forced him into his seat. But she was powerless to do anything about what he said. "You can force me down, but I'm still standing up inside."
—FRED L. BROWNLEE in *These Rights We Hold,* Friendship Press.

579. Once an old Negro, speaking of a man he knew, said, "Bill went clear to the bad. He got to drinkin' and gamblin' and roysterin' around an' squandered all his children." Squandered resources usually bring failure. But when people squander their children, arrest their development, warp and shrivel their children's souls, how immeasurable is that failure!
—SAMUEL W. MARBLE in *The Upper Room Pulpit.*

580. A man who had been condemned to die in the electric chair was asked if he had a final statement to make. He looked at the many reporters, photographers, and officials who surrounded him and then said bitterly: "If I had been shown so much attention when I was a boy, I would not be here today."
—E. PAUL HOVEY

581. Clifford Hood, speaking to a church group, recently told of a twelve-year-old boy who wrote to the Library of Congress requesting two books, one on sane living and the other on space travel. The letter concluded: "If I can't have both books, please send me the one on space travel, for I am more interested in that." Our generation seems more interested in space travel than in sane living, although space travel, like the rest of our future, must depend on sane moral living now.
—ROGER J. SQUIRE

TRAIN UP A CHILD

582. When John Colet founded St. Paul's School in England in 1510, he placed over the headmaster's chair a beautifully wrought figure of the Child Jesus. Above the figure was the inscription, "Hear ye Him." What better hearing? When all scientific and philosophical probing has been done, and all our clever theories have been aired, what better than that we should hear Him? John Colet would say to his class: "Lyfte up your lytel whyte handes for me, whiche prayeth for you to God; to whom be al honour and imperyal majeste and glory. Amen." Our pedagogical brilliance seems tinsel beside that simple reverence. John Colet's pedagogy must return, or our world will disappear in its own violence.
—GEORGE ARTHUR BUTTRICK in *Christ and Man's Dilemma,* Abingdon Press.

583. They had erected a scaffold about the entrance to a big church on the boulevard, and workmen were busily engaged in a remodeling job when a stranger stopped to watch. "What are you doing to this church?" he asked of the man who seemed to be in charge of the operations. "Well, you see," the foreman replied, "they had some front doors here which were very heavy, and we are putting up some that are easier to operate." Then with a peculiar twinkle in his eye he added, "No church has a right to put up doors that little children cannot open."
—ROY L. SMITH in *New Light from Old Lamps,* Abingdon Press.

584. An English artist was sketching outdoors in the Barbizon District in France. He was at work at his easel set up along a stream, when a group of four children appeared in front of him and watched every stroke of his pencil. Finally one

said, "Mister, please get us in the picture!"
—HALFORD E. LUCCOCK in *Communicating the Gospel,* Harper & Bros.

585. Katherine Anne Porter in her substantial yet delightful volume of essays entitled *The Days Before* has an essay on Willa Cather. Remarking that she knew little of Willa Cather's life save that of her childhood, Katherine Porter considered that no great loss. She said: "I have not much interest in anyone's personal history after the tenth year, not even my own. Whatever one was going to be was all prepared for before that. The rest is merely confirmation, extension, development."
—EVERETT W. PALMER. Quotation published by Harcourt, Brace & Co., Inc.

586. From the services in which I joined as a child I have taken with me into life a feeling for what is solemn, and a need for quiet and self-recollection, without which I cannot realize the meaning of my life. I cannot, therefore, support the opinion of those who would not let children take part in grown-up people's services till they to some extent understand them. The important thing is not that they shall understand but that they shall feel something of what is serious and solemn. The fact that the child sees his elders full of devotion, and has to feel something of devotion himself, that is what gives the service its meaning for him.
—ALBERT SCHWEITZER in *Memoirs of Childhood and Youth.* Copyright 1931. Used by permission of The Macmillan Co.

587. Though few children are geniuses, all children, I discovered, possess gifts which may become their special distinction. A thousand talents await recognition! In the able ones who decline to push into first place; in the slow worker who eventually does a superior job; in those with special interests beyond school demands, like entomology or stamp collecting; in those with a flair for decoration or design; in the natural housekeeper. The young inventor may be so absorbed in his work that he neglects important studies; the skillful user of tools may need adult appreciation to protect him from the snobbishness of the book learners, including teachers. . . . Often it is the seemingly unimportant gift which is most useful in life.
—HUGHES MEARNS in *The Reader's Digest.*

588. A New England Bible Institute has published a letter written by one mother to other mothers. It reads in part: "How are we to train our children to steer past all the dangers of their hour? We must not stuff their ears with the wads of our convictions, nor tie them to the masts of our principles. Each child's soul is a thing apart and must realize itself. To force it into certain channels, however good, is to impoverish it at least and to impede its growth. It is ours to teach it to be strong, to choose the best. It is ours to advise, to warn, to guide and encourage. We cannot expect to hand on our accumulated worldly wisdom and have it accepted by our young people without question or test."
—Reprinted with permission of publishers from *The Power of Faith* by LOUIS BINSTOCK. Copyright, 1952, by Prentice-Hall, Inc., 70 Fifth Avenue, New York 11, New York.

589. Parents necessarily exercise authority over their young children and often claim it later; become in this way veritable tyrants. But tyrants are seldom free; the cares and the instruments of their tyranny enslave them. The child that cries is your master; and he is your

master again when he smiles. Your love makes you work for him, and at the same time besets and belabours him in order that he may turn out not as he wishes but as you wish. . . . Nature kindly warps our judgment about our children, especially when they are young, when it would be a fatal thing for them if we did not love them. This fond blindness is itself a slavery; a hard slavery, when you think of it, to feel a compulsory and sleepless affection for a perfectly average creature, and this quite apart from any merit or promise in the child.
—George Santayana in *Dominations and Powers,* Chas. Scribner's Sons.

590. Under the leadership of three or four boys the student body in a private school became restive and threatened to destroy everything they laid hands on. The headmaster notified the boys' fathers. One father sent a telegram to his son which read: "If you do not stop this nonsense, I will take you out of school and put you to work." Another father wrote: "If you do not stop this, I'll thrash you within an inch of your life." Other boys were threatened with the discontinuance of their allowances. One father, wiser than the rest, sent this telegram: "Steady, Son, steady." That is what we need. Not threats but someone to put his hand upon our shoulder from time to time and say: "Hold on awhile longer. Pull yourself together. Don't fly apart." This is the desperate need of our lives.
—Frank A. Court

591. There is a story of a great physicist who with a friend watched a violent electric storm. "So much electricity," he remarked, "and we know so little about it." His friend was surprised and said, "That's strange. I thought I knew all about electricity when I was twelve." "Yes," answered the physicist, "when I was twelve, so did I."
—Arnold H. Lowe in *Power for Life's Living,* Harper & Bros.

592. An old village philosopher said gently to a youth forty years younger than himself who had just made some dogmatic affirmation: "My boy, when I was your age I knew far more than I do now." It often happens that we gain the proper perspective in life only with maturity.
—Fred R. Chenault

THROUGH CHILDREN'S EYES

593. A little girl was on a train with her mother. As she looked out of the window she would cry: "Look, mama, a horse," "Look, cows," "Oh, mama, houses." This kept up until the mother was embarrassed and she turned apologetically to those seated nearby and said: "You know, she still thinks everything is wonderful." Of what tremendous value it would be if we could carry over into adult years the marvelous ability to see that which is really wonderful in life.
—Reprinted with permission of publishers from *You Can Master Life* by John H. Crowe. Copyright, 1954, by Prentice-Hall, Inc., 70 Fifth Avenue, New York 11, New York.

594. "Do you like dollies?" a little girl asked her house guest. "Yes, very much," the man responded. "Then I'll show you mine," was the reply. Thereupon she presented one by one a whole family of dolls. "And now tell me," the visitor asked, "which is your favorite doll?" The child hesitated for a moment and then said, "You're quite sure you like dollies, and will you please promise not to smile if I show you my favorite?" The man solemnly promised, and the girl hurried from the room. In a moment she re-

turned with a tattered and dilapidated old doll. Its hair had come off; its nose was broken; its cheeks were scratched. An arm and a leg were missing. "Well, well," said the visitor, "and why do you like this one best?" "I love her most," said the little girl, "because if I didn't love her, no one else would."
—R. E. Thomas

595. The story has been told of the housewife who asked the grocery boy his name. "Humphrey Bogart," was the reply. "That's a pretty well-known name," responded the housewife. "It darn well ought to be," the boy heartily agreed, "I've been delivering groceries in this neighborhood for four years." To look at oneself and one's place as the grocery boy did at his, to see it as unique and valuable, to keep the gentle, deft touch that can smile and say, "Well, the world is probably glad there is only one of me, but there is one—and while I'm here, I'll live with dignity and good grace," is a warranted and healthy antidote to a feeling of insignificance.
—From *Personal Security Through Faith* by Lowell Russell Ditzen. Copyright, 1954, by Henry Holt and Company, Inc. Reprinted by permission of the publishers.

596. A small boy stood in a little pool of sunlight in a darkened, old-fashioned parlor where a tiny hole in the closely drawn shade permitted a bit of light to pour down upon the carpet in a golden stream. "Look, Mother," he exclaimed as his mother glanced into the room, "I'm standing in the smile of God!"
—Gwynn McLendon Day in *Path of the Dawning Light,* Broadman Press.

597. One summer day an anxious mother could not find her five-year-old son. When at last she located him, he was up near the top of the tallest tree near their home. "Johnnie," she cried, "what are you doing up there? Come down this very minute." There was a mumbled reply which she didn't understand. After a few moments he emerged upon the lowest bough, slid down the trunk, and walked over to her side. Both arms were scraped, and his trousers plainly showed the trials to which they had been subjected. But to her surprise there was none of the deviltry she expected to see in his eyes. He was sober as a judge, positively pious. Taken aback but still indignant, she seized him by the arm and scolded, "What were you doing up there?" He stood away from her, turned up his face, set his big, dark eyes upon her with a seriousness she had never seen in him before. Then he answered, "Why, Mommy, I went up there to look for God."
—Everett W. Palmer

598. A friend of mine tells of driving with his family through the mountains of North Carolina. Along the highway were signs, reading, "The Land of the Sky." Reading these signs, his little boy asked, "Daddy, does God live here?" "Yes, son," the father replied, "God lives everywhere." As they drove along, they passed an old man with a flowing white beard and a long staff. The little boy excitedly shouted, "Look, daddy, I see God." And as the father looked around at these mountains, he said, "Yes, son, I see God too."
—Charles L. Allen in *In Quest of God's Power,* Fleming H. Revell Co.

599. Visiting a friend who was ill in Mayo's Clinic in Rochester, I went over to the main building, where the human body has been reproduced in all its exactness, with the muscles revealed, liquid pulsating through the body, a mechanical heart. While I was looking at

it, a mother and two children came in. As they saw the marvelous mechanism, the boy turned to the mother and exclaimed, "Gee, Mom, I didn't know I was made like that!" But the young lad had not even begun to see the hidden forces of his life. No mechanical reproduction is able to reflect the imagination, the conflicting emotions, the struggle of the will, the delicate impulses, that move across the tissue of the mind.
—Frank A. Court

600. One day a father gave his son a globe of the world, and the boy was so intrigued that night he did not want to turn out his light and go to sleep. The father finally had to go in and take the globe. As he walked out of the room, the boy called out excitedly, "Daddy! What are you going to do with my world?"
—Roy A. Burkhart

601. One glorious summer evening I was standing on the shore as my daughter scooped down into the water and tossed some water toward me as she laughed, "Here, Dad, here's your handful of stars." What an art it is to be able to look down and see the reflected beauty, joy, laughter, high hope, of God's living beauty everywhere and to be able to reach out and fling to all of life just a handful of stars!
—Frank A. Court

602. A Chinese boy once defined [conscience] as a triangle that turns within you every time you do wrong. Its sharp points hurt, but, if you pay no attention, after a while the sharp points wear off.
—Charles Ray Goff in *A Better Hope,* Fleming H. Revell Co.

603. Last fall two university football teams met on the gridiron, and the underdog team defeated the opponents on the opponents' field. When the victorious team upon its return home was greeted at a rally, one of the players explained the reason for the victory: "We outhearted them!"
—Thomas S. Kepler in *A Journey into Faith,* Abingdon Press.

A CHILD SHALL LEAD

604. A little boy was leading his sister up a mountain path. "Why," she complained, "it's not a path at all. It's all rocky and bumpy." "Sure," he said, "the bumps are what you climb on."
—J. Wallace Hamilton in *Ride the Wild Horses!* Fleming H. Revell Co.

605. A family decided that, in order to have something in their new home that would be distinctive of their Christian convictions, they would have a little altar of scented wood. The problem arose as to where the altar should be placed. The young man in the family said, "Why, I think it should be out here in the hall, in the reception room, where everybody will see it when they come in." The father said, "No, it ought to be in here with the books in the library." The mother said, "Maybe it ought to be out in the kitchen where most of my problems are." Finally the debate become so acrimonious that the father said, "Well, let's take it in and give it to our little girl and see what she says." They found her in front of the open fire looking into the dancing flames. The father asked, "What do you think ought to be done with this?" and placed the altar in her hands. She looked up in bewilderment and then put it on the flames. At once it was consumed, but the fragrance of the altar filled every room in the house.
—Charles Nelson Pace

606. One afternoon a father took his small daughter for a walk. It was a glori-

ous day, but he was blind to it all. The glories of that wondrous day were wasted on him. But not so for her. Suddenly he was shaken from his thoughts by hearing her cry, "Oh, Daddy, look!" He turned and saw her kneeling beside a bed of daffodils. She turned a swift glance in his direction and then returned to feast her eyes again upon the flowers. Gently she took one blossom in her hands and moved it about slowly, observing its utter grace and loveliness. Then with the tenderness of a mother she kissed it. As that father saw his little daughter kneeling there in awesome ecstasy before the daffodils, her golden curls and white dress blending so perfectly with the scene, her spirit caught up in wonder, his conscience stabbed him broad awake. He prayed for forgiveness from the Creator of it all that he had allowed his soul to become so dead and asked that once again he could look out upon life through the open and unshuttered windows of childlike wonder.
—Everett W. Palmer

607. A teacher, anticipating a visit to the school from the school board prepared the children so that they might give a good account of themselves. She decided that each should recite by telling what he wanted to be when he grew up. One boy wanted to be a doctor, another a lawyer, and another a teacher. When the board arrived, the teacher was worried about what one boy might say. He was a retarded child and simply unable to keep up with the other members of the class. When his time came to tell what he wanted to do when he grew up, he put on his best smile and said brightly, "I want to lead a blind man!"
—Clarence J. Forsberg

608. In "Pippa Passes" Robert Browning tells of a simple insignificant mill girl as she strolls through the village with a song on her lips. Yet the strains of her song are carried to the ears and the hearts of various people who have come to a crisis in their lives; and all who hear her song, though Pippa is unaware of her influence, are inspired with new strength, new beauty, and new hope.

Each of us has met Pippa. I met her one day many years ago, and her song still sings in my heart. She was a little girl of eight. Her natural, childlike cheerfulness made the whole day bright. Then one day I learned that she had a malignant growth in her throat. She was rushed to one of the world's great medical centers where intense treatment was given, but the disease persisted. She knew what was going on and realized the probable outcome; but still she sang and smiled and played and prayed, never complaining. Sometimes the tension in her parents' hearts became almost unbearable and would be revealed, though ever so slightly, upon their faces. So the little girl scribbled these lines to cheer them:

When your life seems hopelessly tangled
And in the utmost disorder,
It isn't so terribly mangled
That you can't find some carefree border;
And if you look, before long
You're sure to find some hidden song;
So if your life is in disarray,
You don't have to *keep* it that way.
—Homer J. R. Elford

FATHER'S DAY

THE GUIDING HAND

609. Mary by Sholem Asch deals with the mother of Christ. It begins with the wandering tribesman Joseph returning to Nazareth to find himself a wife. Asch makes it natural for Jesus to have many attitudes of good will and graciousness as Joseph in turn reveals these attitudes in his relationships with others. Joseph encounters first of all the resentment of the other villagers in his coming from afar to marry the home-town girl Mary. When Mary cradles the Child beneath her heart before the villagers believe it is time, Joseph meets their resentment and ridicule with the calmness and serenity of spirit that later are reflected in the attitude of Christ. There is a vinedresser who is not a Nazarite, one who is outside the inner circle of regard; yet Joseph becomes a friend of his, and in this one can read the future attitude of Christ toward all who believe God has no inner circle but a circle only of love for all. Is it not psychologically sound for Sholem Asch in the background of his book to suggest that these attitudes we admire so much in the Christ were all reflected in the Nazareth home and in the attitudes of Joseph and Mary as they nurtured the Boy?
—Frank A. Court

610. I remember that as a child it was necessary for me to return from school by way of an old stone quarry. On winter evenings I frequently became terrified by odd-shaped boulders which seemed to me like horrible human monsters. On one particular evening I became so frightened that I ran back to the school master. He contacted my father, who came for me. Taking me by the hand, he walked with me past the fearsome objects. When I walked with him, I had no fear. Whenever during later years I have become fearful of the dangers along life's road, I have remembered that there is a Guide who cares for me along the way.
—J. Calvert Cariss

611. When as a boy our family visited old Fort Marion in St. Augustine, Florida, I was always fascinated by the dungeon where Osceola, the Seminole chief, was held captive. The damp and eerie cell was so black that I could not see my hands, but I was never fearful for my father would hold my hand securely. The remembrance of my hand firmly clasped in my father's grip is like a parable of life for me. Sometimes quite suddenly darkness shrouds all life. No one is exempt from the dark shadows which cross the soul. Yet at our side is the heavenly Father, whose hand is steady and secure.
—William Goddard Sherman

612. During the blitz of London the ladder into a dug-out had been broken, so that the father stood in darkness as at the foot of a well, and his child stood uncertain on the upper edge. He could see her dimly against the night sky; she could not see him at all in the depth. But she could hear his voice: "Jump!" he said, "Daddy can see you. Now, right into my arms!"

There are such times. No preacher can explain sorrow, much less the tragedy that follows human folly. The only resource then is the leap of faith. Every man who leaps, half-fearing, half-hoping, is caught and held: "Underneath are the everlasting Arms."
—George A. Buttrick in *Pulpit Digest.*

613. A little fellow was sweating as he carried a large stone across the yard. "Why don't you use all your strength?" asked his father. The little fellow felt hurt and said, "Daddy, I am." And the father replied, "You haven't asked me to help you." There stood his resources in the person of the father, but uncalled on, for the lad was centered in his own. Conversion puts God at the center.
—E. Stanley Jones in *How to Be a Transformed Person,* Abingdon Press.

614. An American man of letters challenged the Almighty: "I do not believe in God. If there is a God, I give him sixty seconds to strike me dead. If he refuses, that is conclusive proof that there is no God." Suppose my little son came to me and said: "Daddy, if you really are my daddy, I give you sixty seconds to prove it by striking me dead. If you really are my father, prove it that way." That is one thing a father would never do. He would strike himself dead first. And how much greater is the patient love of our heavenly Father!
—Ernest K. Emurian

WORDS OF ENLIGHTENMENT

615. Channing Pollock tells of the influence his father had upon him. His father while a young man died heroically at his post of duty. When Channing was fourteen years old, his father was U.S. consul at a place where the yellow fever was raging. His vacation was due. He had bought the steamship tickets to travel home. But he refused to use them. Pollock says that when his mother learned of the decision, she pleaded desperately for him to leave. She asked, "Have you no fear?" His father answered, "Yes, but none so great as the fear of not doing what I believe to be right." That very day his father contracted yellow fever. Pollock says, "Because I remember what he said, I hope I might do that thing or its equivalent under equivalent circumstances, and that my son might, and my son's son."
—Everett W. Palmer

616. As a boy [Rufus Moseley] was raised in the backwoods of the southern mountains, but received a scholarship to go to college. On the eve of his departure his father summarized his anxieties and expectations by saying, "Son, I don't know much about the world into which you are going, but I trust you." The boy never forgot these words, and strove always to be worthy of the confidence his father had expressed in him. That mountaineer may not have traveled extensively, but he had the vision of what it means to live by one's hopes.
—Howard Conn in *The Hope That Sets Men Free,* Harper & Bros.

617. Willie Keith in the novel *The Caine Mutiny* by Herman Wouk is on the mine sweeper "Caine" when he receives a letter from his doctor father conveying the information that, when the letter is received, the father will be dead from an incurable disease. The father offers to his son three bits of advice. First, "There is nothing, nothing more

precious than time. . . . Wasted hours destroy your life just as surely at the beginning as at the end." Second, "Religion. I'm afraid we haven't given you much, not having had much ourselves. But I think, after all, I will mail you a Bible before I go into the hospital. . . . Get familiar with the words. You'll never regret it. I came to the Bible as I did to everything in life, too late." Third, "Think of me and of what I might have been, Willie, at the times in your life when you come to crossroads. For my sake, for the sake of the father who took the wrong turns, take the right ones. . . . Good-by, my son. Be a man. Dad."
—Copyright 1951 by Herman Wouk, reprinted by permission of Doubleday & Co., Inc.

AS FATHER DOES

618. There is a saying, "Until a boy is about fourteen years old, he does what his father *says;* after that he does what his father *does.*"
—From: *Spiritual Revolution,* by PIERCE HARRIS. Copyright 1952 by Pierce Harris, reprinted by permission of Doubleday & Co., Inc.

619. A church school teacher once asked her class of small boys if their fathers were Christians. One little fellow answered, "My father is a Christian but he is not practicing it at present."
—ROBERT GRAHAM CLARKE in *The Upper Room Pulpit.*

620. In James Baldwin's *Go Tell It on the Mountain* there is a deeply moving scene. John Grimes lives for the day when his father will die and he can curse him on his deathbed; for as long as he can remember, his father has been a minister, pretending one thing while in his vestments but repudiating in behavior all that he proclaims from the pulpit. John has suffered a thousand deaths because of his father's brutality, and in agony of soul he cries: "And I hate you. I hate you! I don't care about your golden crown. I don't care about your long white robe. I seen you under the robe, I seen you!" Children are quick to detect sham and pretense; they respect honesty. Cervantes wisely said: "He preaches well that lives well. . . . That's all the divinity I understand."
—CHARLES F. JACOBS. Quotation published by Alfred A. Knopf, Inc.

621. A certain New York columnist told about how one New Year's Eve his high-school-age son had asked for the car. All that night he and his wife stayed home, turning down invitations, because they were so worried about their boy. Then about midnight the telephone rang. "There has been an automobile accident," the girl at the desk of a local hospital said. "One of the persons involved wanted me to tell you not to worry. He is going to be all right!" "Thank God!" sighed the columnist. Then he heard her continue, "It is your father!" He adds in his column, "Apparently we had been worrying about the wrong generation!"
—CLARENCE J. FORSBERG

NATURE SUNDAY

LESSONS FROM THE SOIL

622. "I would finish hoeing my garden." These words were St. Francis' answer when someone asked him, while working in his garden, what he would do if he were suddenly to learn that he would die at sunset that day. . . . If the future looks dark, so did it on the morning before the first Christmas—and in the year 5,000 B.C. And however dark it seems today, however dark it is, we shall meet life better if we have fulfilled the present to the best of our ability. Today is still ours, along with the obligation to live it to the full.

—DOROTHY VAN DOREN. Reprinted from *This Week* Magazine. Copyright 1948 by the United Newspapers Magazine Corporation.

623. A man should do his share of the honorable work of our world. In a novel by Jozua M. W. Schwartz [*My Lady Nobody*], Ursula hears that Otto van Helmont, son of the baron of the nearby castle, had broken the custom of his rank and is now earning his daily bread. "It seems so ridiculous, a van Helmont earning his living!" she exclaims. Her father, the village pastor, replies: " 'Give us this day our daily bread.' That means: We would accept it, Lord, from no other hands but Thine." She asks, "As manna?" And he answers again, "No, child, as the harvest of toil."

—GEORGE ARTHUR BUTTRICK in *So We Believe, So We Pray,* Abingdon Press.

624. On Louis Bromfield's farm in Ohio the eroded, leached soil was replenished by planting crops with long roots that went down deep to hidden reserves of mineral riches. The soil had become sterile and the shallow-rooted plants had not the power to bring us the elements that would give the ground new life. Today we need more people with deep spiritual roots that will sink into God's inexhaustible riches and bring up elements which will restore health to our society.

—GRAHAM R. HODGES in *The Pulpit.* Copyrighted by the Christian Century Foundation and used by permission.

625. We do not grow physically by standing on tiptoe and stretching ourselves or by anxiously exercising our muscles. Neither do we grow in grace by troubling ourselves with rules and anxiously observing mottos. The gardener puts a plant into the ground hoping to reap a beautiful rose. But he does not grab the plant and stretch it up to make it grow. He rather attends to the conditions surrounding the plant, conditions which are normally conducive to the health of the plant and which seem to encourage growth. He cultivates, irrigates, and nourishes the plant; and he prunes it. By the mysterious processes of nature God gives the growth, and anon the beautiful rose appears. Our growth in grace is like that. We do not grow

in godliness by groaning within ourselves and anxiously keeping the commandments outwardly. We only attend to the conditions of growth, and God through the mysterious ministries of his Spirit gives the increase, and in time a beautiful character unfolds.
—S. L. McKay

626. The late Bishop Quayle was an intimate friend of John Burroughs, the famous American naturalist, who was not a Christian as we measure Christians. One day John Burroughs passed into the eternities, and when Bishop Quayle heard of the death of his friend, he said, "Poor John, he loved the garden, but he never met the Gardener."
—Arthur J. Moore in *The Mighty Saviour,* Abingdon Press.

627. If I had to choose a building to stand for America, it would not be one of those tall silver monoliths of New York City, though. I would go to the country, to the green carpet, for my symbol. It would be barns. The barn is America at its fragrant and warmest best. It stands for the genius of a nation built of rich soil and fat cattle.
—From *On the Green Carpet,* by Robert P. T. Coffin. Copyright 1951. Used by special permission of the publishers, The Bobbs-Merrill Company, Inc.

MOUNTAINS TO CLIMB

628. A young doctor talked with John Dewey just prior to the philosopher's ninetieth birthday. The skeptical young medico blurted out his low opinion of philosophy. "What's the use of such clap-trap?" he asked. "Where does it get you?" To which Mr. Dewey replied: "The good of it is that you climb mountains." The doctor was unimpressed. "Climb mountains! And what's the use of that?" Mr. Dewey answered, "You see other mountains to climb. You come down, climb the next mountain, and see still others to climb. When you are no longer interested in climbing mountains to see other mountains to climb, life is over."
—Charles M. Crowe in *The Years of Our Lord,* Abingdon Press.

629. Among the noted painters of the Alps was Giovanni Segantini. An interesting feature of his career is the fact that as his genius unfolded he climbed higher and higher among the mountains. He was born on the plains of Lombardy. He died on the summit of the Schafburg, nine thousand feet above the sea. The higher he climbed the more his power of interpreting Alpine scenery developed.
—Lucius H. Bugbee in *The Sanctuary,* 1944, Abingdon Press.

630. Many people ask: "What is the use of risking life and limb in attempting to climb Mount Everest?" . . . The real reason behind an expedition is the same spirit of inquiry and adventure that lies behind all mountaineering and exploration. Were man not an inquirer and an adventurer, he would never have risen to his present status. . . . In mountaineering, and on Mount Everest in particular, a man sees himself for what he is. He learns the value of comradeship and of service. . . . Out of [Nature's] strength we gather our own strength. And it is good to be strong, to be able to endure, not as a brute beast, but as a thinking man imbued with the spirit of a great ideal.
—Frank S. Smythe, *The Adventures of a Mountaineer,* J. M. Dent & Sons, Ltd.

631. A man climbs because he needs to climb; because that is the way he is made. The key to the mountaineering spirit is not far to find. . . . It lies not in what men *do,* but in what they *are*—in the raising of their eyes and the lifting of their hearts. . . . For it is the ultimate wisdom of the mountains that a man is never more a man than when he is striving for what is beyond his grasp, and that there is no conquest worth the winning save that over his own weakness and ignorance and fear. "Have we vanquished an enemy?" asked [George] Mallory. And there was only one answer: "None but ourselves." It is not the summit that matters, but the fight for the summit; not the victory, but the game itself.

—From *High Conquest,* by James Ramsey Ullman. Copyright 1941, by James Ramsey Ullman. Published by J. B. Lippincott Co.

632. On August 5, 1952, a group of young mountaineers climbed for the first time to the peak of Nevado Salcantay, the "most savage mountain" of the Peruvian Andes. Recalling their experience, George I. Bell wrote: "To climb such a mountain, however much you fall short of the goal, is an adventure of the spirit, a test of the soul and a challenge to the human will. . . . My finest memory was of the last day at base camp, before we left the mountain to itself. Most of the time, Salcantay was hidden by clouds. Usually it could be seen fleetingly at dawn. That final day I rose very early. In the deep valleys and over the silent jungles there was a brooding mantle of darkness. But far above, flaming in the first rays of the sun, I could see the summit ridge of Salcantay, master of itself no longer. Now the mountain belongs to six of us."

—*Saturday Evening Post*

633. The Crawford Bridle Path is one of the favorite trails to the summit of Mt. Washington in the White Mountains of New Hampshire. At the foot of the trail prospective climbers find a sign which announces that it is 9.7 miles to the summit. It warns that many lives have been lost on the trail, that it is wise for the climber to prepare himself for any emergency which may arise before he attempts to climb. The first two miles are through dense woods and underbrush. In the summer season the path is often damp and muddy. Mosquitoes and flies are a constant irritation. But at length the climber reaches the first ridge. From that place of vantage he can again get a full view of the stately summit. From then on the vistas of the peak are more frequent, and there are deeper satisfactions in the climbing.

Here we have a parable which illustrates the experience of many of those who approach God through the path of faith. It reminds us that before we begin that adventure we will need to remember that many have lost their lives in following the Christian way. It is no easy affair, this pattern laid down by Christ for his followers. It is not to be entered lightly. . . . But for the one who perseveres on the path of faith there comes a glorious moment when a vista is opened through which he catches a glimpse of the face of God. From then on, as he climbs higher, the fellowship with God becomes a more frequent experience.

—George Ernest Thomas in *How to Live Your Faith,* Fleming H. Revell Co.

634. Mountain climbers tell us it isn't getting any easier to climb Mount Everest. A Swiss expedition which got within nine hundred feet of the top reported that, because of movement in the earth's crust, the peak is getting higher every year. According to the Swiss leader, the world's highest mountain, which used to be 29,002 feet, had already reached

29,610 feet and was still growing. He recommended that "anybody who wants to reach the top better hurry." Not long after, a British party took his advice and made it!
—CHARLES M. CROWE in *Sermons from the Mount,* Abingdon Press.

635. A student pastor, calling on families in his parish in the Adirondack Mountains, took a short cut to his home one evening and became lost. For a few moments he was panicky, but then he remembered that he had been telling his church people of their need for an absolute dependence on God. He turned to God in prayer, and there came to his mind the familiar words "For thou art my rock and my fortress; therefore for thy name's sake lead me, and guide me." The word "rock" helped him to find his way, for the bald, rocky peak of Crane Mountain, rising to a height of thirty-two hundred feet, was ahead and served to guide him, until he finally reached safety. Amid the entangling paths of life there is always a Rock to guide and direct.
—FREDERICK L. ANDERSON

RIVERS TO THE SEA

636. A brook is going somewhere. It is water-on-a-mission. About to present itself to other waters at its destination, it never neglects little wayside opportunities. On its way to make its final offering, it gaily gives itself all along the way. Deer drink of its refreshing coolness with a deep content. Boys of seven years and of seventy probe its pools and eddies with their lures and return home at day's end with the brook's gift of speckled trout. Fish, crustaceans, mollusks, and water insects are given a home in its swirling currents and tranquil pools. From its birth in bubbling springs to its arrival at its final goal the brook is selfless and a happy appearing thing. Service and happiness belong together.
—HAROLD E. KOHN in *Feeling Low?* Wm. B. Eerdmans Publishing Co.

637. Those who have entered Yellowstone Park by the east gate recall how the Yellowstone River follows the road all along the long motor drive from the lake to the canyon. The road and the river continue for many miles side by side. If the road turns, the river turns. If the river changes its course, the road turns with it. Side by side the two of them cover the miles. There is not a place, as I remember, on that long journey where one could not stop the motor, step down, and slake his thirst with the laughing waters of the Yellowstone River. That is the picture of God's love. It never leaves us.
—ARTHUR J. MOORE in *The Mighty Saviour,* Abingdon Press.

638. On U. S. Highway No. 78, approaching Atlanta from the northeast, is a modern wonder, Stone Mountain. From some distance one can see the bald dome standing like a man's head above the rolling hills that surround it. As he goes nearer, he can see distinct crevices running up and down the mountainside. They show where during many centuries the rushing waters have flowed. In much the same way the thoughts of a man leave distinct marks on his mind and determine the character of his life.
—S. L. MCKAY

639. Wendell Johnson recalls that the old Greek Heraclitus said: "You can't step in the same river twice." The river changes, and the man also changes. In endless and almost imperceptible quietness the river flows on in rhythmic splendor to the sea. It is the same river, yet it is never the same. It has its origin

in the heights; and as it journeys, it deepens and broadens and is enlarged by the waters of the mountains, the uplands, and the lowlands. If the river stood still and failed to continue its course to the sea, it would become a menace to the health of the communities through which it passes. The fact that it moves continually is a sign of its healthful and life-giving waters. So it is with the physical, mental, and spiritual life of man. Futile inactivity is stagnation. Creative work and divine aspiration mean growth toward divine excellence.
—FRED B. CHENAULT

640. To go fishing . . . is the chance to wash one's soul with pure air, with the rush of the brook, or with the shimmer of the sun on blue water. It brings meekness and inspiration from the decency of nature, charity toward tackle-makers, patience toward fish, a mockery of profits and egos, a quieting of hate, a rejoicing that you do not have to decide a darned thing until next week. And it is discipline in the equality of men—for all men are equal before fish.
—HERBERT HOOVER in *Collier's.*

SOWING AND REAPING

641. In the early 1800's there was a strange figure to be seen among the frontiersmen of the Ohio Valley. This man was recognized by his ragged dress, by his eccentric ways, and by his religious turn of mind. His name was John Chapman. Chapman had started a nursery in Pennsylvania. He visited the cider presses; and there he gathered the refuse, sifting out the apple seeds and sorting them. He urged the people going west to take the seeds with them. For forty years he himself went up and down the estates in the Ohio Valley and planted apple orchards. For this reason he was called "Johnny Appleseed." One can hardly imagine a man doing that kind of thing if he believed the end of the world was coming in the next decade. That willingness to provide for generations yet to come represents the kind of confidence in the future that we need in spite of the threats that are present among us.
—ROLLAND W. SCHLOERB

642. A group of tourists were one day admiring a lovely English garden on a magnificent country estate in Norfolk. They came upon a groundsman caring for a century plant. He explained in affectionate tones that his father had made the planting nearly forty years earlier. "He never saw the blossom, but he tended this plant with great care. I shall never see the blossom either; but if I do my work well, perhaps my son some day will." This is the long-range expectation that is among the many distinguishing characteristics of man.
—HOWARD CONN in *The Hope That Sets Men Free,* Harper & Bros.

643. Howard Thurman watched an eighty-one-year-old man planting a small grove of pecan trees. "Why did you not select larger trees so as to increase the possibility of your living to see them bear at least one cup of nuts?" he asked. The old man replied: "All my life I have eaten fruit from trees that I did not plant, why should I not plant trees to bear fruit for those who may enjoy them long after I am gone? Besides, the man who plants because he will reap the harvest has no faith in life."
—*Deep Is the Hunger,* Harper & Bros.

644. When Captain James Cook, distinguished eighteenth-century English navigator, sailed around the world, he carried with him a package of seeds of

flowers common in English gardens. As his ship touched the shores of countless islands of the seas, and Captain Cook disembarked, he sowed the seeds, leaving reminders of England sprouting everywhere he went.
—HAROLD E. KOHN in *Feeling Low?* Wm. B. Eerdmans Publishing Co.

WONDERS OF CREATION

645. The vastness of God's creation should ever keep us humble. The new telescope at Mt. Palomar enables man to photograph planets over one billion light years away. This distance in miles amounts to a total of 186,000 (miles per second) x 60 seconds x 60 minutes x 24 hours x 365 days x 1,000,000,000 (years). How many billions of planets there are, no one can guess. One astronomer, when asked how he could believe in a God, replied, "I keep enlarging my idea of God."
—OBERT C. TANNER in *Christ's Ideals for Living,* Deseret Sunday School Union Board.

646. A college student once remarked to his instructor that he believed the universe was nothing but a vast machine which made, repaired, and ran itself. The teacher asked him, "Did you ever hear of a machine without a pedal for the foot, a lever for the hand or an outlet for connection with some outside power?" The student of course admitted he had not. "Then," said the instructor, "we had better not think seriously of the universe as a machine."
—ROGER HAZELTON in *On Proving God,* Harper & Bros.

647. Once I spent most of an afternoon watching a tall, lone tree out at the end of a point of land near our summer cottage in Wisconsin battle against a severe windstorm. How the wind would tear at that tree, trying to topple it over; and there seemed to be a joyous encounter as the pine would bend before the wind and then spring back ready to battle again with the next onslaught. Walking over, I placed my hand on a root as the wind battled with the tree and felt there only tautness, solidness. There was no giving to the exposed root, for its end reached down out of sight into the earth to coil around a rock, which enabled this tall old pine, which had stood for many years, to battle against the elements of life. It had roots that went down to the things that abide.
—FRANK A. COURT

648. After a severe electrical storm I looked with dismay at the many broken, twisted, and uprooted trees. Many of them had withstood the ravages of nature for generations but had finally submitted to the fury of a storm. At the center of so devastating a wreckage I saw a small vine that clung tenaciously to the walls of a large building. It was unharmed and as beautiful as ever. Even man is no stronger than that to which he clings. When the storms of life beat with violent destructiveness, we will stand fast if we hold by faith unto the Lord.
—W. A. KUNTZLEMAN

649. Allan A. Hunter speaks of passing a tiny weed which was growing vivaciously in a crack in the well-worn pavement of busy Los Angeles. In part he said about the weed: "Defenseless, unsupported by high-powered promotion, the undaunted weed was quietly exhibiting a commodity which our frightened world craves, but neither Hollywood, nor Wall Street, neither the Kremlin nor Rome, is able to produce, conscript or impose; and that is the radical audacity of faith."
—JOHN M. SYKES in *The Upper Room Pulpit.*

650. Love all God's creation, the whole and every grain of sand in it. Love every leaf, every ray of God's light. Love the animals, love the plants, love everything. If you love everything, you will perceive the divine mystery in things. Once you perceive it, you will begin to comprehend it better every day. And you will come at last to love the whole world with an all-embracing love.
—Fyodor Dostoevski in *The Brothers Karamazov.*

651. Some time ago on the golf course my caddy, a young boy, picked a violet and asked, "Did you ever see the queen on her throne?" When I said that I hadn't, he proceeded to pick the petals from the violet in just the right manner until turning the center of the flower about so that I could see, I saw the throne and a queen with a crown of gold above her head. How like the manner of Jesus! He touched the shepherd's robe, pointed to the birds of the air, picked a flower of the field, held a little child in his arms, and people beheld God in all his glory. Seldom did Christ say, "Believe in God," but always, "Behold the works of God!"
—W. Ralph Ward, Jr.

652. The turtle is a fortunate fellow. When he squirms and struggles from the rubbery egg shell that for weeks has been his home, he is uniquely ready to face the world. He is armored. A shell, composed in part of his own greatly flattened and fused ribs, covers his vital organs. Into this armor he can withdraw his head, his tail and his feet so that a cruel world cannot get at him nor harm him. The turtle is well equipped to enjoy a painless existence. But what an odd and unsatisfying existence it must be!
—Harold E. Kohn in *Feeling Low?* Wm. B. Eerdmans Publishing Co.

653. The frog, it is said, is so easily adapted to its surroundings and so unaware of slight changes that if it is put in a dish of water and the water is slowly heated, the frog will stay there until it is killed by the hot or boiling water, although it could have jumped out at any of the early stages in the heating process. . . . Some persons grow and are alert to new conditions; hence they are able to control those conditions, rather than be controlled by them.
—Harold H. Titus in *Living Issues in Philosophy,* American Book Co.

INDEPENDENCE DAY

SPIRIT OF LIBERTY

654. The spirit of liberty is the spirit which is not too sure that it is right; the spirit of liberty is the spirit which seeks to understand the minds of other men and women; the spirit of liberty is the spirit which weighs their interests alongside its own without bias; the spirit of liberty remembers that not even a sparrow falls to earth unheeded; the spirit of liberty is the spirit of Him who, near two thousand years ago, taught mankind that lesson it has never learned, but has never quite forgotten; that there may be a kingdom where the least shall be heard and considered side by side with the greatest.

—LEARNED HAND

655. In an invocation prayer at the United States Senate, Peter Marshall said: "Lord Jesus, Thou who art the way, the truth, and the life, hear us as we pray for the truth that shall make men free. Teach us that liberty is not only to be loved but also to be lived. Liberty is too precious a thing to be buried in books. It costs too much to be hoarded. Make us to see that our liberty is not the right to do as we please, but the opportunity to please to do what is right."

—*The Congressional Record*

656. The American Way of Life meant to have been born free, and to be so recognized—and therefore not to talk about it much. It meant to *live* democratically, in the simplest and most human sense of noticing, caring about and encouraging people. . . . It doesn't mean a 300-billion-dollar national income, or the statistics of production, or being the "leading world power." It doesn't mean "the world's highest standard of living." It means the most human standard of life and relationships; it means hard work—even, if it comes to it, austerity. It means belonging to a nation of friends, and doing as you would be done by.

—DOROTHY THOMPSON in *Ladies' Home Journal.*

657. What constitutes an American? Not color nor race nor religion. Not the pedigree of his family nor the place of his birth. Not the coincidence of his citizenship. Not his social status nor his bank account. Not his trade nor his profession. An American is one who loves justice and believes in the dignity of man. An American is one who will fight for his freedom and that of his neighbor. An American is one who will sacrifice property, ease and security in order that he and his children may retain the rights of free men. An American is one in whose heart is engraved the immortal second sentence of the Declaration of Independence.

—HAROLD L. ICKES

658. The whole story of America—a story worth the telling and worth the understanding—began with an idea. This idea is actually the political expression of a basic law of nature—that there is strength in diversity. According to this idea, America is a place where people can be themselves. It is a human experience rather than a purely national or cultural experience. It is built upon fabulous differences—religion, race, culture, customs, political thinking. These differences, or pluralism, as the sociologists call it, are actually the mortar that hold the nation together.
—NORMAN COUSINS in *Who Speaks for Man?* Copyright 1953. Used by permission of The Macmillan Co.

659. In 1639, more than three hundred years ago, Stephen Daye, an early settler in this country who established the first printing plant in the colonies, expressed a creed, "The Oath of a Free Man," which every citizen should take to heart today: "I do solemnly bind myself in the sight of God that when I shall be called to give my voice touching any such matter of this state in which freemen are to deal, I will give my vote and suffrage as I shall judge in my own conscience may best conduce and tend to the public weal of the body, without respect of person, or favor of any man."

660. In 1842 Charles Dickens visited America, but little in the land of promise appealed to him and he returned to England disgusted with what he had seen. "The truth was that he did not understand the scenes he witnessed. What was really going on was a great epic in the history of mankind. It was the advance of civilization down the rivers, and through the forests, and out upon the silent prairies of the West. The woods bowed beneath the age, the forests echoed with voices, the savannahs murmured and rustled to the touch of life. In the mind's eye one could see already the log cabins rising into cathedrals, the villages spreading into great cities, and the swamps and cane-brakes changing to the park and meadowland of a smiling civilization. It was a wonderful epic, this advance of the frontier, moving westward day by day. As beside it the ravaging conquests of early Europe, leaving a track of slaughter, seem things of horror."
—From: *Charles Dickens:* His Life and Work, by Stephen Leacock. Copyright 1933, 1934 by Doubleday & Company, Inc.

DOCUMENT OF FREEDOM

661. We Americans say that the Constitution made the nation. Well, the Constitution is a great document and we never would have been a nation without it, but it took more than that to make the nation. Rather it was our forefathers and foremothers who made the Constitution and then made it work. The government they constructed did get great things out of them, but it was not the government primarily that put the great things into them. What put the great things into them was their home life, their religion, their sense of personal responsibility to Almighty God, their devotion to education, their love of liberty, their personal character. When their government pumped it drew from profound depths in the lives of men and women where creative spiritual forces had been at work.
—HARRY EMERSON FOSDICK in *Vital Speeches.*

662. Devotion to God and country epitomizes the life of John Adams, who like Thomas Jefferson was both a signer

of the Declaration of Independence and a President and who like Jefferson died on July 4, 1826, the fiftieth anniversary of American freedom. Adams' two loyalties are expressed in these words from his grave tablet in the First Parish Church in Quincy, Massachusetts: "On the Fourth of July, 1776, he pledged his Life, Fortune and Sacred Honour to the Independence of his Country. . . . On the Fourth of July, 1826, he was summoned to the Independence of Immortality and to the Judgment of his God."

663. The great seal of the United States, printed on all one dollar bills, carries the Latin inscription *Novus Ordo Seclorum.* The designers of the great seal knew that behind the actual accomplishments and failures of the political and economic life of this country there is a dream. Somehow the basic principles of American democracy are felt to be related to the eternal scheme of things. Implied in the motto "The New Order of the Ages" is the belief that this country in its social life demonstrates a fundamental revision of man's traditional way of conducting his affairs, and his change places him in tune with the universe.
—Charles Duell Kean in *Making Sense Out of Life.* Copyright, 1954, by W. L. Jenkins, The Westminster Press. Used by permission.

664. A foreign diplomat once offered this Independence Day toast to the United States: "Let me congratulate you on the second greatest date in history." When friends asked him what he considered to be the greatest date in history, he replied: "December 25, for had there been no Christmas, there would never have been a Fourth of July.'
—E. Paul Hovey

THIS NATION UNDER GOD

665. He who penetrates the depths must sooner or later discover that the most impressive thing in America is her Christianity. The good in this country would never have come into being without the blessing and power of Jesus Christ. Despite every external appearance of materialism and secularism, this is a profoundly religious land. Whoever tries to conceive the American word without taking full account of the suffering and love and salvation of Christ is only dreaming. I know how embarrassing this matter is to politicians, bureaucrats, businessmen, and cynics; but, whatever these honored men think, the irrefutable truth is that the soul of America is, at its best and highest, Christian. When the tears and joy of Christ come to perfect fruition in this land, then America will utter her word.
—Charles Malik in *The Journal of General Education.*

666. The President of the College of New Jersey, the Reverend John Witherspoon, was the only clergyman to sign the Declaration. He is too much forgotten in our history books; John Witherspoon had a far-reaching influence on our democracy. He had taught several of the signers of the document, and nine of them were graduates of the little college over which he presided at Princeton. When he took up his pen to put his name to this document, Witherspoon declared: "There is a tide in the affairs of men, a nick of time. We perceive it now before us. To hesitate is to consent to our own slavery. That noble instrument upon your table, that insures immortality to its author, should be subscribed this very morning by every pen in this house. He that will not respond to its accents, and strain every nerve to carry into effect its provisions, is un-

worthy of the name of free man. . . . For my own part, of property, I have some; of reputation, more. That reputation is staked, that property is pledged on the issue of this contest; and although these grey hairs must soon descend into the sepulcher, I would infinitely rather that they descend thither by the hand of the executioner than desert at this crisis the sacred cause of my country."
—EDWARD L. R. ELSON in *America's Spiritual Recovery,* Fleming H. Revell Co.

667. As late as 1892, the Supreme Court of the United States rendered its opinion in the *Church of the Holy Trinity* case, (143 U.S. 457), wherein it said: "This [the United States] is a religious people. This is historically true. From the discovery of America to this hour there is a single voice making this affirmation." Then the Court reviewed the basic documentary history of the Republic, the charters, commissions and official proclamations and finally the Constitution itself. It then said: "There is no dissonance in these declarations. These are not individual sayings or declarations of private persons; they are organic utterances; they speak the voice of the entire people. . . . There is a universal language pervading them all having but one meaning; they affirm and reaffirm that this is a religious nation."
—O. R. MCGUIRE in *Vital Speeches.*

668. I believe no one can read the history of our country without realizing that the Good Book and the Spirit of the Savior have from the beginning been our guiding geniuses. . . . Whether we look to the first Charter of Virginia . . . or to the Charter of New England . . . or to the Charter of Massachusetts Bay . . . or to the Fundamental Orders of Connecticut . . . the same objective is present: a Christian land governed by Christian principles. . . . I believe the entire Bill of Rights came into being because of the knowledge our forefathers had of the Bible and their belief in it. Freedom of belief, of expression, of assembly, of petition; the dignity of the individual, the sanctity of the home, equal justice under law, and the reservation of powers to the people. . . . I like to believe we are living today in the spirit of the Christian religion. I like also to believe that as long as we do so, no great harm can come to our country.
—EARL WARREN

669. Sincere Christianity and true patriotism have much in common. Our finest patriotic hymn, "My Country, 'Tis of Thee," was written in 1832 by a Baptist clergyman, Samuel Francis Smith; and the pledge of allegiance to the flag was written in 1892 by another Baptist minister, Francis Bellamy.
—ERNEST K. EMURIAN

670. The words, "In God We Trust," carried on many of our coins, are traceable to the efforts of the Rev. W. R. Watkinson of Ridleyville, Pennsylvania. His letter of concern, addressed to the Hon. S. P. Chase, was dated November 13, 1861. Seven days later Mr. Chase wrote to Mr. James Pollock, Director of the United States Mint, as follows: "No nation can be strong except in the strength of God, or safe except in His defense. The trust of our people in God should be declared on our national coins. Will you cause a device to be prepared without necessary delay with a motto expressing in the finest and tersest words possible, this national recognition?"
—G. CURTIS JONES in *What Are You Worth?* Copyright 1954. The Bethany Press.

671. On the courthouse of Cuyahoga County at Cleveland, Ohio, are inscribed these words: "Obedience to Law is Liberty." One of the judges pointed out that there is a significant omission in the inscription. It comes from Richard Hooker, the sixteenth-century author and stylist; and what Hooker wrote was this, "Obedience to *Divine* Law is Liberty."
—Clarence Edward Macartney

672. There are some Old things that made this country. There is the Old Virtue of religious faith. There are the Old Virtues of integrity and the whole truth. There is the Old Virtue of incorruptible service and honor in public office. There are the Old Virtues of economy in government, of self-reliance, thrift and individual liberty. There are the Old Virtues of patriotism, real love of country and willingness to sacrifice for it. These "Old" ideas are very inexpensive. They even would help to win hot and cold wars. I realize that such suggestions will raise the cuss word "Reactionary." But some of these Old things are slipping badly in American life. And if they slip too far, the lights will go out of America, even if we win these cold and hot wars.
—Herbert Hoover

673. In the [concluding chapter] of an important biography of the life of Dwight L. Moody, the evangelist, the biographer Gamaliel Bradford, writing from the point of view of a man of letters, says: "Surely we may end as we began, with the insistence that God is the one supreme universal need of all humanity, and that need was never more pronounced than in America today."
—Hugh Thomson Kerr in *Design for Christian Living*. Copyright, 1953, by W. L. Jenkins, The Westminster Press. Used by permission. Quotation from *D. L. Moody, a Worker in Souls*. Used by permission.

674. In *Remembrance Rock*, by Carl Sandburg, Judge Windom, a man rich in thought and great in years, has what he calls a remembrance rock in the very center of his yard. He has gathered around this remembrance rock precious dust, and he likes to go there to meditate. He has taken a bit of dust from beside Plymouth Rock and from Valley Forge. He has been to Gettsyburg. He has traveled to France and brought back some of the soil that reminds him of the price his son paid in the First World War. There around that rock he has gathered the precious dust, and in this book it becomes for him his remembrance rock. He does not want to forget the traveled road over which his great nation has come into being. But he does not face backward. As he talks about patriotism, he knows that every day there are those who try to escape, who have as their motto, "What's the use?" They're the ones he calls the great deceivers because, instead of using remembrance rock as a steppingstone, they somehow build it as a great monument. Not only is our religious faith a monument to God; it is a living movement that in our day has taken individuals and placed their feet upon the great way that leads at last to the kingdom of God.
—Frank A. Court

675. The United States of America is today second to none among the nations of the world. How did it reach this summit? It became supreme because it placed itself second to One. That one was God. When you read the Declaration and the Constitution, you will be convinced that this nation was founded by men who took God as their partner. In the middle of the nation's history a

crisis was reached when the nation was divided in civil strife. Then a wise leader, taking our nation again to God, said, "This nation *under God* shall have a new birth of freedom." Our allegiance to God and our dependence on him have always been so pronounced that unashamedly we stamped on our coins for the whole world to see: "In God We Trust." So long as we place our nation second to One, we shall be second to none.
—J. R. BROKHOFF

AMERICA IS BEFORE US

676. I think the true discovery of America is before us. I think the true fulfillment of our spirit, of our people, of our mighty and immortal land, is yet to come. I think the true discovery of our own democracy is still before us. And I think that all these things are certain as the morning, as inevitable as noon. I think I speak for most men living when I say that our America is Here, is Now, and beckons on before us, and that this glorious assurance is not only our living hope, but our dream to be accomplished.
—THOMAS WOLFE in *You Can't Go Home Again*. Copyright, 1934, 1937, 1938, 1939, 1940 by Maxwell Perkins as Executor.

677. An American clergyman was picking his way down the main street of a Polish village only a few weeks following the cessation of hostilities in Europe. The little town had been terribly battered by gunfire, and the road was littered with débris and fallen walls. At one point, as the preacher and his interpreter were clambering over a pile of rubble that blocked the doorway of what had been the town hall, they came upon a little group of men who were trying to clear away the entrance and restore some semblance of order. The villagers were very evidently interested in the American and watched his every movement with great gravity. When the two of them were fifty feet or more along their way, the interpreter said, "I wish you could have understood what one of those men said about you as you passed." "What did he say?" the preacher asked, greatly interested. "You must remember," the interpreter said, "that you are the first American these men have seen for perhaps as much as ten years. You may have been the first American one or two of them have ever seen. That is why I was sure you would be interested in knowing that one of them said, 'There goes the United States.' You see, you are all they know about the Americans."
—ROY L. SMITH in *Stewardship Studies*, Abingdon Press.

678. For many years the famous and now fortunately discarded motto which a leading newspaper blazoned across its editorial masthead, "My country, right or wrong!" was the accepted philosophy of too many patriotic Americans. Today the truly patriotic American accepts John Sutherland Bonnell's revised version: "My country, when wrong, to be made right; when right, to be kept right."

679. We here in America have the vitalizing idea and the promising hope for which men live. The idea is not fully planted in fertile ground. Our conception of democracy is a democracy that puts its trust in the people. It is based on the worth of the human personality against deadly invasions of power. It stresses human dignity and individual diversity. It holds that a free society must not tolerate differences but blend them in an inner strength. It knows that national unity cannot come from an imposed conformity. Its faith has a univer-

sal appeal, deeply rooted in human necessities and in human aspiration. It is predicated on the age-old principle that no prison can confine the human spirit. A freedom-thirsty world cannot be kept permanently in chains. Ultimately for all tyranny comes the final death knock on the door. Sooner or later the resurgent forces of the human spirit break through the barriers.
—RAYMOND B. FOSDICK in *Within Our Power,* Longmans, Green & Co., Inc.

680. America's greatest contribution to human society has come not from her wealth or weapons or ambitions, but from her ideas; from the moral sentiments of human liberty and human welfare embodied in the Declaration of Independence and the Bill of Rights. We must cling to these truths, for these are everlasting and universal aspirations. In the words of Lincoln: "It was not the mere separation of the colonies from the motherland, but the sentiment in the Declaration of Independence which gave liberty not alone to the people of this country, but hope to all the world. It was that which gave promise that in due time the weights should be lifted from the shoulders of all men, and that all should have an equal chance." Throughout its history, America has given hope, comfort and inspiration to freedom's cause in all lands. The reservoir of good will and respect for America was not built up by American arms or intrigue; it was built upon our deep dedication to the cause of human liberty and human welfare.
—ADLAI E. STEVENSON in *Call to Greatness,* Harper & Bros. Copyright, 1954, by Adlai Ewing Stevenson.

681. Men who have served well their day and generation somehow become one with the heritage their lives have helped to shape. This is illustrated by Esther Forbes in her biography *Paul Revere and the World He Lived In,* in which she describes the famous midnight ride of the patriot with these words: "So away, down the moonlit road, goes Paul Revere and the Larkin horse, galloping into history, art, editorials, folklore, poetry; the beat of those hooves never to be forgotten. The man, his bold dark face bent, his hands light on the reins, his body giving to the flowing rhythm beneath him, becoming, as it were, something greater than himself—not merely one man riding one horse on a certain lonely night of long ago, but a symbol to which his countrymen can yet turn. Paul Revere had started on a ride which, in a way, has never ended."
—Houghton Mifflin Co.

RESPONSIBILITY OF FREE MEN

682. The late Gutzon Borglum, who sculptured the gigantic masterpiece which is Mt. Rushmore today, used to say that figures of Washington, Jefferson, Roosevelt, and Lincoln had been there in the mountain for the whole 40,000,000 years of its existence. All he had to do, he said, was to dynamite away 400,000 tons of granite to bring the heroic figures into view!

Integrity, faith in freedom and the common man, private morality in public office, and statesmanship above politics are the eternal qualities of mind and spirit that make any nation great. May we here dedicate ourselves to blasting away all that which obscures them from view!
—RAYMOND E. BALCOMB in *Pulpit Digest.*

683. J. B. Priestley once said: "We should behave toward our country as women behave toward the men they love. A loving wife will do anything for her husband except stop criticizing and trying to improve him. We should cast the same affectionate but sharp glance at our country. We should love it, but also insist on telling it all its faults. The noisy, empty patriot, not the critic, is the dangerous citizen."

684. A recent writer on political theory dropped into the middle of his erudite discourse this true and homely statement: "A man should not say: 'I live in a democracy,' but rather, 'I experienced democracy last Tuesday afternoon.'" How do we experience democracy on a snowy Tuesday afternoon? I experienced democracy the other evening when I met a man voluntarily and honestly seeking a solution to a difficult civic problem. Nobody demands it of him, but he is so fine that he demands it of himself. I experienced democracy not long ago when I visited with a labor leader, honestly considering the problems of labor and in dustry with fair-minded courage.
—Harold Blake Walker in *The Presbyterian Tribune.*

685. Carl Sandburg when presented the Gold Medal for history and biography by the Academy of Arts and Letters said: "We find it momentous that Lincoln used the word 'responsibility' nearly as often as he used the word 'freedom.' The free men of the world of arts and letters can well ask themselves, every day and almost as a ritual: 'Who paid for my freedom, and what the price, and am I somehow beholden?' The question is not rhetorical. It is a burning and terrible historical question."
—From *Home Front Memo.* Copyright, 1943, by Carl Sandburg. Reprinted by permission of Harcourt, Brace and Company, Inc.

686. In the Constitutional Convention, Benjamin Franklin stressed the necessity of prayer and emphasized that if this nation did not place its trust in God, it could not endure. When Franklin came out of the Convention, it is related that a lady asked him, "What shall it be, Mr. Franklin, a monarchy or a republic?" Franklin responded, "A republic, if you can *keep it.*" To keep our republic we must keep our religious faith strong.
—Luther W. Youngdahl in *Great Preaching Today,* Alton M. Motter, editor, published in 1953 by Harper & Bros. Used by permission.

687. A Dutch boy said to me in Amsterdam, "I don't like the English. Wherever an Englishman stands, he thinks that is England." Well, this is both irritating and admirable. It means that an Englishman never stands alone but feels that he has the backing of his people and a responsibility to them.
—Gerald Kennedy in *Go Inquire of the Lord,* Harper & Bros.

688. A young woman visited the battlefield of Gettysburg, and her comment was that it was the first time in her life she had ever thought of the Civil War as anything more than reading matter. It is a healthy experience to discover that the great struggles of the past for democracy, liberty, decent economic conditions, and equality of opportunity have been more than reading matter; they have demanded and still demand qualities of wisdom, courage, farsightedness, self-sacrifice invested in social causes, that make the good life in terms of them a long way from simple.
—Harry Emerson Fosdick

689. During the hearings [of the Senate Crime Committee] one of the questions I asked [Frank] Costello was, "Realizing all that America has done for you, what have you ever done for America as a good citizen?" He didn't have the re-

motest idea what I meant and, after deep thought, he lamely answered, "Well, I . . . I paid my taxes!" We all know that there are many things, besides paying taxes, that we can do as individuals, as good citizens, to uphold the magnificent traditions of America.

—From: *The Return to Morality,* by CHARLES W. TOBEY. Copyright 1952 by Charles W. Tobey, reprinted by permission of Doubleday & Company, Inc.

690. A certain dairyman objected to having his cows inspected for tuberculosis and ran the inspector off with a shotgun. In justification of his drastic action, he said, "I am free, white, and twenty-one, and no government official is going to tell me how to run my business." He forgot something. He forgot that his freedom to sell milk ends where the rights of babies to health begin. He needed to be told: "Ye have been called unto liberty; only use not your liberty for an occasion to the flesh, but by love serve one another." Without a keen sense of social obligation liberty is dangerous.

—W. B. SELAH in *The Upper Room Pulpit.*

691. Professor Muehl of Yale Divinity School tells of visiting a fine old ancestral home in Connecticut. The aged owner was the last of a distinguished New England family and she was proudly showing him through the house. Over the fireplace he noticed an ancient rifle that piqued his interest. He asked if he might take it down and examine it. She replied: "Oh, I am afraid that wouldn't be safe. You see, it is all loaded and primed to fire. My great-grandfather kept it there in constant readiness against the moment when he might strike a blow for the freedom of the colonies." Professor Muehl said, "Then he died before the Revolution came?" "No," she answered, "he lived to a ripe old age and died in 1802, but he just never had any confidence in General Washington."

—RALPH W. SOCKMAN

CHALLENGE OF OUR HOUR

692. On December 15, 1952, a new shrine of freedom was dedicated in Washington, D. C. The Declaration of Independence, the Constitution of the United States, and the Bill of Rights were unveiled in their new home, the National Archives Building. By day they are now on public display in helium-filled cases covered with amber glass to prevent deterioration. At night the entire shrine descends into the protective custody of a fifty-ton, fireproof, bombproof vault. . . . Recent decades have witnessed a new affirmation, on a world scale, of fundamental rights and expanded effort in their behalf, but also widespread threats to their preservation and drastic curtailment of their free exercise. . . . Yet at this very time, in many lands freedoms once enjoyed are deteriorating or being buried in the darkness of totalitarian repression or democratic fear.

—S. PAUL SCHILLING in *The Church and Social Responsibility,* J. Richard Spann, ed., Abingdon Press.

693. Those who know the totalitarian society only by hearsay cannot even imagine what it means to be eternally immersed in fear, dependent on the tricks of protective hypocrisy. Under the Soviets, schizophrenia is almost a way of life. There is the outer and public self, conforming with the official rules, and under it is another self, revealed only to trusted friends or hidden even from them and from yourself.

—EUGENE LYONS in *Our Secret Allies,* Duell, Sloan & Pearce, Inc.

694. Dr. Umphrey Lee, in an address at Drew University, once said, quite pointedly: "The democracies believe in the truth that wakes you up so that you will do something. The totalitarian states believe in propaganda that seeks to make you do something before you wake up." Only in democracy are men challenged to enter into fullness of life with minds alert and spirits free. In the last analysis the advocates of tyranny disguised as security make men into puppets, whereas the advocates of democracy transform puppets into men.
—LOWELL M. ATKINSON in *The Upper Room Pulpit.*

695. There is more good life to the square inch [in America] than any place else in the world [but] we need the Three Ps the Communist have: a philosophy, a program and a passion. . . . We must learn to wage peace as boldly as we wage war. . . . We are noted for salesmanship but we sell the wrong things. . . . We have kept silent about our spiritual possessions, which really have the power to kindle human minds.
—ELTON TRUEBLOOD

696. Maxwell Anderson's play, *Barefoot in Athens,* concerns the last days of Socrates and portrays the courage of a man when he is true to his highest convictions, when he has a cause which demands his highest devotion. With these words Socrates pleads that Athens, famed for her righteousness and justice, not do this unjust deed of condemning him to death: "I have been called Socrates the Wise in mockery sometimes. But if this judgment is carried out I shall be called Socrates the Wise in earnest. . . . And so for me this death would be great good fortune, but I cannot welcome it because in just so much as it brightens my name it blackens the name of Athens. And quite simply and honestly, citizens, I love Athens more than myself." In the preface Mr. Anderson writes: "Things came about as Socrates had anticipated—his death made him famous, made his city infamous."
—WILLIAM SLOANE ASSOCIATES

LABOR DAY

WORKERS WITH GOD

697. Over every composition Johann Sebastian Bach wrote the words "To the Glory of God." Whatever we do, regardless of our occupation we must learn to glorify God in our work. Life becomes significant when we do our work in terms of God. Our purpose in life is not just to make a living, for life is far too precious to waste in just making our bread and butter. We must glorify God in the way we make our bread and the way we use the energy which bread offers.

—KARL H. A. REST

698. The way a man looks upon his work will have a decisive influence on whether he does it as his vocation. Sir George MacLeod, of the Iona Community, relates a conversation between a Scotch clergyman and a workman riding together on a train. The cleric managed to guide the conversation into religious topics, and finally asked the man beside him, "As a Christian, what do you do?" "I bake bread," the man replied. "Yes, I know. But as a *Christian,* what do you do?" "I bake bread," was the steady response.

—JOHN L. CASTEEL in *Rediscovering Prayer,* Association Press.

699. The late Dr. H. R. Mackintosh of Scotland, in one of his sermons, tells the story of a visitor who attended the prayer meeting of Robertson of Irvine (a Scottish divine of a bygone generation). He was impressed by one of Robertson's elders. "Who is that man who has just offered prayer?" he asked. "That," replied Robertson, "is an elder of mine who lives in communion with God and makes shoes."

—JOHN SHORT in *Triumphant Believing,* Chas. Scribner's Sons.

700. When someone asks: "What's your racket? What do you do for a living?" what will be your answer? I lay brick, I sell pants, I perform operations? I make thirty-five dollars a week, fourteen dollars a day, 100,000 dollars a year? Or will it be, may it be, "I am helping God build a better world."

—ROBERT I. KAHN in *Pulpit Digest.*

701. During morning watch at a summer conference I looked and listened as a train moved in the distance. I thrilled to the throbbing of the power of the diesel motors. I thought of the tracks upon which the train moved. They were made from ore, taken by man from the earth, refined and fashioned into rails. I thought of the elaborate system by which a dispatcher miles away controlled the movements of many trains. I thought of the cargo being carried in the cars. There was food, clothing, and the tools by which men work. "Yes," I mused, "this is a magnificent world, created by God to be discovered and used by man."

—LEWIS R. ROGERS

702. One of Murillo's paintings shows the interior of a convent kitchen. Angels are busily engaged doing the work of cooking and dishwashing. All is done with such heavenly grace that you forget that pots are pots and pans are pans, and you only think how beautiful kitchen work is, just the sort of work angels would do. The humblest duty is a bit of God's will and shines with heavenly radiance.
—J. R. MILLER

703. A Vermont editor said of Warren Austin as he struggled with the heavy and perplexing problems of the United Nations, "He ain't a hero. Warren's just a Vermonter doing the job that God laid out for him."
—CHARLES M. CROWE in *On Living with Yourself,* Abingdon Press.

704. Let us imagine that on the grounds of "The Hermitage," near Nashville, a few generations ago there was stacked a cord of wood cut neatly into logs. The logs did not get there by accident; they did not put themselves there. What was the cause of their being there? You see at once that there are two possible answers: one, the scientific, in terms of haulage; the other historical, in terms of human activity. But let us analyze the situation in more detail. In order to make a tree into logs you must have a saw. It is a saw that makes logs. The saw, then, was the cause of the logs under discussion. But, as we know, a saw does not make logs of its own initiative; the hand and purpose of a sawyer are required. And while it seems accurate to say that the saw causes the logs, it is more adequate to say that the sawyer causes them. But, after all, the sawyer acted upon instructions; the tree was not his; he had no particular desire to saw logs; he would much rather have been idle in his cabin. The real cause of the logs, then, was General Jackson himself, who instructed the sawyer to cut down the tree and saw it up. And why did General Jackson act as he did? I suppose because he regarded it as his duty to society, to his dependents, and to God that he should take care of his plantation, keep his buildings warm in winter and exercise the responsibilities of his calling. He acted in the way of duty. Thus the cause of the logs, in the end, was General Jackson's sense of duty, his duty to society, to his dependents, and so to God.
—NATHANIEL MICKLEM in *Ultimate Questions,* Abingdon Press.

705. During the war I remember seeing the picture of an altar set up for Holy Communion, which was simply an actual work-bench. After it ceased to be used for obviously religious purposes, it went back to being a work-bench again. I like to think that the boards which upheld the sacred vessels later felt the hammer-blows of men making doors and window-frames and shelves for houses.
—SAMUEL M. SHOEMAKER in *Pulpit Digest.*

706. Above the Mersey River at Liverpool, England, stands what remains of St. Nicholas Parish Church, badly damaged by bombs in World War II. Formerly those who entered it had to turn their backs on the marketplace, the harbor, and the wheat ships anchored there, and then found themselves facing the communion table in semidarkness at the far end. After the war, as George MacLeod graphically tells, a prefabricated hut was built on the ruins, but facing the other way. What had been the porch became the sanctuary, and the tall doors became windows which with-

out stained glass afforded an unobstructed view of marketplace and river. Communicants now see the bread of the common meal on the holy table in the same frame of reference as the wheat produced in men's common life. In such a setting worship gives new meaning to work, and work brings deepened reality to worship. He who knows God as Holy Spirit sees all life in just such a setting.
—S. PAUL SCHILLING in *Religion in Life.*

707. [An] eager young man . . . visited the aged James Russell Lowell at the turn of the century. Thrilled again at his stories of the struggle against slavery, the young man exclaimed, "How I wish I could have stood at your side then!" The aged warrior for righteousness stepped to the window, pulled aside the curtain to reveal the smoking stacks of a great industrial plant with wretched hovels housing its workers, and he asked, *"What more do you want?"*
—HAROLD A. BOSLEY in *Preaching on Controversial Issues,* published in 1953 by Harper & Brothers.

JOY IN WORK

708. If you observe a really happy man you will find him building a boat, writing a symphony, educating his son, growing double dahlias in his garden, or looking for dinosaur eggs in the Gobi Desert. He will not be searching for happiness as if it were a collar button that has rolled under the radiator. He will not be striving for it as a goal in itself.
—W. B. WOLFE in *How to Be Happy Though Human,* Rinehart & Co., Inc.

709. So much unhappiness, it seems to me, is due to nerves, and bad nerves are the result of having nothing to do, or doing a thing badly, unsuccessfully, or incompetently. Of all the unhappy people in the world, the unhappiest are those who have not found something they want to do. . . . True happiness comes to him who does his work well, followed by a relaxing and refreshing period of rest. True happiness comes from the right amount of work for the day.
—LIN YUTANG in *On the Wisdom of America,* John Day Co., Inc.

710. L. P. Jacks tells how he saw a remarkably beautiful astrolabe in a collection of ancient instruments. It was the work of an ancient artificer in India. Round the edge of the fine brasswork there ran an inscription in delicate Arabic characters: "This astrolabe is the work of Hussein Ali; mechanic and mathematician and servant of the Most High God. May His name be exalted throughout the universe." When men come to regard their work in this way, they have at last found joy in it. For the sake of him whom they reverence they put forth their best efforts. The result is good workmanship. More important still, they themselves are better characters.
—T. R. DAVIES in *The Upper Room Pulpit.*

711. Work is doing what you don't *now* enjoy for the sake of a future which you clearly see and desire. Drudgery is doing under strain what you don't now enjoy and for no end that you can now appreciate.
—RICHARD C. CABOT in *What Men Live By,* Houghton Mifflin Co.

712. Joseph Jefferson, the famous actor, spent a great deal of time in his garden. When asked why, he said that with the coming of old age many of the hopes and expectations of life faded, but when he planted things in his garden, he could at least look forward to their flowering and fruition.

—CLARENCE EDWARD MACARTNEY in *You Can Conquer,* Abingdon Press.

MINISTRY OF WORK

713. The word "vocation" has been debased in the modern world by being made synonymous with "occupation," but it is one of the gains of our time that the old word is beginning to regain its original meaning of "calling." "Behold your calling, brethren," is the old text which is now achieving new significance. On the purely secular basis the term "vocation" is practically meaningless, since, unless God really is, there is no one to do the calling, but, on the Christian basis, it is a reasonable word. It still refers, in many cases, to occupation, but the conception is that each occupation can and must be conceived as a *ministry.*

—ELTON TRUEBLOOD in *Your Other Vocation,* Harper & Bros.

714. If ours is God's world, any true work for the improvement of man's life is a sacred task and should be undertaken with this aspect in mind. . . . No religion is irrelevant if it helps people to see the hidden glory of the common things they do. . . . People with no sense of the glory of their work, people from whom has departed the whole idea of work as sacramental, will not long do a good job. Our civilization which ceases to advance is already . . . in full decay.

—ELTON TRUEBLOOD in *Personal Security Through Faith* by Lowell Russell Ditzen, Henry Holt & Co., Inc.

715. F. O. Matthiessen in *The Achievement of T. S. Eliot* says there was in Eliot the realization that nothing great has ever been created without the creator's "surrounding himself wholly to the work to be done," without a continual self-sacrifice "of himself as he is at the moment to something which is more valuable."

—THEODORE PARKER FERRIS in *This Is the Day* (Greenwich: The Seabury Press, 1954), p. 52. Used by permission of the publisher.

716. Several brothers I knew in New England were in a very prosperous engineering and textile business. When reversal of fortune came, one of them through his experience in philanthropic enterprises was made the superintendent of a hospital. He said to me, "It's a joy not to have to work for profit." He was thereafter exempted from that necessity, but I could not help thinking that his philanthropic hospital could not be sustained without the equally Christian vocation of some who stayed within the profit system and with ethical responsibility and social concern made it possible for such enterprises to be supported. Both were phases of Christian vocation.

—CHARLES L. SEASHOLES

717. A weekly magazine recently carried a cartoon of . . . a sleek, pampered visitor . . . in an artist's studio. The studio is bare save for finished and unfinished pictures, an easel and a table. The visitor is looking at the pictures; the artist is staring out of the window. The visitor is saying "What's lacking in your pictures, Carter, is lacking in you. You haven't suffered enough!" Someone other than this well-padded tycoon could have made the observation with greater consistency. But it stands, nevertheless, as an observation concerning us all. What is lacking in our work, whether artists, doctors, lawyers, preachers, businessmen, secretaries, clerks, is first lacking in *us*! Our work is as competent or incompetent, as good or as bad, as

magnificent or puny, as ourselves: no more, no less!
—ALBERT E. DAY in *An Autobiography of Prayer,* published in 1952 by Harper & Brothers.

718. One day in the heat of the African summer, Dr. Albert Schweitzer was working on his hospital. He was lifting boards, nailing them on, when he saw a native standing in the shade of a tree, dressed in a white suit, watching. Dr. Schweitzer said to this man, "Would you give me a hand with this timber? Would you carry that end for me?" The man dressed in his white suit said, "I can't, I'm an intellectual. I have been away to school. It is not fitting for me to do this kind of work." Dr. Schweitzer, looking at him, smiled a little bit, and said, "I used to be an intellectual, too, but I couldn't live up to it." We must never become too proud to do honest work, to accept a useful responsibility.
—Reprinted with permission of publishers from *You Can Master Life* by JOHN H. CROWE. Copyright, 1954, by Prentice-Hall, Inc., 70 Fifth Avenue, New York 11, New York.

719. Bernanos' terse epithet "Our civilization builds machines and destroys people" was illustrated when a builder of prefabricated houses decided that he would demonstrate how swiftly a home could be constructed. Work began on a bare city lot at eight in the morning. With precision and efficiency each workman did the tasks assigned to him. By midafternoon two large cranes began to lift the slab walls of the house into position. As the walls were eased into place, a hapless workman was crushed between the slow-moving partitions. The walls had to be pulled apart to let the man escape. In the speed, complexity, and magnitude of modern technology too often man is the victim.
—HARRY K. ZELLER, JR.

THE DIGNITY OF LABOR

720. The idea that there is more dignity in mental work than in manual work has no basis whatsoever in scripture or in the Christian faith. It is rather like the situation I found on a campus where I had come to lecture on Christian vocation. My young guide, taking me to a class, said gaily, "I can't imagine what you are going to say to *this* class: they are sanitation engineers." Nineteen centuries of culture lay behind that remark —the idea that Christianity has more to do with liberal arts than with engineers. And yet, there is nothing more intimately related to Christianity than sanitation engineering, if you think of it as a medium for maintaining the health of the community.
—ALEXANDER MILLER in *The Intercollegian.*

721. Connie Shaklin, a character in *Round the Bend* by Nevil Shute, says: "We [engineers] are men of understanding and of education, on whom is laid responsibility that men may travel in these aeroplanes as safely as if they were sitting by the well in the cool of the evening. We are not men like camel drivers or shepherds, and God will demand much more from us than from them."
—Copyright 1951 by William Morrow & Co., Inc.

722. An ancient story relates that Solomon upon the occasion of the dedication of the Temple said that the artisan who had contributed most to the noble structure should reign for a day. When the workers were led into the throne room the king was surprised to see a black-

smith in the seat of honor. "I fashioned the tools with which the others labored," he explained.
—WILL A. SESSIONS, JR.

723. One of the world's greatest paintings is *The Angelus* by Millet. The word "angelus" means a prayer and that picture is of two people praying in the field. On the horizon is the church steeple and we presume the bell is ringing a call to prayer. To understand the true significance of the picture, however, you must study where the rays of the afternoon sun fall. They are not on the bowed heads of the men and women, neither do the rays fall on the church steeple. They fall on the wheelbarrow and the common tools. It is the artist's tribute to the dignity of work.
—CHARLES L. ALLEN in *When the Heart Is Hungry,* Fleming H. Revell Co.

724. The labors of James Henry Breasted, the great Egyptologist, must have been monotonous and rigorous as he translated the hieroglyphics of ancient Egypt. In addition he suffered many personal troubles and was beset by nagging worries. Here, however, is what he said about his work: "I am always thankful for work, which does not destroy feeling nor render it callous, but is like a faithful friend who gently leads one into a lovely garden of consolation and noble interest where aches and anxieties are soothed into sweet forgetfulness."
—JACK FINEGAN in *Clear of the Brooding Cloud,* Abingdon Press. Quotation from *Pioneer to the Past,* Chas. Scribner's Sons.

725. If a man could look at himself and the work he had done at the end of a day, and say, it's been good today . . . it's been as right and as fine and as good as I could make it . . . it's taken the best there is in me to do it, and it's made me bigger and better to do it . . . then that man was at home, wherever he was.
—JANICE HOLT GILES in *The Enduring Hills.* Copyright, 1950, by W. L. Jenkins, The Westminster Press. Used by permission.

726. Elbert Hubbard, the brilliant eccentric, once printed on the front cover page of his magazine, *The Philistine,* this wholesome advice: *Remember the Weekday and Keep It Holy.* This is to say that there is a sanctity about labor which is as real and as significant as any worship.
—ROY L. SMITH in *Stewardship Studies,* Abingdon Press.

727. A great American industrial statesman, Clarence Francis, once said: "You can buy a man's time, you can buy a man's physical presence at a given place; you can even buy a measured number of skilled muscular motions per hour or day. But you cannot buy enthusiasm; you cannot buy initiative; you cannot buy loyalty; you cannot buy the devotion of hearts, minds and souls. You have to earn these things."
—CHARLES H. PERCY in *This I Believe.* Copyright, 1954, by Help, Inc. Reprinted by permission of Simon and Schuster, Inc.

WORLD-WIDE COMMUNION

ONE CHURCH IN CHRIST

728. Voldi in *The Big Fisherman* by Lloyd C. Douglas says: "The man [Jesus] has a compelling voice. I can't describe it or the effect of it. It's a unifying voice that converts a great crowd of mutually distrustful strangers into a tight little group of blood relatives."
—Houghton Mifflin Co.

729. One of the most interesting buildings of the Festival of Britain was called "The Lion & Unicorn" and exhibited Britain's basic culture. At the center on a large podium was a heroic Runic cross with this inscription: "One cross—one hundred ways to God." All the hundreds of ways to God come to one cross.
—William Frederick Dunkle, Jr.

730. David Starr Jordan described the search for the Infinite as a mountain climb. Separate bands of people are struggling up the steep slopes, desperately straining to reach the summit. Each group has chosen its own path; it is certain that it alone travels the right one; is calling to the others: "Come with us. We'll show you the way. We have found the real road." The truth is that from the vantage point of the mountaintop, where only God has a panoramic view of the climbers below, all the paths lead to the summit. All the bands can attain the coveted objective, if they continue climbing upward instead of diverting themselves with petty pleasures and costly conflicts that constantly drag them downward. They need not join each other on the way up. Nonetheless, they will some day find themselves standing on the highest peaks together, *if* they never stop their search after God.
—Reprinted with permission of publishers from *The Power of Faith* by Louis Binstock. Copyright, 1952, by Prentice-Hall, Inc., 70 Fifth Avenue, New York 11, New York.

731. A farmer enlisted the aid of some friends in searching for his small daughter who was lost. Despite her tender years and the fact that she was quite ill, somehow she had managed to leave her home and wander away in the tall weeds and grass which stretched away for some distance from the farmhouse. During several hours the farmer and his friends searched fruitlessly, the farmer growing ever more anxious as it commenced to get darker and colder. Then, one of the searchers came forward with a suggestion. "The grass and weeds are quite thick," he said. "It is easy for us to miss many places and go over other places several times. I suggest that all of us join hands, mark our starting place and go through the undergrowth somewhat like a large rake. Then we'll be sure not to skip any place." All agreed it was a good idea and they started out with joined hands. In less than half an hour they came upon the little girl. But, alas,

it was too late. She was dead. Then the farmer lifted up his voice in an anguished cry, "In God's name, why didn't we join hands before?"
—EDWIN T. SETTLE in *Religion in Life.*

732. A once well-known dean of theology used to say that he scarcely believed that the devil is terrified when he sees a Presbyterian forefinger, or a Lutheran middle-finger, or an Episcopalian thumb, or a Methodist or Baptist third finger pointed at him. It is when those fingers and thumb were doubled up in one compelling fist that his Satanic Majesty began to take notice.
—DAVID A. MACLENNAN in *The Pulpit Digest.*

733. John Wesley once told of a dream in which he stood at the gates of hell. He asked the gatekeeper if there were Catholics there. "Many," was the answer. "And Presbyterians?" "Many," was again the answer. "And Methodists?" "Many." Later he stood before the gates of heaven, where he asked the same questions. "There are no Catholics, no Presbyterians, no Methodists here," was the answer, "only Christians."
—WILL A. SESSIONS, JR.

734. There is in India a community called the Ezhava community, numbering about 800,000 souls. About twenty years ago the leaders of that movement, knowing little of Christianity but seeing what it had done for people in certain situations, decided they would lead their people into the Christian church. It is reported, and I think reliably, that a Hindu politician hearing of that decision went to talk with them. He said that he heard they were going to lead their people into the Christian church and asked which church they would choose. They were startled to know that there is not one Christian church but many, and fearing to lose the unity that did exist within their community, did not seek to make their people Christians. History adds to that record the significant footnote of a recent report on how many members of that community in India today are members of the Communist party.
—EUGENE L. SMITH in *Religion in Life.*

735. Henry Sloane Coffin tells a bracing story about an African slave who became an elder in a Christian church. The slave had frequently been sold and resold. One day he fled from his master to the settlement of the Livingstonian Mission where he heard Robert Laws preach on the great peace verses of Isaiah. He listened as the preacher urged the people to open their hearts to the love of God in Christ which would put an end to war among the tribes. "Put your faith in God," he heard him say. "Obey his Word, and the leopard shall yet lie down with the kid and the lamb in the same kraal in peace." In his heart the slave said, "White man, you lie!" But the slave lived to see the day when the leopard and the lamb were at peace with one another. He saw how Ngoni and Tonga, once bitter enemies, knelt together at the same Communion table. The prayer of Christ "That they all may be one" and "That the world may believe that thou hast sent me" has often been heard.
—ARMIN C. OLDSEN

736. Bishop Berggrav of Norway, the brave and saintly church leader who suffered house arrest during the Nazi occupation of his country, made one of the significant addresses at the World Council of Churches. He pointed out that the spirit of unity in Christ has been at work in the Church although the results

are far short of what they should be. He said: "Our unity in Christ, if taken seriously, prevents us from self-aggrandizement and the feeling of having a monopoly on the truth, or of being entitled to be the judges of our fellow churches, rather than being their brethren in Christ. There exists no master church above the others. What we have got is a church family in Christ. So I think we may say that the unity in Christ has started changing the world's church atmosphere."
—Ralph W. Sockman

737. In the good old horse and buggy days, a boy was driving along a road with a farmer very skilled in the finer flickings of the whip. When a fly settled on the horse's back a swift flick of the whip's cord would remove it without appreciably disturbing the horse. Did a bee settle on a roadside flower? Instantly it would disappear under the accurately aimed blow of the supple lash. Only when the vehicle passed near a tree from which hung a wasp's nest were the driver and his whip impressively immobile. "Why didn't you use the whip on those wasps?" asked the boy. "Well," the whip expert answered, "they're organized." Sects no less than insects multiply their effectiveness when they unite with one another.
—*The Ecumenical Courier*

738. Many years ago Rev. S. Parkes Cadman said, in addressing a conference of ministers, "If you are trying to shut yourself in behind your own denominational walls, I suggest that you climb up occasionally, and look over to see how many splendid people you have shut out."
—Roy L. Smith in *New Light from Old Lamps,* Abingdon Press.

739. Winifred Holtby wrote a short story, "The Voice of God," in which she imagined a man who invented a machine that could pick up voices from the past. It was announced that an attempt would be made to pick up the voice of Jesus. Great crowds gathered in Wembley Stadium in London to hear this wonder. They stood quietly and listened and at last the voice came through. Their silence turned to a puzzled murmur and the murmur turned to angry shoutings, until at last the machine was smashed. The voice spoke not in English but in Aramaic.
—F. N. James in *The Pulpit.* Copyrighted by the Christian Century Foundation and used by permission.

740. During World War I a cartoon pictured the so-called Christian nations of Europe and America engaged in a death struggle in an arena. The Japanese, Chinese, and African people were viewing the bloody spectacle with bewilderment. A grinning Japanese was saying, "How these Christians love one another!" Of course the problem is not that true Christian people do not love one another. The problem is that so few are truly Christian.
—Armin C. Oldsen

741. A wheel symbolizes for me the relation of Christians to the world. The hub in the wheel of faith is God, and the spokes may be thought of in terms of the many devout individuals. They find a common center in God, and their lives reach from God to the rim, which is the world.
—Robert Ora Smith

CHURCH AS FELLOWSHIP

742. One of the symbols which stand for the Apostle Paul is the rayed cross. It is the Latin cross with a sunburst of rays

going off from the center of the cross. It represents the extension of the gospel to the ends of the earth. Paul's ministry extended the fellowship—the Christian fellowship—beyond the confines of Galilee and out to much of the then known world.
—J. MANNING POTTS in *The Upper Room.*

743. When I poke a fire, only the tip of the poker need touch the glowing coal, but every atom in the poker is involved, and so is the strength of my arm. It seems to me that we need to follow closely the training which Jesus gave to the disciples. He welded them into a unity as strong as a poker: a poker, we might say, made of very different metals, and welded into an alloy, by his grace and love, stronger than any one metal was before. That united fellowship went out into the world to preach and to heal. The individual in that fellowship did not heal through any freak endowment as a healer given to him as an individual. Where he healed he was the striking point of the whole poker. The whole fellowship was behind him and behind the fellowship was the supernatural power of Christ.
—LESLIE D. WEATHERHEAD in *Religion in Life.*

744. Some time ago, when I was flying back from North Dakota, I was seated at a window of the plane. It was at the time of the Red River flood. A man who was sitting beside me seemed quite rude as he kept looking over me and glancing down at the water-covered fields over which we were flying. Suddenly, with excitement, he pointed and exclaimed: "That's where I live, right down there!" I looked again—with him. Water covered the entire countryside. Once more it dawned upon me that Jesus' prayer for a world that lives like a family is not a petition of idealism; rather it is the most realistic prayer that has ever been offered. If this man's wheat crop is lost, in some tiny, minute way, I too will pay more for bread. Whether I admit it or not, I am his brother, sociologically speaking. He is my brother whether I confess the truth or not. That about which Jesus prayed . . . is a world in which we sincerely, honestly, and happily say, "Our Father."
—G. RAY JORDAN in *Beyond Despair.* Copyright 1955. Used by permission of The Macmillan Co.

745. Dr. H. Richard Niebuhr, of Yale, has developed the symbol of "trialectic" to indicate that the encounter of a faith never takes place in a vacuum. When man responds to life's demands he always does so in a living context, which both colors his understanding of the demand itself and also frames and supports his response. The Christian faith involves a three-way relationship—God and man, God and the fellowship, man and the fellowship. Without the triple character, the whole relationship tends to become abstract or mechanical.
—CHARLES DUELL KEAN in *Making Sense Out of Life.* Copyright, 1954, by W. L. Jenkins, The Westminster Press. Used by permission.

746. Richard Llewellyn in *How Green Was My Valley* offers this remarkable description of the work and influence of the Welsh pastor: "When Mr. Gruffydd started his sermon, he always put a few sheets of paper on the ledge by the Bible, but never once was he seen to use them. He started to speak as though he were talking to a family, quietly, in a voice not loud, not soft. But presently you would hear a note coming into it and your hair would go cold at the back. It would drop down and down, until you could hear what he said only from the shapes of his mouth, but then he would throw a rock of sound into the quiet and bring your blood splashing up inside you, and keep it boiling for minutes while the royal thunder of his voice proclaimed again the Kingdom of God, and the Principality of Christ the Man. That is how we came from Chapel every Sunday re-armed and re-armoured against the world, re-strengthened, and full of fight."

—Copyright 1940. Used by permission of The Macmillan Co.

747. A man was once impressed by the courtesy of the conductor toward the passengers on a streetcar. After the crowd had thinned out, he spoke to the conductor about it. "Well," the conductor explained, "about five years ago I read in the paper about a man who was included in a will just because he was polite. 'What in the world?' I thought. 'It might happen to me.' So I started treating passengers like people. And it makes me feel so good that now I don't care if I never get a million dollars." This is both an example and a picture of the life that assures rewards. Ours is a faith that goes beyond rewards as a part of a bargain or rewards as a lure to virtue, to rewards as the satisfying experiences that follow Christian living.

—Rolland W. Schloerb

THE EMERGING WORLD FELLOWSHIP

748. In 1648 when our Confession of Faith was written, not a word was put into it about Christian missions. How could there be? Few then knew anything about Asia, Africa, South America; even North America had only begun to be populated. The world as we now know it was simply not in the thoughts of the men who wrote our creed. Now, these are different times. The man who says, I believe in Christianity for Americans but I do not see any use in it for Africans or Asiatics, is just as foolish and behind-the-times as the man who says, I believe in Christianity on Bardstown Road but not on Jefferson Street. . . . A man of the 17th century could afford to shut his eyes to the needs of far-off lands. You cannot do that now because there are no far-off lands any more. . . . I say 20th century Christians must have a 20th century horizon. We must take note of the facts of 20th century geography.

—Kenneth J. Foreman in *The Upper Room Pulpit.*

749. God was on an island off the coast of New Guinea which we attacked during World War II. The natives who rowed out to our ship in their dug-out canoes wore crosses about their necks, and on the shell-riddled beach of that little-known and malaria-infested island we found a lonely bamboo church. Half of it had been blown away, but the steeple still stood. The cross at the top was for each of us a symbol and a promise that the creative power of God is greater than the destructive power of man.

—Frank R. Snavely

750. One day I was riding in a jeep with a small convoy along one of the jungle trains in New Guinea. We came to a native village. A crowd of curious people soon gathered. One little fellow, about twelve years of age, came closer than any of the others. He seemed to be particularly interested in the uniform I was wearing. Touching me lightly on the sleeve, he pointed to the cross which as a chaplain I wore on my collar. Speaking in broken English, he said something

I shall never forget. He said, "Me Jesus man, too!"
—LEE EDWIN WALKER

751. The preaching of missions today must seek to expand the horizons of Christians in such fashion that they will have a vivid sense of being part of an emerging world fellowship. The tragedy is that the world of so many Christians is so small. They are like Nathaniel Hawthorne, who wrote during the Civil War to his friend Bridge: "If compelled to choose, I go for the North. New England is quite as large a lump of earth as my heart can take in." The problem of many Christians is that the "lump of earth" they take in is so small. By every means at the disposal of the preacher, he must seek to bring a sense of the reality of the world Christian fellowship to his people. This fellowship is, as William Temple said, "the great new fact of our time."
—ROBERT G. MIDDLETON in *Missions,* Vol. 151, No. 10, p. 35.

752. Dr. Samuel M. Zwemer once declared of William Borden, the saintly young missionary who gave his life for Christ in Egypt: "Borden kept the faith, but he did not keep it to himself." The man who walks with God feels most strongly the urge to share that blessed experience with others.
—SANDFORD FLEMING in *The Upper Room Pulpit.*

753. Sooner or late, if all goes rightly, God himself will, as it were, take [the Christian] gently but firmly by the shoulders and turn him round to face the world, bidding him find therein the work which is to be his service.
—LEONARD HODGSON in *Christian Faith and Practice,* Basil Blackwell.

754. The Chamber of Commerce at Evanston, seeking to prepare the community for the privilege of receiving delegates from the entire Christian world for the World Council assembly, insisted that the citizens and particularly those who were to receive guests into their own homes should "forget their prejudices for seventeen days." The Christian, however, is responsible for more than seventeen days; he must forget his prejudices forever.
—LAWRENCE E. FISHER

UNITED NATIONS WEEK

WORLD-MINDEDNESS

755. With all its defects, with all the failures that we can check up against it, [the United Nations] still represents man's best organized hope to substitute the conference table for the battlefield. It has had its failures, but it has had its successes. Who knows what could have happened in these past years of strain and struggle if we hadn't had the United Nations? I think it is far more than merely a desirable organization in these days. Where every new invention of the scientist seems to make it more nearly possible for man to insure his own elimination from this globe, I think the United Nations has become sheer necessity.
—Dwight D. Eisenhower

756. Man is born for co-operation, not for competition or conflict. This is a basic discovery of modern science. It confirms a discovery made some two thousand years ago by one Jesus of Nazareth. In a word: it is the principle of love which embraces all mankind. It is the principle of humanity, of one world, one brotherhood of peoples. The measure of a person's humanity is the extent and intensity of his love for mankind.
—Reprinted by permission of the publisher, Abelard-Schuman, Inc., from *On Being Human* by Ashley Montagu, copyright 1950.

757. There was ever a wistfulness in Jesus' voice. A wistful look was in his eyes, a wistful mood was in his tears, a wistful cadence gave his words a rainy sweetness of tears and laughter intermingled. His custom was compassion. . . . Christ was wistful for a world; he dwelt among races of provincials. Christ whispered, trumpeted, wept, sang, preached, lived, died—all framing a wide, unprovincial word—the world.
—William A. Quayle in *Today Is Mine,* T. C. Clark, ed., Harper & Bros.

758. Our growth in our relations with mankind may be described by using three common words. The first is "harmony," which, derived from a Greek word meaning "concord," implies agreement and consideration. The second is "sympathy," originally meaning "with suffering," and suggests affinity and interrelationship, the recognition that what affects one man affects another. The sympathetic person not only shows pity and concern but shares in the joys and sorrows of another. The third word, "empathy," derived from the Greek words "in suffering," is defined as the "imaginative projection of one's own consciousness into another being." To show empathy toward another is more than to cast a sympathetic glance or to offer a helping hand; it means to enter so into another's experience that, when he is hurt, you feel pain and, when he is praised, you too are praised.

759. There was an employer who startled applicants for jobs by breaking in, apropos to nothing, with this question: "By the way, would you like to build a bridge?" If the man in sudden surprise would reply, "What? Me? Why, yes, as a matter of fact I would like to build a bridge," he was hired on the spot. For the man who wanted to bring together two separated places was sure to have imagination and constructive ideas. So it is that our Lord comes to us with that same question: "Would you like to build a bridge across the chasms separating mankind? Would you like to unite a divided world?" And if we answer in the affirmative, then we are called at once into close fellowship with him in this mighty task of healing the breach and building the new community.
—GERALD KENNEDY in *With Singleness of Heart,* Harper & Bros.

760. A small boy who was not yet a correct speller wrote on the blackboard "Untied Nations" instead of "United Nations." Unwittingly he made a mistake which the teacher promptly corrected in an unusual manner. "You will remember how to spell 'united,'" she said, "if you remember first that, before people can be united, they must be 'untied.' We must untie ourselves of selfishness and prejudice; then we are free to unite with other people."
—E. PAUL HOVEY

761. At a college convocation the president spoke of the loyalties to which each student pledges his life. These loyalties were symbolized by the four flags which flanked the speaker's stand. First, there was the flag of the United Nations. This flag is a constant reminder of the co-operative endeavor essential to peace and harmony of all men. Second, there was the American flag, expressive of the heritage and meaning of our native land. Third, there was the school flag, representing the primary loyalty to the local college community, its traditions and aspirations. "In your hearts there will be a conflict of loyalties with one flag claiming supremacy," the president said, "unless these loyalties are measured in terms of the fourth flag, the banner of Christianity. When the spirit of Christ and his Church possesses a man's heart, all loyalties are made one. Through allegiance to the Christian flag a man seeks for his home and school Christian standards. The Christian is concerned that his nation be Christlike. The Christian believes that the love of Christ will bring unity and harmony, peace and good will, to men of all nations."

762. The featured speaker at a local meeting celebrating American Education Week spoke with keen and incisive language on the kind of education the world needs today. He pointed out that our schools tend to lift our national aspirations above those of other peoples and to glorify the flag with a degree of reverence. But, he added, the atomic and hydrogen bombs offer possibilities for universal destruction, and in the future "we shall have to think of our nation as an equal unit with other nations in a world family and our flag on a par with other flags of the nations of the world. We must begin to teach these concepts in the schools of the nations, or we shall perish." There was a general agreement with the logic of his thoughts. "But—" he paused long and ominously. "But if ever the school authorities attempted to teach this in your city, you men who have today elected school leaders would be the first to join every patriotic civic group in the community and bend every effort to drive these leaders out of town!"
—HARRY K. ZELLER, JR.

763. When Norman Cousins asked Jawaharlal Nehru for his definition of democracy, the prime minister replied: "I do not presume to define anything, because to define anything that is as big as democracy is to limit it. Nevertheless, if I may vaguely suggest something, I would say that democracy is not only political, not only economic, but something of the mind, as everything is ultimately something of the mind. It involves equality of opportunity to all people, as far as possible, in the political and economic domain. It involves the freedom of the individual to grow and to make the best of his capacities and ability. It involves a certain tolerance of others and even of their opinions when they differ from yours. It involves a certain contemplative tendency and a certain inquisitive search for truth—and for, let us say, the right thing. Democracy is a dynamic, not a static, thing, and as it changes it may be that its domain will become wider and wider. Ultimately, it is a mental approach applied to our political and economic problems."
—*Who Speaks for Man?* Copyright 1953. Used by permission of The Macmillan Co.

764. In *Beyond the High Himalayas,* William O. Douglas speaks of a conversation he had in Pakistan with a Mongolian prince. The prince said that America has wealth and military power, but Russia has ideas, and "ideas usually win." Douglas asked, "But what ideas does Russia have?" and the Mongol answered, "Ideas of liberty." Douglas then described the American traditions of liberty and contrasted the Russian and American concepts of liberation. Finally the prince said: "That's wonderful, very wonderful. But the peasants of Asia do not know these things. America in their eyes is identified with their feudal lords. America is not to them the advocate of social justice." After a pause he added, "Why does not America try to set up bases in the hearts of these people rather than on their lands?"
—Copyright 1952 by William O. Douglas, reprinted by permission of Doubleday & Co., Inc.

765. In the United States Senate, Peter Marshall prayed: "Help us, our Father, to show other nations an America to imitate—not the America of loud jazz music, self-seeking indulgence, and love of money, but the America that loves fair play, honest dealing, straight talk, real freedom, and faith in God. Make us to see that it cannot be done as long as we are content to be coupon clippers on the original investment made by our forefathers. Give us faith in God and love for our fellow men, that we may have something to deposit on which the young people of today can draw interest tomorrow."
—*The Congressional Record*

766. Odd Nansen, the son of the famous Norwegian explorer, has written a day-by-day chronicle of his life in Nazi concentration camps. Here is how the book finishes: "Dear Reader, I shall stop now. This book has turned out long enough, and it may have been heavy going. But when you go to your bookseller for a new one, don't say to him as so many do, 'Now I've had enough of those wretched prison books. Give me some better kind of thing. I can't stand any more of that misery.' . . . The worst crime you can commit today, against yourself and society, is to forget what happened and sink back into indifference. What happened was worse than you have any idea of. And it was the indifference of mankind that let it take place." Nansen's warning should not go

unheeded. If we build a screen between ourselves and the great agony of the world, we are only paving the way to new miseries.

—ROBERT J. MCCRACKEN. Quotation from *From Day to Day*. Copyright 1949 G. P. Putnam's Sons.

THE PRESENT PERIL

767. Man has been more successful in making machines than achieving the will and wisdom to use his engines for humane purposes. This is the predicament of Western man. He has built up a complex civilization, but he may lose it because, in his proud hour of achievement, he has so largely lost or never developed the inner resources that are needed to keep a possible boon from becoming a calamity.

—ELTON TRUEBLOOD in *The Predicament of Modern Man*, Harper & Bros.

768. Ours is a paradoxical world. The achievements which are its glory threaten to destroy it. The nations with the highest standard of living . . . exhibit the least capacity to avoid mutual destruction in war. It would seem that the more civilized we become the more incapable of maintaining civilization we are.

—F. S. C. NORTHROP in *The Meeting of East and West*. Copyright 1946. Used by permission of The Macmillan Co.

769. For centuries we have enjoyed certain blessings: a stable law, before which the poor man and the rich man were equal; freedom within that law to believe what we pleased, to write what we pleased, to say what we pleased. . . . Today we have seen those principles challenged in the fundamentals, not by a few armchair theorists, but by great Powers supported by great armies. We have suddenly discovered that what we took for the enduring presuppositions of our life are in danger of being destroyed. Today we value freedom, I think, as we have not valued it before. Just as a man never appreciates his home so much as when he is compelled to leave it, so now we realise our inestimable blessings when they are threatened. We have been shaken out of our smugness and warned of a great peril, and in that warning lies our salvation. The dictators have done us a marvellous service in reminding us of the true values of life.

—JOHN BUCHAN in *Pilgrim's Way*, Houghton Mifflin Co. Used by permission of Tweedsmuir Trustees. Published as *Memory Hold-the-Door* by Hodder & Stoughton, Ltd.

770. Over a large part of Europe and Asia binding convictions are lacking and there is confusion, bewilderment and discord. The whole complex of traditional belief, habit and sentiment, on which convictions are founded, has collapsed. All over the world indeed the cake of custom is broken, the old gods are dethroned and none have taken their places. Mentally and spiritually most persons today are "displaced persons."

—WALTER MOBERLY in *The Crisis in the University*. Copyright 1951. Used by permission of The Macmillan Co.

771. A number of years ago the people in Los Angeles found tar deposits in which had been preserved for countless generations the bones of prehistoric mammals. These tar pits, as they are called, were traps in which animals of an earlier era were unwittingly caught and held. This tar-pit area has been excavated and landscaped so that men may get glimpses of the nature of life on the earth centuries ago. What better chance has modern man to survive in this world than those prehistoric mammals? Al-

ways we ought to thank God that in our world are those men who discern moral obligation. Sometimes we become irritated when they chastise our behavior. We'd rather go along our easy and stupid jungle paths of hate and war and then tumble at last into a tar pit and human oblivion.

772. The ultimate spiritual significance of the United Nations so far as the Western world is concerned is to compel this world, faced constantly as it is by the challenge of Communism and the challenge of the East, to fall back upon its own spiritual resources. There must be an original conviction and regeneration of the spirit expressing itself in the policies of governments and in the attitude and tone of their representatives. Because of its derivative character, the United Nations cannot provide this spiritual regeneration.

Am I to be told that the world which at its best has assigned infinite worth to the individual human soul; which has not fundamentally repudiated reason and the possibility of objective truth; which has a wonderful living deposit in the theory and practice of the arts; which has not broken away with its continuous, cumulative history; in which the university and the church are free each to obey its own principle; in which the transcendent is still worshipped not as a distant ideal but as a living God; and whose deepest vision is faith, hope and love: am I to be told that a world so burdened and so determined cannot yet awaken in order to develop the necessary universal material, social, intellectual and spiritual message which will enable it to save both itself and the rest of the world? I believe no such thing.

—Charles Malik in *The Christian Scholar.*

AGE OF OPPORTUNITY

773. Having taken full cognizance of the potential danger of the hour, we must not forget that this is also a time of challenge and opportunity. Whitehead reminds us that the creative ages have been the tense, disturbed ages. Creativity always emerges at the point where there is a breaking up of old patterns of behavior. The sentence Dickens used to describe the era of the French Revolution is apropos of ours: "It was the best of times, it was the worst of times, it was the age of wisdom, it was the age of foolishness, it was the epoch of incredulity, it was the season of Light, it was the season of Darkness, it was the spring of hope, it was the winter of despair, we had everything before us, we had nothing before us, we were going direct to heaven, we were all going direct the other way—"

—Charles F. Jacobs in *New World Calling.*

774. There is, thank heaven, more in men's hearts than a mere anxiety about survival. What gives a kind of distinction to our present crisis is the widening sense that the very saving of our skins depends on our securing a quality of life among men. This is the important mid-century news—this growing belief. It is bracing to the spirit when men think that what will save their lives will give also the quality that makes their lives worth saving. . . . The turning point of the history in which it is our privilege to share may well be this growing return of men to their minds and their souls. It is an unmistakable phenomenon of our day. It is much the best thing about us.

—Howard Lowry in *The Mind's Adventure.* Copyright, 1950, by W. L. Jenkins, The Westminster Press. Used by permission.

775. In going through the papers of F. Scott Fitzgerald, his friends found a number of unfinished plots. One had to do with the members of an estranged family who inherited a house. To get it, they all had to live happily in it together. We are in much the same situation. We have all inherited a house—the world. We're a widely separated family of Chinese and Japanese and Africans and Indians and Russians and Europeans and North and South Americans. We've inherited a house, and our task is to learn to live in it together.
—Roy A. Burkhart

776. Douglas MacArthur was asked by a student his belief in regard to a young man's opportunity as he graduated today. MacArthur wrote: "Young man, the new world knows no boundaries. So think the world thought, do the world deed, and be a world citizen. The future is unlimited."
—Frank A. Court

777. In spite of our incredible differences in thinking, our seemingly irreconcilable conflicts in action, we have a unity of spirit, the American spirit. It is difficult to define, and yet I feel it steadfast, the deepening and strengthening expression of a people still in growth, still in the process of welding a new nation out of human material, from everywhere in the world. . . . Our contribution to the solutions of the world's problems will come only from the working of the American spirit. Our approach will be practical, though sometimes impatient; optimistic, though humorously rueful; energetic, though occasionally reluctant. In short, if I am sometimes critical of my own people, it is in excess of love, for I perceive so clearly the needs of humanity and our own amazing ability to aid in fulfilling them, that I grow restless with the delays preventing the realization of ourselves and of what we can do, at home and abroad, to create a sensible and pleasant world.
—From *My Several Worlds* by Pearl S. Buck. Copyright, 1954, by Pearl S. Buck. Published by The John Day Company, Inc.

778. If there is any ethical thinking at all among us, how can we refuse to let these new discoveries benefit those who, in distant lands, are subject to even greater physical distress than we are? In addition to the medical men who are sent out by the governments, and who are never more than enough to accomplish a fraction of what needs doing, others must go out too, commissioned by human society as such. Whoever among us has through personal experience learned what pain and anxiety really are must help to ensure that those who out there are in bodily need obtain the help which came to him. He belongs no more to himself alone; he has become the brother of all who suffer.
—Albert Schweitzer in *Who Speaks for Man?* by Norman Cousins. Copyright 1953. Used by permission of The Macmillan Co.

779. A few men, like Lincoln, belong to the centuries. Simon Bolívar, South American liberator, summarized his achievements with these words: "I have plowed in the sea." His biographer, T. R. Ybarra, in *The Passionate Warrior* said: "No one man could bring into being the United America, founded on the splendid international ideals which shone brightly in his dreams, and few men are endowed with the sort of soul to make even dreaming such a thing possible. Simon Bolívar had such a soul. His dreams may have been extravagant, but they were glorious: they may have been mad, but they were beautiful. . . .

[He] was a dreamer in his youth and in his maturity, in poverty and in prosperity, in misfortune and in power; all his life he nourished himself on dreams, and he lived long enough to know that his dreams were only dreams. But—*he dreamed!* All honor to him!"
—Ives Washburn, Inc.

780. When the H. Allen Smiths were in London they asked an American woman who had lived there many years what she considered the most impressive experience that London offered. She thought awhile. They'd have to wait for a good thick fog, she finally told them, then board a certain bus after dark and ride through mists as thick as cream soup until the conductor sang out: "World's End! Salvation next door!" This fateful cry signifies arrival at a crossroads where stands a "pub" called "World's End." Adjoining it is a Salvation Army hall. Will our world insist on waiting for the "World's End" before looking for salvation?
—Robert J. Searls in *The Pulpit.* Copyrighted by the Christian Century Foundation and used by permission.

SWORDS INTO PLOWSHARES

781. Basil Mathews, walking in the dusty streets of an Arabian village, met a tall young Arab boy playing a flute. He asked to see the flute, for it seemed a heavy awkward thing; on examining it, he found that it was made out of an old gun barrel. The boy explained that he had picked up an old gun on a near-by battlefield, filed it down, drilled holes in it, and out of a weapon of destruction created an instrument of music.
—J. Wallace Hamilton in *Ride the Wild Horses!* Fleming H. Revell Co.

782. After one of the many heartbreaking battles that were fought in the South Pacific during World War II, an American soldier who had been fatally burned by enemy flame throwers was receiving spiritual comfort and strength from a chaplain who knelt at his side. From the lips of the dying man came this profound observation in a whisper, "I guess—we have—too much chemistry—and not enough—Christ." I don't know whether we have too much chemistry, too much physics, too much engineering, too much science; I do know that we do not have enough Christ.
—Armin C. Oldsen

783. Georges Duhamel, who began his life as a surgeon in the French Army over thirty years ago, says in the first of his books written in a military hospital that wars go on because there is no way at all by which one man can feel in his own body the pain which another man suffers. For if each man and all men could feel that pain, there would never be another war.
—Willard L. Sperry in *Sermons Preached at Harvard,* Harper & Bros.

784. In a profound sense the individual who remakes a hostile situation into one of mutual good will and shared experience is a creative artist—and we can best understand him by noting what it is an artist does. In "Abt Vogler," Browning said that the great musical composer is able "out of three sounds" to frame "not a fourth sound, but a star." The composer, in short, makes new unity out of already existing elements; and this is precisely what the genuine peacemaker does. He does not try to make his opponent over in his own image. His concern is to make the situation that includes both himself and his opponent into one where human powers and individual traits that have not been called forth by conflict will be

called forth and made the basis of shared rather than antagonistic action. The sounds with which the musical composer works are neither new nor peculiarly his. As Browning reminds us, they are "everywhere in the world." . . . He does not need better sounds: the old ones will become a new magic if he is able so to feel their intrinsic qualities that he can bring them together into a new, mutually supporting unity.
—HARRY and BONARO OVERSTREET in *The Mature Mind,* W. W. Norton & Co., Inc.

785. At present, everybody is preoccupied by the organization of peace. All are agreed that this is the crucial problem which dominates all the others. But we hear only of "external" solutions . . . of treaties, signatures, understandings, conventions, international police, courts of arbitration, but we never hear anything about the *respect* of these treaties and signatures, the *integrity* of the commissions, the *impartiality* of the judges, the *good faith* of all, without which these instruments lose all their value. Yet we should know by this time that their effectiveness depends entirely on the moral character of the men who have drafted them or participated in them.
—LECOMTE DU NOÜY in *Human Destiny,* Longmans, Green & Co., Inc.

786. Three Chinese characters representing the bases for peace were drawn for me by T. Z. Koo. These were: *"ho*—rice in mouth, the economic basis for peace; *an*—roof over woman, the sociological basis for peace; and *p'ing*—two hearts parallel, the spiritual basis for peace."
—HERBERT BEECHER HUDNUT

787. In almost the exact center of North America, on the border of the Province of Manitoba and the State of North Dakota, in a hilly country called the Turtle Mountains, there is an area of some 2,000 acres called the "Garden of Peace." Beneath the flags of our two nations is a stone cairn on which are the words, "To God in His Glory we two nations dedicate this garden, and pledge ourselves that as long as man shall live we will not take up arms against one another." This is a symbol of the spirit of amity which exists between our two peoples.
—W. J. SHERIDAN in *Vital Speeches.*

788. How much of the distrust and suspicion in the world arises from our display of preparations for war? A banker friend, an outspoken advocate of strong military establishments, told me one day of the manner in which his bank defends itself against burglary. "No employee sounds an alarm while robbers are in the building. That might excite a burglar and cause a shooting," he explained. "Furthermore, no employee is permitted to carry a weapon for his personal defense or to have a gun in his booth." The bank, I observed, followed a policy of nonresistance when attacked by armed robbers. I marveled at my friend's inconsistency, for he wished to protect our nation in a manner which was not desirable on the premises of his bank.
—JOHN EDWARD LANTZ

789. In Caesar's day it cost 75¢ to kill a man in battle. In Napoleon's day the cost had increased to $3,000. By the time of the Civil War it is estimated that it required $5,000 to kill an enemy soldier. It is believed that $21,000 was required to kill a man in World War I, and in World War II America paid $50,000 per capita for its dead enemies. The cost in dollars is staggering; but the cost in potential national leadership, in dedi-

cated fathers, in the loss of teachers, civic leaders, and human benefactors is inestimable.
—G. Curtis Jones

790. A young golfing friend, a fighter pilot during the last war, stood and watched with me a jet plane go by overhead. "How fast is that fellow going?" I asked him. Scanning the sky with an experienced eye, the young fighter pilot said, "About five hundred miles an hour." About that time a much slower plane came lumbering overhead, whereupon I said: "What's that? And how fast is he going?" Taking another look, the young fellow said, "Why, that's one of the old things we used for rescue at sea, and he's going about 150 miles an hour." He smiled and said, "It's silly, isn't it? If you're going out to kill somebody, you go five hundred miles an hour, but if you are just going out to save a life, you knock along at 150."
—From: *Spiritual Revolution,* by Pierce Harris. Copyright 1952 by Pierce Harris, reprinted by permission of Doubleday & Co., Inc.

791. Members of a geology class were on a field trip. During their examination of ancient rock formations a great bomber passed overhead. When the students turned their attention to the flight of the airplane, the teacher said thoughtfully, "All the world today is focused on the latest improvement in engines of destruction; but when these have long since been forgotten, the rock formations will still be here." So it is with Jesus Christ. After the implements of hate and war have become dust, the Rock of Ages will still be a living reality in the hearts and lives of men.
—John B. Schlarb

REFORMATION DAY

AFFIRMATIONS OF PROTEST

792. We should understand the word *Protestant*. "Well," you say, "that's easy; it means 'to protest.'" All right, but what is the meaning of the word *protest*? You will find something like this: "to make a solemn declaration or affirmation." Protestantism is a solemn declaration of some great affirmations about God and man.
—ROBERT E. GOODRICH, JR. in *The Upper Room Pulpit.*

793. With the Reformation came the founding of our particular Protestant tradition in the history of the Church. But we do not think of it as the founding of our tradition; we think of it as a reannouncing of the principles that had been fundamental in Christ's ministry and in the Early Church but that had been lost along the way. The Reformation did not so much see the formation of new churches, as the reformation of the Church of Jesus Christ in something more like its original and primitive form.
—D. CAMPBELL WYCKOFF in *The Task of Christian Education.* Copyright, 1955, by W. L. Jenkins, The Westminster Press. Used by permission.

794. A century ago, President Charles G. Finney of Oberlin College taught that the converted man is not only reformed, but is a reformer: Christians should set forth "with all their hearts," he said, "to search out all the evils in the world, and to reform the world, and drive out iniquity from the earth. Religion is something to *do*," he insisted, "not something to wait for."
—LISTON POPE in *The Intercollegian.*

795. Professor Thomas N. Lindsay, in his *History of the Reformation,* states that Luther's message and movement were democratic in that they, (1) destroyed the aristocracy of the saints; (2) leveled the barriers between the layman and the priest; (3) taught the equality of all men before God, and (4) the right of every man of faith to stand in God's presence whatever be his rank and condition of life.
—EDGAR DEWITT JONES in *Sermons I Love to Preach,* Harper & Bros.

796. When Luther was still in his Augustinian monastery, struggling with his doubts, one of his Roman Catholic teachers said to him: "Brother Martin, let the Bible alone; read the old teachers. They give you the whole marrow of the Bible; reading the Bible simply breeds unrest." Well, I'll say it breeds unrest! It challenges conscience, it upsets complacency, it calls to repentance, it opens doors to personal and social transformation.
—HARRY EMERSON FOSDICK in *The Pulpit.* Copyrighted by the Christian Century Foundation and used by permission.

797. The facts seem to show that the rediscovery of the Bible and the Reforma-

tion grew up side by side, acting and reacting on one another. First one made a move and then the other followed suit. A glance at the dates shows this happening. In 1516, Erasmus published his Greek New Testament and the very next year Luther nailed his thesis to the church door in Wittenberg. In 1522 Luther translated the New Tetsament into German and a few years later German princes and cities began to call themselves "Protestant." Again, in 1525, Tyndale translated the Bible into English and in two years' time Reformation doctrines were being openly advocated in Oxford and Cambridge. Once more, in 1535, Olivétan translated the Bible into French and a year later Calvin published his *Institutes* and Geneva went Protestant. Every new step in biblical discovery or translation seemed to be the occasion, if not the cause, of another development in Protestantism.
—A. M. Chirgwin in *The Bible in World Evangelism,* Friendship Press.

HEROES OF FAITH

798. I shall not forget speaking to a group of Protestant students at the University of the Philippines at Quezon City just outside Manila. There was something different about them, and in some ways it was the most thrilling student group I ever addressed. I said to the young man who directed them, "What is there about this group that is different? Why do I sense here a kind of spiritual excitement?" "Well," he said, "it is because they are a minority. It is because nearly every one of them had to make a deliberate choice to become a Protestant. Nearly every one of them had to sacrifice something for his religion. They have to be better than the majority, for they have to be an example in a critical society."
—Gerald Kennedy in *Here Is My Method,* Fleming H. Revell Co.

799. Some time ago I went to a public meeting where a minister burned a copy of the Revised Standard Version of the Bible. "That is terrible," a friend said to me. I answered that it was not as bad as things used to be, for once they burned men for translating the Bible. Some one wrote to Erasmus: "Firewood in England is getting scarce, because we are using it to burn heretics."
—Roy A. Burkhart

800. At Drew Theological Seminary there is a tradition that, when the late, beloved Samuel F. Upham was dying, friends and relatives gathered at his bedside. Someone, wondering if his life had come to a close, advised: "Feel his feet. No one ever died with warm feet." Upham opened his eyes slowly and said, "John Huss did."
—Ernest E. Thompson

801. [Luther] was the father of a household, the molder of the German people, a new David playing on his harp, an emancipator of certain fetters of the spirit, the divider of the Church, and at the same time the renewer of Christendom. All this he was, and more; but pre-eminently for his own time as well as for ourselves he was a man athirst for God.
—Roland H. Bainton in *Here I Stand,* Abingdon Press.

802. Once Wendell Phillips and a young friend were sitting by the fire. It was a memorable evening. Recollections had flushed the cheeks of the veteran campaigner. Memories of former heroic days had loosened his tongue. He had completely lost himself in the thrilling recital of the past. The young visitor . . .

exclaimed, "Mr. Phillips, if I had lived in your time, I think I should have been heroic too!" . . . His voice was tremulous with indignation as he exclaimed: "Young man, you are living in my time, and in God's time! Be sure of this: No man could have been heroic then who is not heroic now."
—G. Ray Jordan in *Living Joyously* by Kirby Page, Rinehart & Co., Inc.

803. When Queen Elizabeth learned that Emmanuel College of Cambridge University had been founded for the training of Puritan clergymen, she admonished her Chancellor of the Exchequer, Sir Walter Mildmay, saying, "So, Sir Walter, I hear you have erected a Puritan foundation?" "No, Madam," said he, "far be it from me to countenance anything contrary to your established laws; but I have set an acorn which, when it becomes an oak, God alone knows what will be the fruit thereof."
—Fred L. Brownlee in *These Rights We Hold,* Friendship Press.

804. In one of his books Thornton Wilder tells of an aged missionary bishop who was spending the last two years of his life in retirement in France. The pathos of those years is summed up in this line: "His was a fighting faith; and when he no longer had battles to fight, his faith withered away." I mention this because it underscores the fact that a vital faith is always a fighting faith.
—Harold A. Bosley

WORLD TEMPERANCE DAY

WHY MEN DRINK

805. In an address made a few years ago by Dr. A. C. Ivy while he was Professor of Physiology and Pharmacology at Northwestern University School of Medicine . . . speaking on the theme, "Why People Drink," he said: "Alcohol gives temporary relief from worry; abolishes mental tension; disguises difficulties; relieves a feeling of inferiority; makes a weak person feel strong; an ignorant person feel smart; a poor person feel rich; an oppressed person feel free; a bad person feel good; and makes one imagine himself a good driver who may be potentially a motor car murderer."

—Harold A. Bosley in *Preaching on Controversial Issues,* published in 1953 by Harper & Brothers.

806. When the movie "The Lost Weekend," was shown across the country, Seagram's distillery followed the trail of it with advertising, "We have always said that some men should not drink." . . . *Who* should not? No man knows whether he is one who can't until he is caught, and as Dr. Deets Pickett has said, "Neither science nor Seagrams can tell him that."

—J. Wallace Hamilton in *Ride the Wild Horses!* Fleming H. Revell Co.

807. Some time ago *The Chicago Tribune* had a news story about a national tavern owners' convention. The meeting was called because across the nation business in the taverns had been falling off at such a calamitous rate. They were studying the reasons why. According to the newspaper one of the reasons was television in the home. People didn't need to go to the taverns to see television programs. Second, the high birth rate meant that mothers were not free in the evenings. Third, high taxes were taking much of the money that people used to spend for liquor. So in view of all this and to entice people away from their homes, certain resolutions were passed. One was to make taverns more attractive. The owners couldn't do anything about the birth rate, but they consoled themselves with the thought that the increasing population would give them more patrons in later years. They set aside a substantial budget and a committee or lobby to go to Washington to try to reduce taxes, not only for themselves but for all potential drinkers. The church is interested in building up the home, in making homes more attractive, in pointing to the ultimate satisfactions of home life; but the tavern owners' convention seemed concerned only with things that would tear down the home.

—Frank A. Court

808. The moderate drinker is the best friend of the liquor industry. He is the fellow who makes their advertisements appear to be telling the truth. This is

especially so if he is known as a church member. His example tends to make his neighbors and those young men who admire him believe that drinking is respectable, a mark of success, a harmless and happy diversion. He is bait for the trap. For this reason he is upheld and glorified in liquor advertisements. They never picture a skid-row citizen, the one drinker in nine who becomes addicted, the blowzy woman, the crime induced by alcohol, or a drink-destroyed home. Always it is the "man of distinction" drinking in moderation. He is the best friend of the liquor interests and as a consequence the worst enemy of the Church in its fight against such evil.
—Everett W. Palmer

809. A recent cartoon portrayed an elderly woman, half tipsy, sitting at a night club table. A jazz band was beating out "Sparrow in the Treetop"; people were sitting about with dunce's caps and paper horns; an old-faced waiter was standing by with a tray of cocktails, and the old woman was asking, "Waiter, am I having a good time?"
—Orva Lee Ice in *Tomorrow Is Yours,* Abingdon Press.

810. W. F. Russell tells humorously of a new golf game called "Drink and Smell." It calls for two players, two caddies, two bags of clubs, and one large bottle of whiskey. According to the rules the winner of the first hole gets a drink from the bottle, the loser gets only a smell. This is repeated after the second hole and so on. If the same player should win three holes in succession, he is practically sure to lose the next.
—Ralph W. Sockman

REASONS FOR CONCERN

811. A devoted mother pleaded with her pastor to do all he could to help her alcoholic son. The pastor quickly became disgusted with the son, who was a repulsive fellow and not one bit cooperative, and gave up the mother's request as a hopeless task. The mother begged him to try again and put it like this: "If you cannot help him for his own sake, please do it for my sake. Remember, he's my son." There are people in the world so vicious and hateful that I cannot love them for themselves. There are folks in my town who are very hard to love. But when I have stood at the foot of Calvary and have heard the Saviour, who loved me enough to die for me, say to me as he points to every human being, "These are my children for whom I died; love them; preach the gospel to them; pray for them; help them in every possible way," why, that's an entirely different matter.
—Armin C. Oldsen

812. In a western town lived a preacher whose son grew up tall and straight, with a mind keen and clean and wholesome. In that same town lived a foul-mouthed, atheistic, and very brilliant doctor. A strong friendship grew up between the two. The doctor, with his brilliant mind, became a hero to the boy, and gradually there came an estrangement in the preacher's home. Under the father's roof the boy was irritable and unmanageable, contemptuous of his father's faith, resentful of even his mother's kindly concern. And wherever the interest of his father came into conflict with the interest of his friend, the boy consistently chose the latter's way and soon came almost completely under the spell of his atheistic hero, so much so that the people of the church shook their heads sadly and said, "He is getting more like the doctor than like his father. He is more the doctor's son than the son of his own father." One midnight

the preacher, with heavy heart, stole softly into the bedroom of his son, to find the air filled with the fumes of alcohol, and the boy's mother kneeling by his bed, stroking his hair, kissing his forehead, caressing him. Looking up through the veil of tears, she said, "He won't let me love him when he's awake."
—J. WALLACE HAMILTON in *Horns and Halos in Human Nature,* Fleming H. Revell Co.

813. Mrs. Marty Mann, executive director of the National Committee on Alcoholism, has said that the years of her acute chronic alcoholism were the most painful years of her life. "I suffered constantly, not just one kind of pain, but *all* kinds of pain. I suffered physically, mentally, emotionally, financially, and socially—in every department of my life. I tell you, honestly, and on behalf of those three million human beings [alcoholics] that alcoholism is the most painful disease known to man."

814. Almeda C. Adams, author of *Seeing Europe Through Sightless Eyes* and a founder of the Cleveland Music School Settlement, has enlarged the vision of many normal persons. Her life of wide usefulness knows no bitterness toward the physician who under the influence of liquor used too strong a solution of silver nitrate on her eyes when she was a few days old. Yet throughout life she has paid dearly for his folly.
—ROBERT C. NEWELL

815. Spurgeon told one time of a famous tailor who was about to die. His associates asked him to tell the secret of his success in the tailoring business. . . . In a solemn voice he gave them this infallible rule for success in these words: "Always put a knot in your thread." . . . Many a life of large capacities and great promise has been wrecked because in pursuing larger goals men have overlooked smaller habits . . . that destroy.
—CHARLES M. CROWE in *On Living with Yourself,* Abingdon Press.

816. One clear cold March day I stood at the edge of Niagara Falls. The cataract was garbed in her most glorious winter garments. The rapids above the falls sparkled in the afternoon sun. Some birds were swooping down to snatch a drink from the clear water. My host told me how he had seen birds carried over the brink. They had dipped down for a drink and ice had formed on their wings. Then they had dipped for another drink and more ice weighted their little bodies. Another dip or two and they could not rise. Over the falls they went. Sin is as deceptive as the sparkling water of Niagara's wintry rapids. Dip into it once too often and we are not able to "lay aside every weight, and sin which clings so closely."
—From: *How to Believe,* by RALPH W. SOCKMAN. Copyright 1953 by Ralph W. Sockman, reprinted by permission of Doubleday & Co., Inc.

817. A young man went to his physician to have his eyes examined. The examination of the eyes themselves was followed by inquiry into his way of life. Then the physician knew what he had suspected when he looked at the eyes. Faithfully he told the young man that unless he renounced certain practices and changed his way of life, he would be totally blind in six months. The revelation was a shock but not sufficient to break the spell of evil. "Goodbye sweet light," wailed the patient, "I cannot give up my sin."
—ALBERT E. DAY in *An Autobiography of Prayer,* published in 1952 by Harper & Brothers.

818. The righteous Christian institutions of a community can insist on the same standard of morality for all classes of citizens alike. . . . In my town, for example, if a person gets drunk on the north side, he gets hauled home in a station wagon and his name comes out the next morning in the society page. If, however, he makes the mistake of getting drunk on the south side of town, he gets hauled away in a patrol wagon, and next morning his name comes up on the police docket.
—From: *Spiritual Revolution,* by PIERCE HARRIS. Copyright 1952 by Pierce Harris, reprinted by permission of Doubleday & Co., Inc.

MIRACLES OF GRACE

819. A member of Alcoholics Anonymous said that [he had] wanted to buy an unusually fine watch. It combined a chronometer, a stop watch, and a few of the features of a calendar and astronomical observatory; it indicated the day of the month and the phases of the moon. "In fact all it lacked was hot and cold running water." He realized that if it ever needed repair it could not be taken to an ordinary repairman. It would need to be taken to its maker. "Then one day," he said, "it came to me that my life was a very complicated affair like that watch. It had broken down, and was running out of control. I decided that my only chance was to take it back to its Maker."
—DAVID A. MACLENNAN in *Joyous Adventure,* published in 1952 by Harper & Brothers.

820. Bishop Azariah of Dornakal, India, whose diocese grew in his twenty-five years as bishop to almost a quarter of a million outcaste Christians, tells how he taught recent converts to give their witness. "I used to have them place their hands on their heads as if in the act of baptism, and repeat after me: 'I am a baptized Christian. Woe is me if I preach not the Gospel.' One of us protested that these were illiterate outcastes —how could they preach? 'I will tell you,' said the Indian bishop. 'A caste villager asked one of our outcastes: "Have you seen God?" He answered: "Sir, you knew me two years ago. I was a drunkard. You know me now. I do not think I should have all this change if I had not seen Jesus Christ." Is there any better way,' concluded the bishop, 'of witnessing for God'? The answer in the early centuries and today is none."
—JOHN FOSTER in *After the Apostles.* Copyright 1951. Used by permission of The Macmillan Co.

821. A group of businessmen were talking about the most significant questions they had ever asked. One after another recalled the questions which had changed their lives: "Which school shall I attend?" "Will you marry me?" "Will you lend me five thousand dollars?" "Which stock should I buy?" At last a bank president, a man of high standing in the community and the most successful member of the group, told his story. "The most important question I ever asked," he said, "had nothing to do with money." He related the day long before when the village drunk, shunned by society, a burden to his family and well on his way to a drunkard's grave, entered the bank with a request for a loan. "In the course of our conversation I simply asked, 'Why don't you come to church, Frank?' He was surprised and confused, but the following Sunday he attended church with me. The whole congregation was amazed to see him there and even more so when he became a believer and a new man in Christ. From then on he lived and at last died

a faithful disciple. I've asked many questions, but none equals those simple words, 'Why don't you come to church, Frank?' "
—W. A. KUNTZLEMAN

822. A young man was overly protected by the too fond ministrations of his mother so that he was not quite able to withstand the abrasions of mature life. So he sought the protection of the crowd: the boys at the bar. There was the magic of alcohol which like Aladdin's genie filled a palace of joy and for the moment vanquished his fears in the convivial fellowship of the tavern. But his flight from fear and loneliness was temporary. One day in a fit of sober depression while kneeling before a small altar in my study the young man went into a fit of trembling and said desperately: "Oh, don't leave me alone, not for a minute. Don't leave me alone." I tried to tell him that God would never leave him alone and that he would know that companionship if he did what pleases God. How the idea penetrated his drugged mind is a miracle of grace. Later when he was sober and happy and rebuilding life, he told me: "I'm never alone any more. Even when I go to call on some of my biggest customers, Christ goes with me; and I'm trying to please him in whatever I do."
—ENSWORTH REISNER

823. An able-bodied man in the prime of life came to my door. His breath was strong with the smell of liquor as he demanded money. I suggested that there was something he needed more than money, and he immediately became abusive. He wanted cash, he said, not talk. Resentment welled up within me. But as I looked at him, a new appreciation of all life came to me. He stood before the parsonage door. The wood panels which held the squares of glass in place seemed to suggest the form of a cross. I was then able to talk with him more calmly, for I remembered One who always spoke with sympathetic understanding to those whose lives had been made wretched through sin.
—ARTHUR A. WAHMANN

824. We recognize [Alcoholics Anonymous] as an organization of desperate people fighting a desperate battle. Historically, religion itself was born out of desperation. The modern Church, as is true of medicine, is failing to help the alcoholic; we are breaking our hearts, often, but we are helping very little. We have moved too far from the point of desperation in too many instances.
—RUSSELL L. DICKS in *A Sober Faith* by G. Aiken Taylor. Copyright 1953. Used by permission of The Macmillan Co.

825. A century and a half ago Thomas Jefferson said: "Were I to commence my administration again, with the knowledge which from experience I have acquired, the first question which I would ask with regard to every candidate for public office would be, 'Is he addicted to the use of ardent spirits?' "
—L. L. DUNNINGTON

826. A child's life is greatly influenced by the lives of persons he admires and imitates. But a small child may sometimes become a determining force in the life of a parent. At a wedding reception the guests were offered beverages to toast the bride and groom. A five-year-old boy watched his father and mother take glasses from a tray. "Mother," he said, "you can't be my mother if you drink that. Daddy, you're no longer my daddy if you drink that." The mother immediately returned her glass to the tray, and the father sheepishly hid his. One by one the guests put their glasses aside.
—FREDERICK L. ANDERSON

STEWARDSHIP DAY

GOD'S OWNERSHIP

827. The word "steward" in the Old Testament meant "the man who is over." A similar connotation is conveyed in the New Testament reference to "an overseer, one to whom something has been entrusted." In practically every instance the English word "steward" conveys the idea of responsibility to another. In fact, almost every English word ending in "ship" implies relationship. God, then, is the master; man is the servant. God is the owner; man the overseer, the steward. Stewardship, then, implies and demands total accountability. As Dr. Riley Montgomery says, "A person cannot be a steward of what he owns but only of that which is another's."
—G. Curtis Jones in *What Are You Worth?* Copyright 1954. Bethany Press.

828. A capitalist and socialist were arguing about the relative merits of their positions when a third person stepped forward and interrupted them and said, "I am a theist." They immediately ridiculed him and asked, "What do you mean?" He replied, "A capitalist believes that individuals own and should own the wealth of the world. A socialist believes that all the people should own the wealth of the world and create a great commonwealth. A theist believes that God owns the world and that man is merely the custodian, the steward of its wealth. A theist believes that everything begins with God and everything belongs to God. 'The earth is the Lord's, and the fulness thereof.' I am a theist."
—Albert A. Chambers in *Successful Fund Raising Sermons,* Funk & Wagnalls Co.

829. Sir William Blackstone, compiler of the commentaries on English law that bear his name, rests the institution of private property on the ultimate ownership of God: "This is the only true and solid foundation of man's dominion over external things, whatever airy metaphysical notions may have been started by fanciful writers on this subject. The earth therefore, and all things therein, are the general property of all mankind . . . from the immediate gift of the Creator."
—Costen J. Harrell in *Stewardship and the Tithe,* Abingdon Press.

830. An old Danish proverb reminds us that there are no pockets in our shrouds. On one occasion the late Bishop Edwin Holt Hughes had delivered a sermon on "God's Ownership." Later in the day his host, a man of considerable means, was conducting him over his plantation. At one point, looking over his broad acres and remembering the morning's sermon, he asked, "Do you mean to tell me, Bishop, that this land does not belong to me?" In a flash the answer came, "Ask me that one hundred years from now."

—COSTEN J. HARRELL in *Stewardship and the Tithe,* Abingdon Press.

831. I have a friend, a businessman in Toronto. He came one day driving a great black Cadillac. I looked at him and jokingly said, "You're very prosperous these days." He turned and in sudden seriousness said, "Why, God gave me this Cadillac." I said, "That's interesting." He said, "I think God wants his children to have the best." I said, "You know, it's interesting that God gave you a Cadillac; he gave his only begotten son a cross. He gave his first and best disciple decapitation, imprisonment, stoning, shipwreck and all the thousand other troubles that he faced."
—CHARLES B. TEMPLETON in *Great Preaching Today,* Alton M. Motter, editor, published in 1953 by Harper & Bros. Used by permission.

BURIED TALENTS

832. Banks are required by law periodically to advertise in newspapers those accounts in which there are unclaimed deposits. Hundreds of persons apparently forget that banks are holding money in trust for them. Occasionally an advertisement will remind a depositor of his forgotten wealth. When men and women give their lives and talents into the keeping of God, many lose faith in their creator and act as though they had never entrusted any treasure to him. They live pauperized lives when they might be spiritually rich.
—GLENN H. ASQUITH

833. This sentence by one of our informed Christian leaders is provocative: "The history of Christianity could be written in terms of the ingenious and fatal ways in which Christians have tried to make their faith and practice easy."
—DAVID A. MACLENNAN in *Joyous Adventure,* published in 1952 by Harper & Brothers.

834. An eager youth, employed during his summer vacation in a shirt factory, worked hastily so that he might receive the bonus offered to those who put out the largest quantity of work. In his haste the youth destroyed much good cloth. When the superintendent reprimanded him for his haste, the boy said: "Only a few shirts were poorly cut. Eighty-five per cent were all right. In school a grade of eighty-five is pretty good." But his boss replied: "A grade of eighty-five may be good enough in school, but I'd soon go out of business if fifteen per cent of my material is spoiled. When you work quickly, you must work more skillfully."
—E. PAUL HOVEY

835. A seminary student after his senior sermon came anxiously into the professor's office asking, "It will do, won't it?" and the answer was a cold, "It will do—*what?*" Sermons should do something as well as say something. We shall expect a dud once in a while, but an alert preacher will be concerned if, Sunday after Sunday, he preaches and all go home. . . . After a sermon by Saint Francis a friar sought him out saying, "Father, I fain would take counsel of thee concerning the welfare of my soul."
—GEORGE MILES GIBSON in *Planned Preaching.* Copyright, 1954, by W. L. Jenkins, The Westminster Press. Used by permission.

836. A sign on a radiator in a hotel room said: "Please turn the radiators all the way on or all the way off. If they are turned only partially on, they will leak and be noisy." A lot of Christians have lives that are squeaky and noisy and

they can't hold happiness and joy for long—they leak.
—E. STANLEY JONES in *How to Be a Transformed Person,* Abingdon Press.

837. Some Christians are like the citizen who had his house built across the Arkansas-Missouri line. The county officials in Missouri thought he paid taxes in Arkansas, while the officials in Arkansas thought he paid taxes in Missouri. . . . It is a rule in law that a man must pay taxes according to where he sleeps. One night officers of each state stole up to the house to find where the citizen in question had his bed located. To their amazement, they found that this crafty individual had placed his bed directly across the state line. . . . This illustrates pretty well the status of many a man in the church. A part of his life he gives to God, and the other he gives to the world.
—C. GORDON BAYLESS in *And Be Ye Saved,* Fleming H. Revell Co.

838. One evening I watched a young man move mysteriously from one side of a car to another. On closer examination it appeared that he was removing some very large and shiny hub caps. When he noticed me, he explained, "I just got these new hub caps, and I don't intend to have them stolen." He placed the hub caps in his car, locked the car door, and then went on his way. In my mind I could imagine that, each time he left his car, he took time to replace the hub caps. What a ritual! Yet for how many of us life has become little more than the protection of chrome.
—R. A. PANZER

839. "I myself," says the narrator in *Embezzled Heaven* by Franz Werfel, "have at very rare moments, which are not my worst ones, a strong inclination to faith—even to faith in the strict sense." To this another replies: "Inclination! It is like having an inclination to be a singer. A person can possess a voice. That is a gift which comes from Heaven. But what are you going to do with your voice if you do not study and practise and work hard, without allowing yourself a single day's remission? Faith, too, is an art that must be studied and practised and practised and studied, like singing."
—Viking Press, Inc.

840. The young doctor in A. J. Cronin's *The Citadel* came to his time of reckoning. When politics defeated his health measures in a Welsh mining town, he sold his standards for money. After his wife's tragic death he found in her handbag snapshots of himself in those heroic days, and letters of gratitude from impoverished miners, and other mementos she had which reminded her of the man he might have been. He shouted to himself in a drunken stupor. "You thought you could get away with it. You thought you *were* getting away with it. But by God! you weren't."
—WALLACE FRIDY in *A Lamp Unto My Feet,* Abingdon Press. Quotation published by Little, Brown & Co.

841. John Galsworthy portrayed all humanity through the moving drama he called *Loyalties,* in which a crime was committed and the characters then attempted to defend that to which each recognized allegiance—one, his family; another, his regiment; and others, a social set, a race, a business firm. With the best of intentions they were thus thrown into hopeless conflict. Finally one of them committed suicide, leaving a note which remarked, "A pistol keeps faith." Reading that sentence, one of the other characters paused to muse, "Keeps

faith! We've all done that. It's not enough." Much of the pathos of our humanity is there. Made for a high allegiance, we give our loyalty away to something less than the highest; out of this springs our conflict.
—MERRILL R. ABBEY in *Creed of Our Hope,* Abingdon Press. Quotation from *Plays, Fifth Series* by John Galsworthy, Chas. Scribner's Sons.

842. The standards of the world do not summon man to great heights of living, for the world is the great leveler. It puts everyone on the same plane. "What everybody says must be true," it maintains. "Whatever everyone does must be right." Be like your neighbor and you'll be a good fellow. Christ challenges man to rise above the average plane. Nothing less than Godlikeness can satisfy the Christian, who is called to live on loftier heights than the world knows and to call all men to rise with him.
—KARL H. A. REST

843. There is an apocryphal story of the days when the British were in control of India and a drunken, wizened government analyst tested milk in a certain province. One day he called at a house, and in the doorway stood a woman with a beautiful baby. "My word," he said admiringly, "you have got a bonny baby." She looked for a moment at the thin, little man and said, "Well, you see, you test the milk, but my baby drinks it." There is all the difference between a knowledge which sifts and analyzes and discusses, and that saving knowledge whereby a man commits himself to God.
—MALDWYN EDWARDS in *The Upper Room Pulpit.*

844. When I was a small boy, my mother's friends applauded politely when they recognized the tune of "Home on the Range" which I played with two fingers on the piano. Years later I heard Ignace Paderewski improvise upon that same tune with ten greatly expressive and talented fingers. What a vast difference there was between the spotty playing of my childhood and the rendition of the master! Our Christian life, when lived by minimum standards only, may be recognizable; but how glorious is our witness when we express our faith in a complete surrender of talent and devotion.
—QUENTIN T. LIGHTNER

845. While waiting for a bus one day I engaged in conversation with a boy who carried an old, battered music case. "Did you ever take piano lessons?" he asked. "Yes," I answered, "many years ago." "Did you quit?" he questioned. "Yes, I quit during the first year." The boy was silent for several moments before asking, "Are you sorry you quit?" I was glad that the bus came just then, but I could not forget the question. How many joys we miss through our lack of perseverance! God gives us many opportunities, but we must do our part or there is no profit.
—GLENN H. ASQUITH

STANDARDS OF VALUE

846. An American tourist traveled all over France with only one French word in his vocabulary. Only one word in French, yet it worked for him like magic. "*Combien?*" "How much?" That was all he knew. There are many people who have but one standard of values, who know only one word in any language. "How much?" In dollars and in cents —"How much?"
—J. WALLACE HAMILTON in *Successful Fund Raising Sermons,* Funk & Wagnalls Co.

847. A minister soliciting for a worthy cause was turned down by a curt letter which ended, "As far as I can see, this Christian business is one of continuous give, give, give." The clergyman wrote back, "Thank you for the best definition of the Christian life I have ever heard."
—Arline Boucher and John Tehan in *Guideposts*. Copyright by Guideposts Associates, Inc. Published at Carmel, N. Y.

848. In Germany following World War II there was a slogan that achieved some popularity, *"Ohne mich,"* which means, "Without me." If the nation wanted to go somewhere, it had to go "without me." We had a similar slang expression in my youth, "Let George do it." In our community there are people who take this attitude toward the church. They believe churches are a good thing, but they are unwilling to accept any responsibility in keeping them going.
—Rolland W. Schloerb

849. Bishop John Hines of Texas tells of an experience, common to us all, of parking in a space with unused time on the meter. One time I did this very thing. Just a few minutes was needed in the library to return a book. When I faced the choice of several parking spaces, I did as you would have done: I parked in the space which had a little time left. I parked on someone else's nickel. . . . "Yet," as Bishop Hines points out, "thousands of church people do just that every year. They never give a cent to build a church, but they use the churches which others have built, to educate their children in religion and morals. They are parking on another's nickel."
—Wallace Fridy in *A Light Unto My Path,* Abingdon Press.

850. Years ago I bought a book on *How to Publicize a Church* for a dollar. I do not remember much about it, and I don't even know where the book is. There was one little thing in it that I shall never forget. It said, "You cannot spell the chUrch without you." It was written in block letters with a great big *U* in it.
—Richard I. Porter

851. The story is told of a man who was asked to purchase a ticket for a benefit concert. "I'm sorry," he said, "but I'm busy that night. However, I shall be with you in spirit." His friend replied, "Splendid, and where would you like your spirit to sit? I have tickets for two, three, and five dollars."
—Richard K. Smith in *Successful Fund Raising Sermons,* Funk & Wagnalls Co.

852. An "inactive" church member, when approached by a canvass worker, commented: "Well, I don't go to church any more, but here's a dollar just to keep me active." Can a begrudged dollar keep a man "active" in the work of God's kingdom?

853. In Lancaster County, Pennsylvania, where I have lived for the past thirty years they tell a story about a Pennsylvania Dutch minister who had no regular charge, but who supplied vacant pulpits around the countryside as opportunity offered. One Sunday, accompanied by his little son, he boarded a trolley car and journeyed several miles to a small town where he was scheduled to conduct the service of the morning. As he entered the church he noticed a box in the vestibule bearing the legend, "For the poor," and although he was himself not blessed with a superfluity of this world's goods, he produced a quarter from his pocket and dropped it in the

receptacle. At the conclusion of the service he was escorted from the pulpit by one of the officers of the church who thanked him for his sermon and stated that it was the custom of the congregation to give their supply preachers the contents of the poor box. When he unlocked it, out dropped nothing whatever save the poor minister's own quarter. He pocketed it with a wry smile, and as he and his little son walked back to the trolley station, the boy looked up into his face and said: "You would have gotten more out if you had put more in, wouldn't you, Pop?"
—H. W. Prentis, Jr., in *Vital Speeches.*

854. An Arab fed faithfully a beggar who was at his gate, but one day the Arab was in extreme difficulty and needed someone to run an errand for him immediately. He summoned the beggar and asked him to do the service, but the beggar drew himself up to his haughty height, and said, "I ask alms; I do not run errands!"
—Louis H. Evans in *The Kingdom Is Yours,* Fleming H. Revell Co.

855. A committee went to see [a] rich man in New York, asking for a gift of one thousand dollars for a certain charity, and he said "No." He was even rude about it. As the committee started away, he said, "Go to that young attorney at the end of the hall, and tell him I said to give you one thousand dollars for this cause." "But you yourself have given nothing!" they exclaimed. "No," he replied, "that is the tragedy. I have it all right, and there was a time when I could have given it to you and would have been glad to do so, but I have loved it so long that the springs of philanthropy have dried up."
—Arthur J. Moore in *The Mighty Saviour,* Abingdon Press.

856. I saw two flies walking beside a ten-acre field this past summer. At least it looked like a ten-acre field to them; it was a piece of Tanglefoot. The younger fly said to the older, "What do you think of this stuff called Tanglefoot?" "I am opposed to it," the older said. "What is the matter?" came the reply. "Is it poisonous?" "Not a bit of it." "Is it bitter?" "No, it is rather sweet." "Then, what are your objections?" About that time a friend of theirs settled down in the middle of that flypaper. "My flypaper," he said proudly. But the flypaper said, "My fly." Then his friend remarked sadly, "You will never see him in church anymore. He possesses wealth, but he is more possessed by his wealth."
—Clovis G. Chappell in *In Parables,* Abingdon Press.

857. An anxious father, fearful that his son had lost all interest in the church, asked the minister to speak with the boy. At the first opportunity the minister said to the boy, "I should think you would want to keep your interest in the church if for no other reason than that your father is so interested." "You don't know my father," the boy replied, adding, "By the way, how much does Dad pledge to the church each year?" The minister thought for a moment and said: "I'm not sure what he gives, but I know he is one of our most generous members. I should say he gives five dollars a Sunday." The boy figured a bit. "That makes $260 a year. But it costs him $600 a year to belong to the country club, and he gave $5,000 to help elect his friend the mayor. You say I ought to attend church because Dad is so interested. I don't think he is as interested as you think. Go ask him to give $500 a year to the church and then come and talk with me."
—Arthur V. Boand

CONSECRATION OF MONEY

858. A man who supported his church and the work of missions very liberally was asked how on his limited income he could afford to give so generously. "When I served the devil," he answered, "I did it on a grand scale. When I received the knowledge of Jesus Christ, I promised him a portion of every day's achievement. I intend to serve Christ on a grander scale."
—E. Paul Hovey

859. Back in the days when Chicago was growing into the metropolis it now is, Armour, a Presbyterian and a generous civic benefactor, said: "I work for God and pack meat simply to pay the bill."
—Frank A. Court

860. In going over the report of the past year a woman remarked: "But we didn't give to the One Great Hour of Sharing." She was corrected and the amount given was stated. "Well, then," remarked another, "if we didn't remember that we gave, we didn't give enough."
—Margaret McCord Lee in *The Presbyterian Tribune.*

861. After a church-wide stewardship campaign the church officers met to discuss the results. The success of our efforts, we discovered, was measured not by charts or figures but rather in the relating of how a little girl in the Sunday school, having heard that the church was raising money, came forward with her most prized treasure—seven Indian-head pennies.
—R. A. Panzer

862. A four-year-old had gone to the store with his mother. There his attention was attracted by a display of packages of candy especially designed for tiny tots. The little fellow was fascinated, and his mother, in a hurry as always, grew impatient while he lingered unable to make up his mind. "Hurry, hurry, son! Spend your money! We must be going." To which the little chap replied, "Don't hurry me, Mommy. I've only got one penny, and I have to spend it carefully."
—Roy L. Smith in *New Light from Old Lamps,* Abingdon Press.

MONEY TALKS

863. We sometimes say that money talks. To be sure it does. Get to know two things about a man—how he earns his money and how he spends it—and you have the clue to his character, for you have a searchlight that shows up the inmost recesses of his soul. You know all you need to know about his standards, his motives, his driving desires, his real religion.
—Robert J. McCracken in *On Living with Yourself,* by Charles M. Crowe, Abingdon Press.

864. Money has decisive significance because it is an instrument for good or evil. With a ten-dollar bill we can buy enough liquor to paralyze our intelligence and become a moron, blunt our sense of propriety and behave like a fool, loosen our inner controls and become a criminal. Or with a ten-dollar bill we can buy the works of Plato and the Bible, making available for ourself the supreme wisdom, righteousness, and joy of the ages. With our money we can pamper ourselves with some unnecessary comfort, or we can be a partner with Christ in his work. By means of our money we can support business which exploits human weakness, strengthens the underworld, and attacks all that the church seeks to defend; or we can support the agencies which serve and up-

lift mankind. Money is an instrument by which we do good or evil.
—Everett W. Palmer

865. If you believe in something, you support it. If you support something, the time comes when good wishes and cordial words are not enough and your hand reaches for your pocketbook. Then the fun begins. For giving is fun. If you refuse to give, your support is wavering; and if your support wavers, it can't be that you believe in that something in any strong way. Maybe our account books, after all, offer the honest list of those things in which we really believe.
—Kenneth Irving Brown in *Not Minds Alone,* Harper & Bros.

866. William Allen White gave the city of Emporia a public park of fifty acres as a memorial to his daughter. He directed that it was not to bear his name. When he handed the deed to the mayor, he said: "This is the last kick in a fistful of dollars I am getting rid of to-day. I have always tried to teach you that there are three kicks in every dollar, one when you make it. . . . The second kick is when you have it. . . . The third kick comes when you give it away. . . . The big kick is in the last one." It was a blunt way of saying that the successful, happy life is the giving life.
—Charles M. Crowe in *Sermons on the Parables of Jesus,* Abingdon Press.

867. Persons who have given priority in life to the acquiring of personal possessions may well find counsel in the lives of truly great men who have never been intimidated by an unworthy love of money. "Einstein could have become a very rich man in a short time if he had been willing to capitalize his fame on the lecture platform and in the newspapers," writes H. Gordon Garbedian in *Albert Einstein: Maker of Universes.* "But to him an inexpensive glass dish was as good as one of silver, so why become excited about money? He believed that wealth only appealed to selfishness and always tempted its owners to abuse it. To friends who remonstrated, pointing out the good that money could do, the scientist cut in: 'I am absolutely convinced that no wealth in the world can help humanity forward. The example of great and fine personalities is the only thing that can lead us to fine ideas and noble deeds. Can you imagine Moses, Jesus or Gandhi armed with the money-bags of Carnegie?' "
—Funk & Wagnalls Co.

868. Money buys everything except love, personality, freedom, immortality, silence, peace.
—From *The People, Yes* by Carl Sandburg. Copyright, 1936, by Harcourt, Brace & Co., Inc.

THANKSGIVING DAY

SPIRIT OF THANKFULNESS

869. One time I rode in the chair lift up Bel-Air Mountain in the Catskills. It had been cloudy in the valley; but as we moved up, the sun shone more brightly. At the top it shone brilliantly, and we enjoyed an excellent view of a vast and endless horizon. The spirit of thankfulness is a spiritual chair lift. When we are low in mood, we need only to think of our blessings and express our gratitude to God, and we are lifted to heights of praise where we gain a new perspective of our circumstances.
—ARTHUR A. WAHMANN

870. When Charles A. Lindbergh sighted the southern tip of Ireland at the close of his first trans-Atlantic flight he recorded: "One senses only through change, appreciates only after absence. I haven't been far enough away to know the earth before. For twenty-five years I've lived on it, and yet not seen it till this moment. For nearly two thousand hours, I've flown over it without realizing what wonders lay below, what crystal clarity—snow-white foam on blackrock shores—curving hill above its valley—the hospitality of little houses—the welcome of waving arms. During my entire life I've accepted these gifts of God to man, and not known what was mine until this moment. It's like rain after drought; spring after a northern winter. I've been to eternity and back. I know how the dead would feel to live again."
—Reprinted from *The Spirit of St. Louis* by Charles A. Lindbergh. Copyright 1953 by Charles Scribner's Sons. Used by permission of the publishers.

871. Moshe Wolfe in *East River* by Sholem Asch says significantly: "Of course man is nothing but dust. As it says in our Bible—What is man that thou art mindful of him? But still the Heavenly Father is concerned over him, watches over him every minute of his life, guards his every footstep. Not only mankind but every individual man and woman is under his watchful care. And every animal, every blade of grass. Our sages have said that under every blade of grass there is an angel, who tends it to make it grow. Thus it is that all creation gives thanks to God. The grass that grows fulfills God's commandment, and the bird that sings, sings only for God. The great and the small, the stars in the sky and the drops of water in the ocean, are all in God's care. There is not a leaf on a tree which does not tremble at God's will, for everything which God has created belongs to God. There is not and there cannot be anything in existence without God."
—Copyright 1946. G. P. Putnam's Sons.

872. At the heart of thankfulness is a sense of appreciation. And God be thanked for those who have increased our awareness. Sherwood Anderson in a

letter to his brother wrote: "I have been to Nebraska, where the big engines are tearing the hills to pieces; over the low hills runs the promise of the corn. You wait, dear Brother; I shall bring God home to the sweaty men in the corn rows. My songs shall creep into their hearts and teach them the sacredness of the long aisles of growing things that lead to the throne of the God of men."
—*Letters of Sherwood Anderson,* Howard Mumford Jones, ed., Atlantic Monthly Press and Little, Brown & Co.

873. Nothing brightens life—our own and others'—so much as the spirit of thanksgiving. A doctor I knew in South Wales prescribed in certain cases of neuroses what he called his "thank-you cure." When a patient came to him discouraged, pessimistic and full of his own woes, but without any symptoms of a serious ailment, he would give this advice: "For six weeks I want you to say 'Thank you' whenever anyone does you a favor, and to show you mean it emphasize the words with a smile." "But no one ever does me a favor, Doctor," the patient might complain. Whereupon, borrowing from Scripture, the wise old doctor would reply: "Seek and you will find." Six weeks later, more often than not, the patient would return with quite a new outlook, freed of his sense of grievance against life, convinced that people had suddenly become more kind and friendly.
—A. J. Cronin in *The Reader's Digest.*

874. I knew a four-year-old girl in Japan who, at the end of a wonderful day of play with her American and Japanese friends, asked permission to say her evening prayers in her own words. Then she said, "Thank you, God, for a pleasant day," hesitated a moment while she thought what should come next, then in complete sincerity added, "I hope you've had a good time too." That prayer implies that if thankfulness is genuine it must be linked to life's actions. It is thankfulness which says to God, "I hope that this day my actions have brought you only pleasure."
—Joe J. Mickle in *This I Believe.* Copyright, 1952, by Help, Inc. Reprinted by permission of Simon and Schuster, Inc.

875. John Henry Jowett said: "Gratitude is a vaccine, an antitoxin, and an antiseptic." This is a most searching and true diagnosis. Gratitude can be a vaccine that can prevent the invasion of a disgruntled attitude. As antitoxins prevent the disastrous effects of certain poisons and diseases, thanksgiving destroys the poison of faultfinding and grumbling. When trouble has smitten us, a spirit of thanksgiving is a soothing antiseptic.
—Clinton C. Cox in *The Upper Room Pulpit.*

OCCASION FOR THANKS

876. It is recorded in the early days at Plymouth: ". . . at noon men staggered by reason of faintness for want of food, yet ere night, by the Good Providence and blessing of God, we have enjoyed such plenty as though the windows of heaven had been opened to us." Elder Brewster, we are told, when often he sat down to a repast of clams, with a cup of cold water, looked up to heaven and returned thanks "for the abundance of the sea and for the treasures hid in the sand." . . . But through these difficulties and many others the Pilgrims worked, prayed, and did their highest sense of right. And they had their Thanksgiving Day.
—Harry C. Kenney in *The Christian Science Monitor.*

877. The place of the Pilgrim Fathers in American history can best be stated by a paradox. Of slight importance in their own time, they are of great and increasing significance in our time, through the influence of their story on American folklore and tradition. And the key to that story, the vital factor in this little group, is the faith in God that exalted them and their small enterprise to something of lasting value and enduring interest.
—Samuel Eliot Morison in *By Land and By Sea,* Alfred A. Knopf, Inc.

878. An epitaph in Middle Cemetery, Lancaster, Massachusetts, which commemorates Lucy Eaton, died 1847, aged 96, reads:

> Descended from the Pilgrims
> She lov'd their doctrines
> And practic'd their virtues.

—*Stories on Stone,* Oxford University Press, Inc.

879. My job makes it necessary for me to travel East on the train several times each year. Sometimes the railroad goes along beside the old Oregon Trail where the pioneers traveled westward a generation or two ago. There are places in western Nebraska where I have walked in the ruts of the old wagon wheels. As I sit in a comfortable, air-conditioned roomette and travel down the rails seventy-five miles an hour, my imagination can see the prairie schooners rocking on their way painfully and slowly a few miles each day. And it comes to me that if they had not made the trip the hard way I could not be making it the easy way. I am the recipient of gifts created out of their courage, their sacrifice, their vision.
—Gerald Kennedy in *God's Good News,* Harper & Bros.

880. There is rather a fine story in the life of the late Edmund Morel. Morel, an extremist in politics and surprisingly bitter, had a curious friendship with the then Prime Minister. In 1923 Morel visited all the European capitals, and, on his return, stayed with Mr. Baldwin at Chequers. There he told his story; where he had been; what he had seen; rags in Poland; prosperity in Prague; hunger in Austria, simmering revolt in Hungary. A dark picture and full of shadow, and the shadow fell upon both their hearts. Then abruptly the Prime Minister turned to Morel and, lifting a bowl of blood-red roses, said, "Do you like roses, Morel?" And Morel said, "Like them—I love them." "Then," cried the Prime Minister, "bury your face in this loveliness and thank God."
—Alistair MacLean in *High Country,* Chas. Scribner's Sons.

881. People give thanks for many reasons, but too often only because the time of the year reminds them that they ought to be thankful. It is the question of whether they really are and really feel thankful. It is one thing to go through the accepted motions of being thankful on Thanksgiving Day, and it is another to feel really thankful. . . . Thankfulness cannot be dedicated to any one day; it must embrace the calendar year and every day in the year. It is only by measuring our year-round thankfulness that we get a true measure of our sincere appreciation.
—H. F. Dunton in "Talking Shop," in *Wilson Library Bulletin.*

882. A physicist, speaking to a civic club on the "Wonders of Electricity," told of man's achievements in the controlling of this mysterious power. When he had concluded, the question was asked, "How do we make electricity to

begin with?" The scientist explained the laws of magnetism and added: "Truthfully, gentlemen, we stand humbly before this fact. Electricity is not something we make. It is given. We begin by accepting it. It's as simple as this: no magnetism, no electricity." Most of the marvels of the world are available to those who humbly and graciously accept them.
—G. THOMAS FATTARUSO

883. In a letter to a friend, Katherine Mansfield once wrote, "I have just finished my new book. Finished last night at 10:30. Laid down my pen after writing 'Thanks be to God.' I wish there was a God. I am longing (1) to praise him, (2) to thank him." Everyone but those whose lives have been strangely and constantly filled with bitterness will understand her meaning. In the joy and elation we feel at having accomplished an aim we had set, in being chosen by our associates for an honor, in hearing the first avowal of love from one we have come to love, on first taking to ourselves for our own a "thing of beauty" that will be "a joy forever," we know ourselves to have been given an unearned blessing. When this happens we are not content until we have shared our happiness with other people, and—if our sense of the source of this good be strong—until we have given thanks to God.
—JOHN L. CASTEEL in *Rediscovering Prayer*, Association Press. Quotation from *The Letters of Katherine Mansfield*, J. Middleton Murry, ed., Alfred A. Knopf, Inc.

SHARING OUR GIFTS

884. Presidential Thanksgiving Day proclamations have often concerned our national advantages and prosperity. Sometimes, however, genuine responsibility has been deemed essential to the spirit of gratitude. Coolidge, for instance, wrote: "We have been a most favored people. We ought to be a most generous people. We have been a most blessed people. We ought to be a most thankful people." Truman suggested: "May our Thanksgiving be tempered by humility, by sympathy for those who lack abundance, and by compassion for those in want."

885. Gratitude is one of the most precious of Christian graces. But it must be gratitude to God, not nationalistic pride, and it must be linked with compassion. Abundant harvests and sufficient resources are a trust. Sharing them with . . . "the needy and helpless . . . the hungry and homeless . . . of other lands" is a privilege as well as a duty. The faith that links occasions for thanksgiving with imperatives for sharing found expression five centuries ago in the writings of Jan van Ruysbroeck, Flemish monk. He said: "When man considers the wealth and the marvelous sublimity of the divine nature, and all the manifold gifts which he grants and offers to his creatures, amazement is stirred up in his spirit at the sight of so manifold a wealth and majesty; at the sight of the immense faithfulness of God to all his creatures. This causes a strange joy of spirit and a boundless trust in God. . . . Christ had nothing of his own, but all was held in common."
—*The Christian Century*. Copyrighted by the Christian Century Foundation and used by permission.

886. In the distance could be heard music from the county-fair caliope. A small boy, eager to join his friends at the fair grounds, begged his father, a hardworking farmer, for money to go. Finally the father went into the kitchen and took an old coffee can from the shelf. He reached into his savings and brought out

a shining silver dollar. "Son," said the father, "there is one thing I want you to remember when you spend this silver dollar. Think of the long, hard hours required to earn it. When you spend it, remember you are spending a part of your father's life." The material blessings which our heavenly Father offers to his children are a part of himself, his labor, and his love.
—Carlton Van Ornum

887. Late one night when I was driving along an isolated road, the motor of my car stopped. A friendly traveler came along, took a rope from the trunk of his car, and towed my stalled car nearly thirty miles to a garage. When I insisted that he accept pay, he refused. He rejected my offer to fill his tank with gas. "Well," I said, "I must in some way return your kindness." The stranger replied, "If you really want to show your gratitude, buy a rope and always carry it in your car."
—Robert C. Newell

888. "There is no lovelier way to thank God for your sight," Helen Keller has written, "than by giving a helping hand to someone in the dark."

BREAKING BREAD GRATEFULLY

889. A girl in college . . . sat down at a cafeteria table with five other girls, and began by saying grace silently with her head down. The others laughed. When she raised her head, she said to them in a nice but firm way: "What were you laughing at?" They said: "You know," and went on snickering. "Aren't you grateful?" she asked. "For what? We paid for the food," they said. "Where did you get the money?" she queried. "Family," they said. "Where did they get it?" she asked. "Worked for it," they said. "Where did they get the strength—where does it all come from?" she asked. That evening at supper, two more of them said grace. Next day all six of them said it with her. And now she's got the whole lot in a prayer-group!
—Samuel M. Shoemaker in *Pulpit Digest.*

890. Margaret Lee Runbeck in *Time for Each Other* records the time when she and her husband offered thanksgiving at their table: "I don't quite know how it started. Maybe because the news broadcasts come immediately before dinner. But anyway, before Peter went away [to war], something began happening in our house. Some unseen presence came in, and after we had listened to the news, it took us each by the hand and led us more quietly into our dining-room. The first time we felt it, we had no words. The second night one of us said with embarrassment, 'Funny thing. Don't laugh, but just now I had a feeling we were all going to bow our heads and say Grace.' 'Grace?' 'Yes. You know, that old-fashioned custom of giving thanks before a meal.' Then Peter said: 'I *have* been giving thanks. Every time I see our table, and us around it, and good food upon it. I say it to myself.' 'Let's do it together.' So that night we did. Later we learned words to say together, but that first night we said our Grace in silence. I didn't know any formal words, but something in me said, 'When danger walks outside the house, those within become reverent. . . . Forgive us for that spiritual mercenariness, please.' And Something answered, 'There is nothing to forgive. Only draw near to Me.'"
—Appleton-Century-Crofts, Inc. Copyright, 1944, Crowell-Collier Publishing Co. Copyright, 1944, Margaret Lee Runbeck.

891. At the close of a church supper the group formed a friendship circle. Since it was Thanksgiving time, the pastor suggested that each one tell what he was particularly grateful for that year. One by one each told of his special blessing. When it came the turn for a little pale-faced girl, she hesitated a moment and then said: "I am thankful that I am thankful."
—J. R. Brokhoff

892. We do good things from a variety of motives. Suppose I am seen opening my wallet and giving a five-dollar bill to a needy person in my office. As to motivation (conscious or unconscious), this can mean a number of things: (1) that I wished my associates to note my generosity; (2) that I decided this would be a quicker way to deal with the man than to go into his problem more deeply and work out permanent solutions for his needy condition; (3) that I hoped he would do me a favor, such as speaking well of my deed; (4) that it made me feel good to do a creditable good work; (5) that it would help make up for the fact that I had slighted someone yesterday; or (6) that I was grateful for the many blessings that had come to me in times of need.
—James A. Pike in *Beyond Anxiety,* Chas. Scribner's Sons.

893. John went to a home where everyone sat down and immediately began to eat. He asked, "Don't you say a blessing before you eat?" The reply was, "No, we don't take time for that." John thought for a moment and then said: "You're just like my dog. You start right in."
—Herbert W. Hansen

SYMPTOMS OF INGRATITUDE

894. A woman once said to her physician, "Doctor, why am I seized with these restless longings for the glamorous and faraway?" The doctor replied, "My dear lady, they are the usual symptoms of too much comfort in the home and too much ingratitude in the heart."
—Wallace Fridy in *A Light Unto My Path,* Abingdon Press.

895. "According to their pasture, so were they filled; they were filled, and their heart was exalted; therefore have they forgotten me." Here is a rich pasturage, and in the enjoyment of it there is born the spirit of forgetfulness. . . . A man's devotion is apt to dwindle as he becomes more successful. Our piety does not keep pace with our purse. Absorption in bounty makes us forgetful of the Giver. We can be so concerned in the pasturage that the Shepherd is forgotten. Our very fullness is apt to become our foe. Our clearest visions are given us in the winter-time when nature is scanty and poor. The fulness of the leaf blocks the outlook and the distance is hid. And the summer-time of life, when leaves and flowers are plentiful, is apt to bring a veil. And the very plentifulness impedes our communion.
—John Henry Jowett in *Things That Matter,* Fleming H. Revell Co.

896. We should ever hold the Pilgrim Fathers in reverence, for their object in coming to this country was exactly the opposite of that which brings hither the majority of modern immigrants. Many modern pilgrims leave poverty and discomfort in Europe in order to find wealth and luxury in America; but the passengers in the Mayflower, in order that they might be free to worship God in their own way, left the refinement and civilization of Europe for the bleak and dangerous wilderness in the New World.
—William Lyon Phelps

UNIVERSAL BIBLE SUNDAY

BIBLE IN HISTORY

897. When a British monarch is crowned, the Archbishop of Canterbury takes a volume and places it in the new king's or queen's hands. "We present you with this book," he says, "the most valuable thing that this world affords. Here is wisdom, this is the Royal Law; these are the lively oracles of God." That volume, of course, is a copy of the Bible.
—DAVID A. MACLENNAN in *Joyous Adventure,* published in 1952 by Harper & Brothers.

898. John Richard Green in *A Short History of the English People* makes this comment concerning the Puritan period: "England became the people of a book, and that book was the Bible. It was as yet the one English book which was familiar to every Englishman; it was read at churches and read at home, and everywhere its words, as they fell on ears which custom had not deadened, kindled a startling enthusiasm. . . . The whole temper of the nation felt the change. A new conception of life and of man superseded the old. A new moral and religious impulse spread through every class."

899. The Time Capsule was the most widely publicized stunt of the New York World's Fair in 1939. It was an eight-hundred-pound torpedo-shaped shell that the Westinghouse Electric and Manufacturing Company dreamed up and buried in Long Island to be dug up five thousand years later. A host of miscellaneous modern articles were put into it: a Lily Daché hat, golf balls, and approximately ten million words of microfilmed printed matter. Beside the published index of the contents of the Capsule, only one full-sized book went into it—the Bible. When Dr. Francis C. Stifler, an American Bible Society secretary, called on the assistant to the president of the Westinghouse Electric and Manufacturing Company to ask him why the Bible had been placed in the Time Capsule, this is what Mr. Pendray said: "The Holy Bible, of all books familiar to us today, will most likely survive through the ages. Therefore, the Bible that we placed in the Time Capsule will be a sort of connecting link between the past, present, and future."
—VIOLET WOOD in *Great Is the Company,* Friendship Press.

900. We sometimes speak of heroes of the Bible; in fact the entire Biblical literature has a single Hero. A variety of interesting and colorful men and women walk across its pages, but everything of lasting significance is done by God alone. It is a library of "the mighty acts of God." The Germans use the word *Heilsgeschichte* for the whole narrative, "salvation-history." There is only one Saviour.
—Reprinted from *Communion Through*

Preaching by HENRY SLOANE COFFIN. Copyright 1952 by Charles Scribner's Sons. Used by permission of the publishers.

901. Emblazoned on a mural in one of New York's skyscrapers, artist Frank Brangwyn puts in words this conviction: "Man's ultimate destiny depends not on whether he can learn new lessons or make new discoveries and conquests, but on his acceptance of the lesson taught him close upon two thousand years ago."
—Reprinted with permission of publishers from *You Can Master Life* by JOHN H. CROWE. Copyright, 1954, by Prentice-Hall, Inc., 70 Fifth Avenue, New York 11, New York.

902. The Christian knowledge of God is not given to any man save in conjunction with the telling of an old, old story.
—JOHN BAILLIE in *Our Knowledge of God,* Chas. Scribner's Sons and Oxford University Press.

903. One of the moving exhibits in the London Missionary Society Exhibition recently held in Bournemouth was the leaves of one of the buried Bibles of Madagascar. The Queen who, for purposes of her own, determined to stamp out the Christian church seemed to have succeeded in her purpose. But some of the Bibles were not destroyed: they were buried in the ground. One day they were brought forth again and the imprisoned light of truth was set free to disperse the heathen darkness. That is a parable of God's ways with men. What God fills with life can never be vanquished by death.
—JOHN SHORT in *Triumphant Believing,* Chas. Scribner's Sons.

904. Says Jude, the brother of Jesus, in *Mary* by Sholem Asch: "The Torah does not abide in heaven; it dwells with us on earth! It lives in every academy and school, and on the lips of the rabbis. It does not come by dreaming, but by earnest effort and ordeal, by sleeping on hard benches, eating dry bread, and imbibing the words of the sages."
—Copyright 1949. G. P. Putnam's Sons.

905. You don't have to read political science or study constitutional law to understand democracy or to realize that, when individuality is suppressed, society suffers; when originality is thwarted, progress is halted. You only have to read the Bible to provide understanding. Let Saul have his heavy armor if he wishes and let David have his slingshot and his five smooth stones. Let each of us be as impetuous as Peter or as slow and plodding as Andrew. From the point of view of a dictator who can rule only as long as individual thoughts and ideas and conduct are suppressed, these are dangerous thoughts to be lurking in the mind of man. Yes, if I were a dictator the first book I would burn would be the Bible.
—QUENTIN REYNOLDS in *This I Believe.* Copyright, 1952, by Help, Inc. Reprinted by permission of Simon and Schuster, Inc.

BOOK WHICH STIMULATES

906. During the last war, a Belgian student who was a member of a Bible-study group wrote as follows to a friend: "We are hungry most of the time and with little to do: but we have formed a group for studying the Bible. It is the only Book which does not tell lies about man."
—D. T. NILES in *That They May Have Life,* Harper & Bros.

907. Two French pastors, who were Christian pacifists, got into trouble with the Vichy regime because of their insistence on taking care of Jewish refugee children. Thrown into a concentration camp, these men also read the Bible. Offered their release if they would pledge allegiance to the Petain Government, they refused. Their Communist fellow prisoners were intrigued that anyone in the modern world should refuse to sign a piece of paper if, by signing, he could gain his liberty. When they found out that it was the Bible that had given these two pastors that sense of honor, the Communists asked to sit in with the pastors in their Bible study.

As a result of what they learned, a spokesman for the Communists said: "We admit that your religion is superior to ours. This way of life that Jesus taught and lived is the way all men ought to live. It is the way all men will live—after the Revolution. But, of course, it isn't practical now."

—J. Carter Swaim in *Right and Wrong Ways to Use the Bible.* Copyright, 1953, by W. L. Jenkins, The Westminster Press. Used by permission.

908. "I do not dare to look at the New Testament," Gamaliel Bradford declared, "for fear of its awakening a storm of anxiety and self-reproach and doubt and dread of having taken the wrong path, of having been traitor to the plain and simple God."

—*The Journal of Gamaliel Bradford,* Van Wyck Brooks, ed., Houghton Mifflin Co.

909. A professor said that in taking an examination the students would sit a seat apart to avoid all appearances of evil, "as the Good Book says." A smart aleck held up his hand and asked, "What if you don't believe in the Good Book?" The professor replied, "Then you will put two seats between you."

—Alfred W. Swan

910. It is reported that in the Viking Museum in Bergen, Norway, there are relics of the great Hanse merchants of the powerful Hanseatic League which during the thirteenth and fourteenth centuries controlled all the seafaring trade from Germany to the Baltic. These men were evidently very pious traders and students of the Word. Prayer books and crucifixes remain, with other reminders of the medieval faith. Also among their relics are two sets of scales, one for buying, the other for selling, with prayer notes of thanksgiving for the means and opportunity of cheating the poor fisherfolk.

—J. Carter Swaim in *Do You Understand the Bible?* Copyright, 1954, by W. L. Jenkins, The Westminster Press. Used by permission.

911. One Korean convert could recite the whole of the Sermon on the Mount. To a surprised missionary he gave the explanation: "At first I tried to commit it to memory verse by verse, but it would not stick. So I tried a new plan. I took just one little bit of the Sermon and said, 'Tomorrow I am going to try that on my neighbor.' "

—David A. MacLennan in *Joyous Adventure,* published in 1952 by Harper & Brothers.

912. Concerning the Ten Commandments a little girl said: "They don't tell you what you ought to do; they just put ideas into your head."

913. In a small country church where Bible verses were painted on the walls, this passage from John was written in an unusual manner; and I believe it gives us the key to the search for life. It was written, "I am the way, the truth, and the life, if you love me."

—Ensworth Reisner

914. When Guy Rowe was asked to do the paintings for the biblical book *In Our Image,* he spent long months in research and planning, and when the masterful work at last was done, he made this comment on his own experience as an artist: "I don't know how to explain it in words. I had to elevate myself to the high places in order to catch the spirit of the prophets."
—Roy M. Pearson in *This Do—and Live,* Abingdon Press.

READING WITH UNDERSTANDING

915. In our reading of the Bible we need to remember that at the center is Christ himself. Whatever leads us to a fuller appreciation and understanding of him is important; all else is secondary. Martin Luther once described the Bible as the "swaddling clothes and the crib in which Christ lies." If our attention is engrossed with the "swaddling clothes" or with the "crib," the precious treasure may be overlooked entirely. In a similar way the attention of some is absorbed so much with difficulties in biblical interpretation that they do not get to the heart of the Bible. They never see Christ and consequently never come into a personal relationship with him.
—Karl H. A. Rest

916. Through faith in God a Christian can believe even that which his mind cannot completely comprehend. Those of us who have little understanding of the science of electricity may sit back and enjoy television. We may read with benefit and inspiration a psalm even though we may not know exactly who wrote the psalm and when and where and how.
—Lewis R. Rogers

917. When General Booth was asked about difficult or perplexing passages in the Bible, he replied: "If I come across a bone, I just put it on one side of my plate and go on till I find the next nourishing mouthful."
—Karl H. A. Rest

918. In spite of its unfathomable depths the essential truths presented in the Bible are so clear and simple that a little child can grasp them. A child can understand something of the majesty, the power, the wisdom, and the love of God. A child can appreciate man's relationship to the world: the world is so great, and man is so puny. A child can understand something of the evil of sin, how it offends God, how it angers God, how God will punish it. A child can appreciate God's fatherly concern for his welfare, especially the forgiveness of sins for Jesus' sake. A child can be stirred by its eternal destiny in heaven with God through Christ after it has by faith lived a life of service to God and neighbors.
—Armin C. Oldsen

919. I remember vividly a moment in my childhood as an event of more than passing importance. Every morning before breakfast we assembled in the sitting room and my father read a passage from the Bible, followed by a prayer. These family prayers did not appeal to me as a child hungry for her breakfast, an absent-minded child, too, whose thoughts were usually woolgathering. But on this particular morning my father started to read the book of Job. The dramatic story caught my attention, and when he would have closed the book, I begged him to read on, so his voice conveyed—doubtless with many skippings—the tale of Job's temptations, trust and woes. But somewhere, as my father read, I became excitedly aware of something more than the story: of the beauty and glory of words; of the images they can evoke

and the thoughts they can enkindle. In short, on that morning, I discovered for the first time inspired literature.
—DOROTHY THOMPSON in *Ladies' Home Journal.* Copyright 1953.

920. Even good motives may be poorly motivated. As a child I was promised by my father that I would be given a shiny silver dollar if I read the Bible through from Genesis to Revelation. The dollar seemed mighty appealing to me, and so with enthusiasm I began to read. I read the first books of the Old Testament but soon became discouraged and finally I gave up. To read the Bible was, of course, a worthy pursuit; but the motivation was unworthy.
—JOHN EDWARD LANTZ

921. Robert Murray McCheyne was once asked whether he wasn't afraid of running short of sermon materials. He replied: "No, I am just an interpreter of Scripture in my sermons, and when the Bible runs dry, then I shall."
—DONALD G. MILLER in *Fire in Thy Mouth,* Abingdon Press.

NEGLECT OF THE BIBLE

922. During my college days I felt fortunate to spend my summers as a Bible salesman, for I had the privilege of travel, of earning money, and of rendering Christian service too. One day I called at a home and asked permission to exhibit my Bibles. The lady of the house resisted my sales talk and finally said: "I believe every word in the Bible! Why should I read it any more?" A few pertinent questions disclosed that, although she apparently treasured the Bible, she did not know its contents nor was she willing to discover its truths.
—JOHN EDWARD LANTZ

923. In a discussion about the Bible a woman said: "I let the preacher read the Bible for me. He understands so much better than I do." "That," another person suggested, "is like buying secondhand clothes or being content with leftover food at a restaurant. Anyone who relies on the preacher to do his Bible reading for him will never have anything but a secondhand religion."
—E. PAUL HOVEY

924. A mother, helping her son to sort his clothing, found in the breast pocket of his old Army uniform the Bible she had sent him. "Did you read it?" she asked. "Yes, Mother." "How far?" "From cover to cover." "Open it to page three," said the mother, thrusting the Testament at him accusingly. There he found a five-dollar bill. "I put it there when I sent the Bible," she said.
—J. CARTER SWAIM in *Right and Wrong Ways to Use the Bible.* Copyright, 1953, by W. L. Jenkins, The Westminster Press. Used by permission.

925. A father of wayward children complained that although a Bible had always lain on the table in the living room his children had not heeded its instructions. But the Bible, a beautifully bound volume, was kept beyond those children in their most formative years, lest their dirty hands should soil the pages. "The soul of a book *can* be separated from its body," says Mortimer J. Adler. "A book is more like the score of a piece of music than it is like a painting. No great musician confuses a symphony with the printed sheets of music. Arturo Toscanini reveres Brahms, but Toscanini's score of the C-minor Symphony is so thoroughly marked up that no one but the maestro himself can read it. The reason why a great conductor makes notations on his musical scores—marks them up again and again each time he returns to study them—is the reason why

you should mark your books. If your respect for magnificent binding or typography gets in the way, buy yourself a cheap edition and pay your respects to the author." Even so the family Bible, whatever its binding, becomes the Family Book when sometimes dirty little hands and sometimes penciled reminders show that respects have been paid to the Author.
—Quotation from *The Saturday Review.*

926. In a museum display case I saw a beautiful Bible. It was exquisitely wrought and showed the care and talent of a devoted craftsman. The skillfully tooled leather binding was a wonder to behold. On the top of the case was a small sign which read: "Hands Off." That beautiful Bible will be tenderly preserved for centuries. Our great-grandchildren will no doubt look at it—through glass. But few hands will touch that precious binding, and no hearts will plumb the depths of its message to find words for life. No tears will stain the pages. No resolutions will be inscribed on the margins. It will rest in the hands of no distraught supplicant who turns in prayer from the Word of God to the throne of grace. That Bible is a rarity, and it is priceless, but it is also no longer serving the purpose for which it was bound.
—Charles L. Allen

927. A sign on a Bible in a large church in New England read: "Not to be taken from the building." From what I know about many churches, the sign was unnecessary—there was little chance that even the smallest word in that book would ever leave.
—Rex H. Knowles in *Pulpit Digest.*

928. One day a woman went into a bookshop to purchase a Bible; there the enterprising young assistant, apologizing for his inability to supply one, said: "I am very sorry, madam, we sold our last copy yesterday; but I have here another book which I can heartily recommend." Another book! Yes, for many the Bible is only another book, and it remains unread.
—John Trevor Davies in *Lord of All,* Abingdon Press.

929. A theological-school professor told his class: "You will go out of this school into a jungle of religious illiteracy, so don't go waving Bible verses around in the air or chanting your belief in the Holy Writ, or you will become another witch doctor rattling the bones of a dead faith. The only way to bring the Word of God to life is to live it."
—Ensworth Reisner

930. A colporteur told the Christmas story to the people of a village in North India, then read it from the Scripture. "How long ago was this great day when God's Son was born?" one asked. "About two thousand years," the colporteur told him. "Then why has the news been so long in reaching us?" the villager asked in surprise. "Who has been *hiding* the Book all this time?"
—Herbert Beecher Hudnut

TRANSLATING THE WORD

931. Whenever we take from our shelves a copy of the Bible, we would do well to pause for a moment of grateful prayer for those consecrated souls of twenty centuries who have made possible our handling of the Word of Truth. Think of the devout men who first recorded for us the story of man's quest for God and God's search for man. Think of the scholars and teachers and scribes and printers who through the years have labored in the transmission and translation of God's Book. We cherish today

the faith of our fathers only because we have received our Father's Book.

932. J. B. Phillips, Bible translator, has written: "No modern translator, and certainly not myself, is in any sense in competition with the Authorized Version that you know so well. What we're trying to do by the help of God and by such skill and imagination as He has given us, is to give you in English as nearly and as accurately as we can what was written twenty centuries ago. 'It's like seeing a famous picture after it's been cleaned,' a well-known English scholar once wrote to me. I treasure those words, for although I know that there will always be those who prefer the mellow patina of age, there are those who are willing and indeed eager to read a conscientious attempt to bring across the centuries the inspired words in all their vividness, directness and lack of decoration."
—*Plain Christianity*. Copyright 1954. Used by permission of The Macmillan Co.

933. According to the statistics published by the French Academy, there are 2,378 languages spoken in the world today. Of these only 190 have the complete Bible and another 937 have some part of it. Fully half the languages of the world do not possess so much as a single sentence of Scripture. Obviously there is still plenty of translation work to be done. And plenty of distribution work too. For with 1,000 million people at present able to read and an additional 50 million each year learning to read, how is it possible to catch up, much less to keep pace with the need? The answer depends to a large extent on the seriousness with which the Church as a whole recognizes its obligation and responds to it.
—A. M. Chirgwin in *The Bible in World Evangelism,* Friendship Press.

934. Referring to the scholars who have given us the Revised Standard Version, [one] man said to me: "Why do these busy-body scholars think they must rob us of the beauty of our choicest English classic? It is nothing but sacrilege. No one would think of changing Shakespeare." Right there is the answer. No one *would* think of changing Shakespeare. We read and study Shakespeare for its literary beauty, its turn of phrase. That is the supreme value of Shakespeare. That is why Shakespeare has endured. But the Bible is more than literature. It has beauty in abundance and unsurpassed, especially in our English versions; but the supreme value of the Bible is in its message, the good news of God's love for man revealed in Christ. And while it is not possible that such news could be given without beauty of expression, nevertheless, as usage changes among the words of any tongue, beauty of expression must give way to clarity of meaning.
—Francis C. Stifler in *Missions,* Vol. 150, No. 7, p. 410.

935. In an art gallery I noticed a student who was seated in front of a magnificent canvas. On a small easel he was reproducing the lines and colors of the original. Through his immature and imperfect efforts he was gaining a fuller appreciation of the skill of the master. Would not each of us reverence more fully the Bible if we might attempt to rewrite Psalm 23, the story of Ruth, the prophecies of Isaiah, or Paul's immortal chapter on love? Only as we imitate, however imperfectly, the bold strokes of the inspired writers of scripture, do we realize their greatness; and only as we attempt to translate their words into our daily lives, do we fully appreciate their noble challenge.
—Friedrich Rest

ADVENT AND CHRISTMAS

GOD WAS IN CHRIST

936. At first [the contemporaries of Christ] may have said, God sent him. After a while that sounded too cold, as though God were a bow and Jesus the arrow. That would not do. God did more than send him. So I suspect they went on to say, God is with him. That went deeper. Yet, as their experience with him progressed, it was not adequate. God was more than with him. So at last we catch the reverent accents of a new conviction, God came in him. That was not so much theology at first as poetry. It was an exhilarating insight and its natural expression was a song. God can come into human life! they cried; God has come into human life! Divinity and humanity are not so separate that the visitations of the Eternal are impossible.
—HARRY EMERSON FOSDICK in *Living Under Tension,* Harper & Bros.

937. The coming of Jesus Christ into the world brought the peace of God into the hearts of men—and with peace came joy. As Joseph Fort Newton beautifully phrased it: "For the first time man was glad about God."
—JOHN C. MIDDLEKAUFF

938. The fact of Christ, writes Dr. Carnegie Simpson, "does not indeed show us everything, but it shows us the one thing we need to know—the character of God. God is the God who sent Jesus." In other words, God must be like Christ. The character of the Creator cannot be less than the highest He has created, and the highest is that babe born to Mary on that first Christmas morning.
—A. IAN BURNETT in *Lord of All Life,* Rinehart & Co., Inc.

939. God does not sound the trumpets before him. He comes quietly, unobtrusively, in a casually begun acquaintance, in the communication of a seminal idea, in a book one happens upon, in a word dropped by a friend, in a gleam that flickers for a moment in the darkness and then vanishes, leaving behind a new hope that there is light and a sure path, opening not far ahead. He comes in a disaster that makes one clutch at any straw only to find, by what seems sheer accident, one has laid hold upon a life preserver; in a demand, too great for one's own wisdom and strength and love, which spurs one to the last research that ends in the long-awaited discovery.
—ALBERT E. DAY in *An Autobiography of Prayer,* published in 1952 by Harper & Brothers.

940. Atoms can reveal mathematics. Flowers and stars and mountains and sunsets can reveal beauty. The biological order can reveal life in its ascending series. Historical events can present a dramatic story that expresses and vindicates a moral order. But it is only through a concrete person who is divine enough to show love and grace in con-

summmate degree, and human enough to be identified with us, that we can be assured of love at the heart of things. Christ is the coming of God in and through the process of history—God revealed to us in the persuasive terms of personal life and loving will.
—RUFUS M. JONES in *Rufus M. Jones Speaks to Our Time,* Harry Emerson Fosdick, ed. Copyright 1951. Used by permission of The Macmillan Co.

941. The meaning of the Incarnation . . . is simply that we do not have to *attain* union with God. Man does not have to climb to the infinite and become God, because, out of love, the infinite God descends to the finite and becomes man. Despite man's refusal of God, despite his pride, his fear, his helpless and hopeless involvement in the vicious circle of sin, God's nature remains inalterably love. . . . The eternal Word, the Logos, becomes flesh, making our nature his nature. . . . In short, God has wedded himself to humanity.
—ALAN W. WATTS in *Behold the Spirit,* Pantheon Books, Inc.

THE PURPOSE OF HIS COMING

942. A little boy, child of missionaries, was in school in the United States at Christmas time. The principal said to him, "Son, what would you rather have most of all for Christmas?" The boy looked at the picture of his father framed on his desk and . . . said, "I want my father to step out of that frame." The little boy voiced the cry of humanity: We want God our Father to step out of the frame of the universe. . . . Jesus is God stepping out of the frame of the universe—God simplified and God personalized.
—E. STANLEY JONES in *How to Be a Transformed Person,* Abingdon Press.

943. Christ did not come to earth to tell us merely what we ought to do; he came to do something for us. He came not merely to exhort but to help. He did not come to give us good advice. That, if it were no more than that, was possibly not a thing of which we stood greatly in need, for there are always plenty of people who are ready with their advice. Advice is cheap, but what Christ offered us was infinitely costly. It was the power of God unto salvation.
—JOHN BAILLIE in *Invitation to Pilgrimage,* Chas. Scribner's Sons.

944. It is told of James the Fifth of Scotland that on occasion he would lay aside the royal robe of king and put on the simple clothes of the peasant. In such a disguise, he would move freely about the land, making friends with ordinary folk, entering into their difficulties, appreciating their handicaps, sympathizing with them in their sorrow. And when as king he sat again upon the throne, he was better able to rule over them with fatherly compassion and mercy. It was this and more than this which the King of Kings did on our behalf. He took upon himself the form of a man, and limited himself to the narrow bounds of mortal frailty.
—A. IAN BURNETT in *Lord of All Life,* Rinehart & Co., Inc.

945. A father . . . lost a son in Japan during the late war. At first he was very bitter against the Japanese. But gradually he came to realize that Japanese boys, like his own son, had been helplessly caught in the war system. His bitterness gave way to charitableness and he contributed generously to the founding of the International Christian University in Japan. When we see charity replacing hate in the human heart—that is Christ coming.
—From: *How to Believe,* by RALPH W.

SOCKMAN. Copyright 1953 by Ralph W. Sockman, reprinted by permission of Doubleday & Company, Inc.

946. Surgeons at the University of Minnesota have performed an operation during which a healthy person "loans" his heart to a patient on an operating table. The surgeons operate on the "idle" heart in the patient while life processes flow into his body through plastic tubes connected to the donor. What a graphic picture of the Christian's opportunity! We meet people each day who have been overwhelmed by life. Their hearts have become heavy and broken. We loan our hearts to them through understanding and sympathy and follow the example of One who has ever loaned his heart to the least and the lost.
—ROGER J. SQUIRE

947. Christ is like someone who lifts us to a high mountain so that we can map the whole surrounding countryside. He is like the dominant, unifying perspective of the landscape artist or writer, without which the canvas or manuscript is a collection of scattered impressions or ideas. C. S. Lewis has said that the Incarnation, the Grand Miracle, is like a newly discovered section of a novel or a manuscript of which we can say, "This is the missing part of the work. This is the chapter on which the whole plot of the novel really turned. This is the main theme of the symphony."
—WOODROW A. GEIER in *Religion in Life*. Quotation from *Miracles*. Copyright 1947. Used by permission of The Macmillan Co.

948. Gabriel Marcel, French philosopher and dramatist, put a play on the French stage that contains an eloquent description of our world. One agent cries: "Don't you feel sometimes that we are living . . . in a broken world? Yes, broken like a broken watch. The mainspring has stopped working. Just to look at it, nothing has changed. Everything is in place. But put the watch to your ear, and you don't hear any ticking. You know what I'm talking about: the world, what we call the world of human creatures. . . . It seems to me it must have had a heart at one time, but today you would say the heart has stopped beating."
—HAROLD A. BOSLEY

THE LIGHT PIERCES DARKNESS

949. The Light which shone in Christ and which continues to shine through the persons who bear his imprint and the institutions which worthily carry his name *is* the Light that shone at Creation. . . . We go forth into days of deepening darkness. It is possible, though by no means certain, that the darkness may close in on most of our world for our generation. Of what can we be confident? Of one thing at least: the one reality which is certain to survive, carrying with it through the darkness much of the accumulated riches of the past, ready to kindle new lights on the farther side of darkness, is the Christian Movement in the World. We may hold that confidence because the Christian Movement, with all its weakness and its pettiness, its failures and its follies and its infidelities, is the bearer of the Ultimate Power of the Universe. It is the bearer of the Light which cannot be overcome because it is lit from the Eternal Light of God himself. Against that Power, no human force can finally prevail. That light, no man-made darkness can ever extinguish.
—HENRY P. VAN DUSEN in *Life's Meaning*, Association Press.

950. [Paul] speaks of seeing "the light of the knowledge of the glory of God in the face of Jesus Christ." Furthermore, "we all with unveiled face beholding as in a mirror the glory of the Lord, are transformed into the same image from glory to glory." What this thought might have meant to the early Christians I never realized until I stood one day on the south rim of the Grand Canyon in Arizona. I had gone out along the rim to the point where one could see the Painted Desert. The guide had said to go first into the Watch Tower erected on the edge of the canyon and look at the art work of the Indians. There were displayed designs in sand and stone in which the thirty-eight different colors of the desert were represented. Going out on the terrace I looked off at the desert itself and tried to discern the colors. But a haze overlay the desert. Then I remembered that the guide had said, "Don't forget to look in the mirror." A large mirror of polarized glass was hung in such a position that it reflected the desert. This glass removed much of the haze. In the mirror I saw the colors. The Painted Desert at last was real.

—Justin Wroe Nixon in *Responsible Christianity,* Harper & Bros.

951. In the city of Rome, there is a palace with a high dome on the inside of which there is a painting known as "The Dawn" by Guido Reni. So high is it that it is very difficult to see. In order that visitors may see this masterpiece clearly and with ease, a table has been placed directly beneath the dome, and on it a mirror. All that has to be done is to look into the mirror. Before Jesus came, it was difficult to see God. But with his coming, it was as if a mirror had been placed before the eyes of men to enable them the better to see and to understand. Indeed, do we not hear him say, "He that hath seen me hath seen the Father"?

—Norman A. McMurray in *The Upper Room Pulpit.*

952. When an old church in Richmond, Virginia, was razed, there was found a stained-glass picture of Holman Hunt's "Christ Praying in the Garden." Generations earlier it had been covered with organ pipes. Nor could it be seen from the exterior of the building, for the brick wall of a neighboring structure obscured it. Almost everybody had forgotten it was there. Behind the façade of modern life the reality of God is still alive in human hearts waiting to be recognized and appropriated. When we tear away the outer veneers of sophisticated civilization, we find God at the center of every life.

—William Frederick Dunkle, Jr.

953. Ralph Adams Cram, the late great architect, was wont to say that the exterior of a church should be secondary to its interior. All too often church builders put up an imposing front to impress the passer-by and then economize by cheapening the furnishings within. But, said Dr. Cram, a church should be like a Christian in that it gets better and richer the farther in you go.

—Ralph W. Sockman in *The Whole Armor of God,* Abingdon Press.

954. I stood once within the cathedral at Chartres looking at a great window as the light poured through it from the sunset sky. The workmanship represented there was supreme. The colors of the window held a secret the greatest artists in stained glass in our own day have longed to penetrate. The window was a human creation. But its glory came not from man. It came from the sky. The light that streamed through the window, and that at once invested it with beauty and enabled the visitor to see it, was a gift to man from beyond.

So with our ideas of God; whether they be wrought in stained glass, in stone, in a poem or in a song, they all say as the mountains, the hills, and the seas said to Augustine, "We are not thy God," but "he made us."
—JUSTIN WROE NIXON in *Responsible Christianity*, Harper & Bros.

955. During World War II a bomb falling near Reims Cathedral shattered the beautiful rose window into thousands of pieces. The villagers, women and children, searched until every broken or splintered piece of glass was gathered up. After the war skillful artisans put the window back to its original beauty as each separate piece was leaded into the perfect whole. It is religion that enables us to pick up life's fragments and redream our dreams, relive our hopes, rethink our faith, until the light of God once again shines through the window of our life.
—FRANK A. COURT

956. In his description of a bomb test in Nevada in the spring of 1952, David Lawrence used a phrase which is an inclusive one in a far deeper sense than the one in which he used it. Describing the tension of the last few seconds before the bomb was dropped he wrote, "Then there was a light out of this world, with the intensity of a hundred suns." A great phrase! In the bombs bursting in air we do get a "light out of this world." Our only hope comes from out of this world—a light not with the intensity of a hundred suns, but with the infinitely greater intensity of God. "God is light," and in his light we have light for reliance and direction for action, "The light of the glory of God in the face of Jesus Christ."
—HALFORD E. LUCCOCK in *Communicating the Gospel,* Harper & Bros.

957. Alfred Noyes, speaking to a gathering of British Commonwealth youth in Albert Hall, London, said: "The whole of our ordered freedom has been built upon the value, the absolute value, of the individual human soul. Those values are not diminished by the size of the physical universe, which, even in the days of Genesis, was considerably taller than the tallest man. They do not depend on the centrality of the earth. They depend on the centrality of their Creator. Rocks and stones may crush us to pieces physically; but, however large, they are not so valuable in the eternal memory, or so near to God, as the smallest human heart that ever sacrificed itself for what it believed to be right, or caught one glimpse of the divine. There is a great saying of Galileo. . . . 'The sun, which has all those planets revolving around it, is able to ripen the smallest bunch of grapes as though it had nothing else to do in the universe.' We need not doubt the power of that infinitely greater Light."
—From *Two Worlds for Memory*. Copyright, 1953, by Alfred Noyes. Published by J. B. Lippincott Co.

958. Lord Kelvin once said, "The last stage of any great discovery is a leap in the dark." The Christian echoes with slight but significant revision, "The last step in any discovery is a leap into the Light," for there is a mystery of Light as well as of darkness.
—WILLARD BREWING in *Here Is My Method,* Fleming H. Revell Co.

959. As I was about to go across a street, a woman pulled me by the arm and said, "Look at the red light." I replied rather weakly: "But look at the people going across," and her reply was: "Don't look at them. Look up at the light and follow it." Good advice. For she put the whole thing in a nutshell. Are you get-

ting your walking signals in life from God, or from the herd? Are you breaking his laws to keep step with them?
—E. Stanley Jones in *Growing Spiritually*, Abingdon Press.

THE DIFFERENCE HIS COMING MAKES

960. I was once asked to teach a course at Nebraska Wesleyan University on the relationship between civilization and Christianity. I called that course "The Difference Christianity Has Made." I remember writing to one of my old professors and telling him what I was trying to do, asking for suggestions. He wrote back: "Above all, don't exaggerate. Understate everything Christianity did for the world, because even then the case will be so tremendous no one can doubt it. You don't need to exaggerate."
—Gerald Kennedy

961. A Jewish soldier who had attended several Protestant services during the [Second World] war went to a rabbi and asked him the difference between the Messiah of the Jews and the Jesus of the Christians. The rabbi explained: "The difference is that we Jews believe the Messiah is still to come, whereas Christians believe he has already come in Jesus." To this, the soldier asked what I assume was an unanswerable question: "But, rabbi, when our Messiah does come, what will he have on Jesus?" Certainly, it would not be purity of life, positive goodness, or perfect righteousness.
—John C. Middlekauff in *The Upper Room Pulpit*.

962. William Lyon Phelps . . . speaking to a small group of us . . . suddenly said, "You know, I am a Unitarian." All of us were greatly surprised, because we knew he was not only a member of the Calvary Baptist Church in New Haven, but also its honorary pastor, having been ordained to the ministry rather late in life. Then, when Dr. Phelps discerned that we were sufficiently shocked, he added, "I mean by that, Jesus is the only God I know." . . . When we have found Christ we feel that we are at the end of our quest. "He that hath seen me," said Jesus, "hath seen the Father."
—Edward Hughes Pruden in *Interpreters Needed*. Copyright, 1951, by The Judson Press. Used by permission.

963. Toward the conclusion of his seven volume *A History of the Expansion of Christianity*, Kenneth Scott Latourette writes: "Types of Christianity which had failed to stress the centrality of Jesus as God's Christ had not shown the power to reproduce themselves through many centuries. The continuing vitality of Christianity was intimately bound with this conviction. So far as the historian could be sure of anything about the future of Christianity it was this: if the Christian faith triumphed it would be through uncompromising loyalty to him through whom it had come to birth and who in all its ages had been the acknowledged master of its flaming spirits. As the most discerning of the disciples of its first century had seen: 'In him was life and the life was the light of men.' In the first century that had been an assertion of faith. By the twentieth century experience had made it demonstrated fact."
—Harper & Bros.

964. Gordon Rupp tells about visiting Berlin shortly after the war. As an Englishman he knew how altogether possible it was that Hitler might have established a Nazi Empire. As he walked down the Wilhelmstrasse he passed the

great German War Ministry which had been blown to bits. In the Cathedral of Berlin the bombs had penetrated even to the very crypt where lay the remains of the Prussian kings who laid the foundation of German militarism. Hitler's own Chancellery was left without one stone upon another. On its step a weary mother sat watching her baby kick and laugh. Then he says: "So another mother and another Baby lie across human history as the empires rise and fall and the captains and kings strut their hour and then depart while God writes history in his own way."
—RAYMOND E. BALCOMB in *Pulpit Digest.*

965. Leslie Stannard Hunter tells this story: "As the threats of war and the cries of the dispossessed were sounding in his ears, Western Man fell into an uneasy sleep. In his sleep he dreamed that he entered the spacious store in which the gifts of God to men are kept, and addressed the angel behind the counter, saying: 'I have run out of the fruits of the Spirit. Can you restock me?' When the angel seemed about to say no, he burst out: 'In place of war, afflictions, injustice, lying and lust, I need love, joy, peace, integrity, discipline. Without these I shall be lost.' And the angels behind the counter replied, 'We do not stock fruits, only seeds.'" A part of our religion is the belief that it does not hand us ready-made fulfillments—it gives us promises.
—*The Seed and the Fruit,* Morehouse-Gorham Co., Inc.

966. A member of the House of Commons who had listened to the wartime speeches of Neville Chamberlain and Winston Churchill made this comment: "When Mr. Chamberlain said the fine, true thing, it was like a faint air played on a pipe and lost on the wind at once. When Mr. Churchill said it, it was like an organ filling the church, and we all went out refreshed and resolute to do or die." And this is the difference between the promises of men and the promises of God. Human promises are like thin pipings which fade away quickly. When God gives us a promise, it comes with the fullness of the organ in the cathedral, filling us with courage and determination. Resting on his promises, men through the years have been made strong again.
—GERALD KENNEDY in *Who Speaks for God?* Abingdon Press.

967. During World War I a Canadian officer, known to be a professing Christian, had just returned from a front-line trench when a brother officer twitted him with the words: "I do not quite see, old man, what your Christ does for you." This was his reply: "Shall I tell you what Jesus can do? He can help you to be a gentleman in hell."
—FRED R. CHENAULT

PREPARING THE HEART

968. Advent is a period of preparation for Christmas. Before her marriage a bride prepares herself in many ways. She counsels with her pastor, her hemstitcher, her volume of etiquette. Friends and relatives come to her with advice, assurance, and aid. It is forethought and preparation which heightens the joy and solemnity of the words she offers and receives at the altar. Advent offers an opportunity to ready the heart and mind for the joy and solemnity of kneeling at the manger of the King of kings.

969. The words "Advent" and "adventure" have a common derivation. Advent should be a season of Christian adventure. Many of the noble visions of the past have become blurred; but as

Christmas approaches, new hope and new faith enter our hearts. The adventure of life is renewed and reinvigorated. We are given, as it were, a new spiritual lease on life; for a spirit of expectancy and enthusiasm comes to those who remember the hope that God in Christ brings to man.

970. Christmas is a still small voice that speaks to the heart as quietly as the Child was born on a silent, holy night. When we are getting ready for Christmas, let us make sure that what we are taking care of are the "preparations of the heart." For only the heart can really celebrate Christmas. The inner heart is the only place fit for entertaining that meaning which could turn our earth to heaven—if we would allow it. So Christmas is to be celebrated in the kingdom within. It cannot approach us as something added from the external world. But here the wonderful paradox occurs. For the promise reads, "Seek ye first the kingdom of God, and all these things shall be added unto you." When Christmas does begin and does reign from within, there materializes around us a wonderful holiday season, visible and touchable—added unto us for all who know us to share.

—Margaret Lee Runbeck in *Fifty Years of Christmas,* Ruth M. Elmquist, ed., Rinehart & Co., Inc.

971. For this wonderful man, whom those of us who call ourselves Christians believe to have been more than man, possessed an attribute which we know from our own experience to be utterly beyond the capacity of human nature. . . . The whole meaning of Christmas, the miracle of Christ's birth—and death—is that once and once only in human history there was such a being. He so loved his fellow men that his whole life was dedicated with the least alloy of self to the relief and service of all those who stood in need of them. He left us two commandments: that we should love God—whose nature he revealed to us by his own—with all our being; and that we should love our neighbor as ourselves. However far we are from fulfilling either, we all of us, as a result of Christ's life, come at Christmas for a moment a little nearer to both.

—Arthur Bryant in *The Illustrated London News* and *The Reader's Digest.*

WONDER AND WORSHIP

972. Charles A. Lindbergh, midway between New York and Paris on his first transoceanic flight, records: "It's hard to be an agnostic up here in the *Spirit of St. Louis,* aware of the frailty of man's devices, a part of the universe between its earth and stars. If one dies, all this goes on existing in a plan so perfectly balanced, so wonderfully simple, so incredibly complex that it's far beyond our comprehension—worlds and moons revolving; planets orbiting on suns; suns flung with apparent recklessness through space. There's the infinite magnitude of the universe; there's the infinite detail of its matter—the outer star, the inner atom. And man conscious of it all—a worldly audience to what if not to God?"

—Reprinted from *The Spirit of St. Louis* by Charles A. Lindbergh. Copyright, 1953, by Charles Scribner's Sons. Used by permission of the publishers.

973. Will Durant in *The Story of Philosophy* has this to say about the God of the ancient Greek thinkers: "Aristotle's God never does anything; he has no desires, no will, no purpose; he is activity so pure that he never acts. He is absolutely perfect; therefore he cannot desire anything; therefore he does nothing. . . . His sole employment is the contemplation of himself. Poor Aristotelian God!—he is a *roi fainéant,* a do-nothing king; 'the king reigns, but he does not rule.'" Many modern people think of God in abstractions: God is truth; God is goodness; God is love. Philosophical thinking is one approach to knowing God, but it is a partial and limited approach. The ancient Greeks came to sense this. The God of abstract supreme ideals was so far removed and inactive that he meant too little in their lives. So they said God must communicate his thoughts to men and does so through the faculty of divine reason, through the world reason which is his Word, the Logos. John began his Gospel, "In the beginning was the [Logos] . . . and the [Logos] was made flesh, and dwelt among us."

—Edward W. Stimson. Quotation published by Simon & Schuster, Inc.

974. Jesus has been the most potent force in history. . . . When we think of all that has come out of his teaching in the impulse to human freedom and dignity; the challenging of ignorance; the relief of suffering; the conquest of disease; the growth of humanitarian concern for the weak, the destitute, and the helpless; the inspiration to great art and literature, architecture, and music; the enlarging of personal horizons; the incentive to more sensitive and concerned moral living; the stabilizing of the inner lives of millions of Christians through the ages and around the world; the fostering of prophetic attack by even a determined minority on such giant evils as race prejudice, human exploitation, and war—when one simply enumerates these things, it seems a travesty to say that Christianity has failed, and a serious error to give up hope.

—Georgia Harkness in *The Modern Rival of Christian Faith,* Abingdon Press.

975. I wonder what happened to those gifts the Wise Men brought to Bethlehem? All records about Jesus seem to indicate that he possessed no rare wealth. Of course I'm just guessing, but I feel reasonably sure that he did with those first gifts what he does with all the countless gifts that believing hearts have brought to his feet ever since. I think he in turn gave them away. The Wise Men had *guarded* them, but Jesus *used* them.

—William Frederick Dunkle, Jr.

976. Those who are wise, wealthy, and well disposed can also come to Christ, pouring out of their treasures gifts such as they have to offer, of gold, frankincense, and myrrh. The artist Sandro Botticelli seems to have had something of the same idea when he painted his famous *Adoration of the Magi.* Those who have made a study of his masterpiece have identified the faces which the artist put upon the men bowing before the Christ. They are the men of high political and ecclesiastical positions of his own day. It has been suggested that in the two different canvasses which the famous Italian painted of the same picture he changed the faces so as to bring his suggestion up to date. With great insight he showed that the wise men represent the men of high estate in every age.

—Gerald O. McCulloh in *The Upper Room Pulpit.*

977. Dr. E. P. Dickie tells how he once had the experience of attending at the same time to two different sermons. One was preached from the pulpit, and the other from a stained-glass window in which a slight defect had obscured a single letter of the theme, so that it read, "Glory to God in the HIGH ST." There is the role of the Church and of

the church member—to see to it that the glory of God floods the common life, and all the activities and institutions of men.
—ROBERT J. MCCRACKEN in *Questions People Ask,* Harper & Bros.

SYMBOLS FOR COMMON MEN

978. It is profoundly significant to me that the Gospel story in Luke reveals that the announcement of the birth of Jesus came first to simple shepherds, who were about their appointed tasks. After theology has done its work, after the reflective judgment of men from the heights or lonely retreats of privilege and security has wrought its most perfect pattern, the birth of Jesus remains the symbol of the dignity and inherent worthfulness of the common man.
—HOWARD THURMAN in *Deep Is the Hunger,* Harper & Bros.

979. We have coined a colloquial expression, V.I.P., meaning "Very Important Person." But Christmas comes every year to remind us that we need not be Very Important Persons to see and know God's glowing glory. Christmas means that every person is very important to a God who first sent the shining of his love to simple shepherds engaged in simple tasks and who gave his only-begotten Son to live the ordinary life of ordinary men gloriously.
—WILLIAM FREDERICK DUNKLE, JR.

980. Until it was pointed out to me, I had missed one of the glories of Raphael's *Sistine Madonna.* The Madonna with the Infant Jesus, the two cherubs, and other details catch the eye first, as they are intended to do. Yet if we see nothing else, we miss the magic of this great sermon in paint. Look closely at the background of grey blue cloud and you will see it is not cloud at all. It is a vast crowd of cherubic faces, so closely linked together that they make a cloud background for the Madonna and Child. The cloud takes shape, it is the "Cloud of witnesses" to the great fact of the Incarnation.
—JOHN HELLON in *The Upper Room Pulpit.*

981. The bedroom windows of a mountain farmhouse were tightly shuttered. On the walls were cheap dime-store lithographs, hung there by poor, ignorant folk who didn't appreciate the real beauty they might have had simply by opening windows to the mountain views outside. So many of us suppose we must decorate our daily living with the clashing colors of commercialized art when we have only to open the windows of our days to see all about us God's glory. We are forever trying to brighten the commonplace ways we live with what is only gaudy and tawdry, neglecting to appropriate the beauty and wonder that God offers.
—WILLIAM FREDERICK DUNKLE, JR.

982. If Christmas means anything, it means that all life is filled with glory and melody and joy, and that fear has forever fled. In one of her remarkable utterances, Jenny Lind, "the Swedish nightingale," summed up the high purpose of her life with these four words: "I sing for God." So the shepherds went back to their task, each one holding his secret in his heart and saying to himself, "I keep sheep for God." That is the spirit that has transformed the world.
—HUGH THOMSON KERR in *Design for Christian Living.* Copyright, 1953, by W. L. Jenkins, The Westminster Press. Used by permission.

983. A deeply suggestive touch has been given to the Christmas portrayal

by a certain artist. He shows the shepherds on the hillside looking up into the heavens whence they hear the angelic chorus singing, "Glory to God in the highest, and on earth peace, good will toward men." But at the shepherds' feet is one of their dogs. The dog is alert, poised, but he is not looking into the heavens with the shepherds. His head is turned in another direction. The dog is aware that something unusual is happening, but he does not know what it is. He is missing the message heard by his masters, the shepherds. In depicting the difference between the dog and the shepherds, the artist was true to the original Gospel portrayals of the Christmas event, for in them there are such differences of observation!
—Ralph W. Sockman in *Now to Live!* Abingdon Press.

984. Christianity is a religion of song. Agnosticism has no Gloria. Confucianism and Brahmanism have no inspiring anthems or soulful hallelujahs. Dreary, weird dirges reveal no glad hope for the present or future to heathen nations. Moral melodies are generated the instant Christ is known, for his love is the source and soul of praise. Faith in Jesus awakens gladness and creates a freeness, fullness and depth of songfulness that the great question with a believer is, "How can I keep from singing?" Christian hope gives birth to a great uplift of cheerful optimism. The believer's face is radiant with gladness, and his speech inevitably flows into chants, anthems and glorious melodies. Where false religions have any music at all, it is generally found to be what one has most truthfully called "plagiarized praise."
—T. DeWitt Talmage. Used by special permission of *Christian Herald* from the book *Fifty Years of Christmas,* owners of copyright.

985. One summer afternoon in 1933 John Jacob Niles heard a band of traveling evangelists in Murphy, North Carolina. Annie Morgan, a member of the group, sang one of the most strikingly beautiful folk melodies that Niles had ever listened to. He requested that she repeat the words which millions now hear each Christmas:

I wonder as I wander, out under the sky,
How Jesus the Savior did come for to die
For poor on'ry people like you and like I,
I wonder as I wander, out under the sky.

Despite his efforts to locate Annie, Niles was never again to find her. Many of us, like Annie, live quietly obscure lives and yet somehow offer to the world influences that will linger on to bless others long after we ourselves are gone.
—Robert C. Newell. Quotation by John Jacob Niles, G. Schirmer, Inc.

986. A great artist once visited a home in which a little girl was celebrating her birthday. As one of her gifts she received a fan. The artist said to her, "Give me your fan, and I will paint a picture on it." She turned away saying impudently, "You shan't spoil my fan." If only the girl had given her cheap fan to the great artist, he would have returned it to her with a beautiful picture; and its value would have been increased a thousandfold. She refused in her contrariness to surrender her fan to an artist. Our lives may be as small and as cheap, and we are still clinging to them when the master Artist asks for them. He wants our lives that we might be friends with him and have fellowship with him. That fellowship is the real meaning of Christmas.
—J. R. Brokhoff

987. Jeanbon St. Andre, a leader in the French Revolution, said to a peasant,

"I will have all your steeples pulled down, that you may no longer have any object by which you may be reminded of your old superstitions." "But," replied the peasant, "you cannot help leaving us the stars."
—WALLACE FRIDY in *A Lamp Unto My Feet,* Abingdon Press.

988. Ernest Poole in his novel, *The Harbor,* describes a lad in Brooklyn Heights whose habit it was to wander out to a secluded spot which gave him a glorious view of the harbor. Almost at his feet, however, were nests of railroad tracks which carried hundreds of freight trains laden with precious cargoes from all over the world. But these trains frequently hid his view of the harbor. Then one night he discovered that by lifting his eyes ever so slightly he "could see the stars above the freight trains."
—DONALD H. TIPPETT in *Best Sermons, 1951-52.* Copyright 1952. Used by permission of The Macmillan Co.

989. A small child who saw the stars for the first time was greatly impressed and intrigued by them. Childlike, she had many questions. Were they there all the time? Why couldn't you see them during the day? Couldn't you see them until it got dark? Her mother replied, "Yes, their beauty is hidden all through the day. You can see them only at night. Aren't they lovely?" And then she added, "Darkness is always beautiful if we will only look up at the stars instead of into the corners." . . . [The stars] tell us that night is the most joyous part of the day. It is the time of homecoming after a hard day's work. . . . Night is the time for rest and for sleep. So it is with death. It is life's night. It is a glorious homecoming. It is a reunion with those who have gone before. It is rest from labor. It is simply to lie back in the Everlasting Arms.
—LESLIE R. SMITH in *From Sunset to Dawn,* Abingdon Press.

THE MEANINGS OF CHRISTMAS

990. The raw materials of the Christmas mood are a newborn baby, a family, friendly animals, and labor. An endless process of births is the perpetual answer of life to the fact of death. It says that life keeps coming on, keeps seeking to fulfill itself, keeps affirming the margin of hope in the presence of desolation, pestilence and despair.
—HOWARD THURMAN in *Meditations of the Heart,* Harper & Bros.

991. Christmas has forever been identified with childhood. The day began with the birth of a Child. God's greatest gift to man was this Child, and his greatest gift to the sons of men is the joy and responsibility of parenthood. Christmas serves to emphasize the fact that Christianity has done more than any culture or religion to make the love and care of children a hallowed responsibility.

992. "Would you like to know," a prosperous businessman asked Leigh Mitchell Hodges, "what I'm giving my boy for Christmas?" Expecting it to be some costly present, Hodges was surprised when the man handed him a paper on which was written: "To my dear son: I give you one hour of each weekday, and two hours of my Sundays, to be used as you wish.—Your Father." "The greatest gift a man can give—yet a gift every father owes to his son," was Hodges' comment.
—IDA A. R. WYLIE in *The Reader's Digest.*

993. Years ago Phillips Brooks said of the first Christmas, "A father and a mother and a child are there. No reli-

gion which began like that could ever lose its character."
—WILLIARD L. SPERRY in *Sermons Preached at Harvard,* Harper & Bros.

994. The track of a three-toed dinosaur has been found on the top of coal strata high up on the cliffs near Grand Junction, Colorado. Men have never seen the animal itself, but they have seen its footprint. Men have never seen God; but he has left his imprint, evidences of his creatorship, upon the face of the world. The Babe of Bethlehem is the greatest evidence of the real character of God.
—JOHN H. BLOUGH

995. In South Carolina a popular football coach was asked to address a civic club on the meaning of Christmas. He used the word "Christmas" as the outline and made each letter represent an aspect of the meaning of Christmas: *C* for charity, *H* for holiday, *R* for reverence, *I* for inspiration, *S* for suspense, *T* for thankfulness, *M* for merriment, *A* for aspirations, and *S* for sincerity. All of these are fine; but if Christ was the heart of Christmas, would it not be reasonable to expect that *C* would stand for child or for Christ?
—J. R. BROKHOFF

996. Emmanuel . . . means "God with us." For large numbers of people this has become a lost meaning of Christmas. How dramatically this was illustrated in the experience *Life* magazine had in preparing its Christmas issue one . . . December. A photographer had been sent to the School of San Roco in Italy to get some pictures of the wonderful Tintoretto murals of the nativity. Arriving in Venice this photographer began his assignment. He tried to photograph these exquisite paintings in natural color. He tried with every conceivable kind of light but the colors would not come clear. Upon minute examination it was revealed that these murals of the nativity had been overlaid with four centuries of varnish, dust, and the accumulation of dirt through which the radiant beauty of the original colors could not shine. Only with polaroid light could the photographer get the paintings to come through in their authentic colors to his camera. This is a perfect analogy to what has happened to the Christmas message itself. The real meaning of Christmas . . . has been overlaid with centuries of sentimental varnish and commercial dust until millions see in Christmas only the sweet story of a baby in a manger for whom we are moved to pity, or the occasion for an organized, commercialized, vulgarized carnival of gaudy splendour.
—ROBERT E. LUCCOCK in *If God Be for Us,* Harper & Bros.

997. Christmas as observed by believers in Iceland has a charm that is peculiarly its own. . . . First of all, everything must be clean for Christmas. Every corner of the house and every bit of clothing must be immaculate. All necessary repairs must be made, however inconspicuous the need. All of this is symbolic and preliminary. The greater preparation is that of the heart. All differences must be adjusted and all hearts reconciled. Then there are gifts, family reunions, and fellowship with friends. And over all, there hovers the sweet consciousness of the coming of Christ into the world and into the hearts of men.
—CHARLES W. KOLLER in *Tents Toward the Sunrise.* Copyright, 1951, by The Judson Press. Used by permission.

998. Harlan Miller said a bit facetiously that he wished it might be possible to

put up some of the Christmas spirit in jars and then open a jar of it every month or so. I devoutly wish that the world would cease to sentimentalize Christ as little more than a beautiful legend and do some careful listening and straight thinking about what he has to say and about what he has done. Christ is not a sentiment to be enjoyed one day out of the year and completely crowded out of everyday living. He is the one and only Saviour, God's own Son, to be embraced by faith and to be served with mind and heart and will every day of our life.
—ARMIN C. OLDSEN

999. A pastor asked his janitor to come to church and the janitor replied, "Have you had any recent news from God?" The Good News had been reduced to musty, stale news. The whole thing was suffering from dry rot.
—E. STANLEY JONES in *How to Be a Transformed Person,* Abingdon Press.

1000. The historian Arnold Toynbee has said that the greatest new event of our time is still the Crucifixion, and the clergyman Ralph W. Sockman meant the same thing by other words, "The hinge of history is on the door of a Bethlehem stable."
—DWIGHT E. STEVENSON in *Faith Takes a Name,* Harper & Bros.

1001. In *The Four Pillars of Democracy,* Edgar J. Goodspeed writes of the Hermes of Praxiteles: "You do not have to be a connoisseur to know when you stand before it . . . that you are in the presence of a masterpiece, one of man's supreme achievements in sculpture or indeed art of any kind. In fact, it helps you to understand what is meant by a revelation. For as you look, a new perspective . . . opens before you, and things you once found satisfying and great fall suddenly into truer proportions. And you instinctively say, 'No one should talk of Sculpture until he has stood before this figure, and looked upon it.'" This Jesus Christ did and does today in the spiritual realm—only multiplied a thousandfold. See what happened to men who were exposed to God through Christ. Like the shepherds who when they had stood by that manger went away to tell abroad the experience of the day "glorifying and praising God for all the things that they had heard and seen," or like the Wise Men who "saw the young child with Mary his mother and fell down and worshipped him," thousands who have stood in his presence have felt the contagion of his power and have been changed.
—FRANK B. FAGERBURG. Quotation published by Harper & Brothers.

INDEX OF NAMES

CROSS INDEX OF SUBJECTS